The Portable Technical Writer

William Murdick
California University of Pennsylvania

Jonathan C. Bloemker
Compunetix, Inc.

Houghton Mifflin Company
Boston   New York

Senior Sponsoring Editor: Suzanne Phelps Weir

Senior Project Editor: Rosemary Winfield

Senior Production/Design Coordinator: Sarah Ambrose

Senior Manufacturing Coordinator: Florence Cadran

Senior Marketing Manager: Nancy Lyman

Cover Design: Len Massiglia/LMA Communications

Printed in the U.S.A.

Library of Congress Catalog Card Number: 00-133837

ISBN: 0-395-98633-8

2 3 4 5 6 7 8 9-EU-04 03 02

Contents

13 *Letters and Reports* 271

14 *Job Search* 295

Preface

The Portable Technical Writer is intended to serve as the only necessary textbook for a college course in technical writing. It covers most major topics typically found in technical writing textbooks, as well as some topics not usually included, and it provides far more writing assignments than can be completed in a semester. Few teachers will get through all the chapters, but many will come close. We designed the book to be cost efficient. At the end of the term, students won't be left holding an expensive, overweight tome, two-thirds unread.

To achieve that efficiency, we have used a lean blunt style that directly tells students what they need to know to understand the subject and do the assignments, and we have dispensed with color photographs, anecdotes, interviews, cartoons, sidebars, and other nonessential filler. Houghton Mifflin has contributed by providing a publishing venue for inexpensive, quality textbooks through its *English Essentials* series.

▲ Audience

The Portable Technical Writer is addressed to

- students majoring in technical writing seeking an introduction to their profession
- students majoring in business who want to know how to communicate technical information in business documents
- students majoring in science, engineering, or technology who want to be able to do their own technical writing
- students majoring in fields with a scientific component—such as nursing, gerontology, or sports medicine—in which professionals are required to communicate technical information and write instructions.

▲ Content

Technical writing is now a fully evolved profession. Accordingly, this book focuses on the methods that professional technical writers bring to their work. Our premise is that anyone handling technical information in the workplace can benefit from learning the skills and adopting the approaches developed by these professionals.

In addition, we provide a selected coverage of business writing. Technical writers and others who communicate technical information need to know how to write certain kinds of letters, reports, and proposals.

Near the beginning of the book is a section called "Big Project Ideas," which provides twenty-six suggestions for month-long to semester-long writing assignments, as well as guidance on how to proceed with such projects.

The book's fourteen chapters are organized under four parts. Part I looks at the social contexts for writing in a high-tech workplace, including collaborative writing processes. Part II covers the basic skills required for technical writing. Part III examines the process of creating large documents, such as technical proposals and manuals. And Part IV addresses marketing and business documents.

Besides the creation of printed texts, *The Portable Technical Writer* addresses online research, online documentation, Web marketing, and Web job search.

▲ Design

Each chapter presents its content in short numbered sections, each of which ends with one or more writing assignments to keep students engaged in active learning.

Throughout the text a fictional telecommunications company, Pittsburgh Telemax, serves as the context for the discussion of professional practices. This artifice provides an extended concrete example of technical writers at work.

▲ Acknowledgments

Thanks to Yoshiko Murdick, who contributed to the artwork and performed many other important tasks.

Thanks also to Assistant Editor Tamara Jachimowicz for her energetic and competent assistance throughout the project, and to Jennifer Roderick and the other Houghton Mifflin editors who helped in the development of the book.

Our gratitude goes out to those who reviewed, and in some cases classroom-tested, versions of *The Portable Technical Writer*. In alphabetical order, they are as follows:

> Karen Carpenter, University of Maryland–Baltimore County
> Jeannie Crain, Missouri Western State College
> Richard Fincham, E-Transport, Inc., Pittsburgh

Julia Galbus, University of Southern Indiana
Robert J. Gill, Rutgers University
Michael Goeller, Rutgers University
Lucy Graca, Arapahoe Community College
Tom Harris, Rutgers University
Karen Holleran, Scott Community College
Clive Muir, University of Baltimore
Shirley Nelson, Chattanooga State Technical College
William Peirce, Prince Georges Community College
Pete Praetorius, Michigan Technological University
Anca Rosu, DeVry Institute of Technology
Sharla Shine, Terra Community College
Ron Smith, University of North Alabama
Bill Stiffler, Hartford Community College

Their comments were extremely helpful.

PART 1

The Social Contexts for Technical Writing

Technical Writing in College

Technical writers produce texts that people use at work and in their private lives to understand technology and to carry out tasks. Students in a college technical writing course can best learn technical writing by creating *useful* texts. This chapter sets up that approach to learning. It begins with a brief orientation to the general nature of technical writing. It then presents a set of twenty-six month-long to semester-long writing assignments, along with advice on how to carry out such projects.

Shorter writing assignments are offered in each of the remaining chapters.

Even if you don't undertake an extensive writing project for your course, much of the information here about collaborative work and about planning and evaluating your writing can be applied to these shorter assignments.

1.1 >——Technical Writing Defined

George Hayhoe, in an editorial in the journal *Technical Communication,* defined technical writing as

> the transfer of specialized information from subject matter experts to those who need to use it.
>
> *(Hayhoe, 1999, p. 24)*

Under Hayhoe's definition, the person doing the transferring would probably not be the subject matter expert but, rather, someone else—a professional technical writer—hired to "transfer" the information.

Other writing experts take a broader view of technical writing, defining it as **any writing that conveys or uses technical knowledge.** Under this definition, most scientists, engineers, and technicians are technical writers, regardless of their job title.

In this book we use Hayhoe's restricted definition of technical writing. From this viewpoint, a technical writer doesn't *do* scientific research, or engineering, or technical work but, instead, *explains* that work and *puts it in a useful form,* such as a set of instructions. We take this perspective in order to focus on the sophisticated methods developed by professional technical writers. These methods include a style and rhetoric appropriate for explaining technical concepts and conveying technical information. They also include project planning, record keeping, using electronic tools, document designing, document testing, and other craft.

We realize that not everyone taking a technical writing course plans to become a technical writer in this restricted sense. But everyone who has to communicate technical information will benefit from learning how professional technical writers do it.

Technical writing should be seen as a social rather than solo activity. Technical writers employed by companies typically work as team members contributing to the planning, documenting, and promoting of new products. Those employed by government agencies or non-profit organizations also work collaboratively with colleagues to advance the interests of their employers. Although some technical writers work alone on small projects, they still work within a social context. They write what their employers want them to write, for readers other than themselves. They may have to use formats created by their employers; they may have to incorporate passages written by other employees; they may have to use technical terms dictated by the organization's style guide.

So we begin this book by examining the social contexts for technical writing. Since you will be doing your technical writing within a college environment, we make that the starting place.

ASSIGNMENTS FOR 1.1

1. *Examine Other Definitions* Find two additional definitions of technical writing. Look in other technical writing textbooks or in technical dictionaries or other reference books available in your library. In class, as these definitions are shared, note any unique ideas that emerge from the definitions. Your instructor may then want you to write a short in-class paper on the range of perceptions that experts have about what constitutes technical writing.

2. *Social Dependence* When we say that technical writing is a social activity, we mean, in part, that technical writers depend on what others have done before them (see the second-to-last paragraph in section 1.1). Write down two ways (not mentioned in section 1.1) in which technical writers are thus dependent.

1.2 >—— Collaborative Work in College Writing Courses

Working as a whole class or within a group, you and your classmates can cooperate in many ways to create better written products. Even when working independently, you can help each other by giving critiques of each other's texts. One suggestion for a structure for peer review was posted by Stephen Bernhardt of New Mexico State University on the Association of Teachers of Technical Writing listserv (ATTW-L). We summarize it here with his permission:

> I like to create a shared network drive on which individual students create their own folders for their classwork. We also create a review folder. When students have a draft for review, they place it in the review folder and let people know (in class or by e-mail) that their work is ready and that they would like it reviewed. Ideally, they identify what kind of review they would like (for organization, content, style, readability, etc.).
>
> Authors password-protect their documents (in Microsoft Word, Tools/Protect). As students review and edit, their comments go right into the file as Track Changes. The authors can then review the comments and accept or reject them.
>
> Everybody has to review three other people's files, and everybody has to get his/her own work reviewed by three people. When they turn in their work, authors write a cover memo identifying from whom they got help and what they changed as a result of the reviews. I give credit to students who do good reviews.

One reason technical writing teachers like Stephen Bernhardt engage students in peer review is that technical writers, because they are professional writers, are often called upon to critique, revise, edit, or proofread the writing of others in their organization. So when you do peer review in a technical writing course, you are not just doing "school stuff," you are doing real technical writing.

Another form that collaborative work takes in college is the group project. For group projects that you carry out in your technical writing course, we suggest the kind of planning approach illustrated in Box 1.1.

In addition to project planning, team writing requires everyone to agree on and follow a set of rules for participation. Otherwise, internal disputes, resentments, or confusion over responsibilities may arise, resulting in missed deadlines or poor-quality work. Box 1.2 provides suggestions on how to organize participation in a team effort.

BOX 1.1 ▼   **Project Planning Table**

Project Title:	
Completion Date:	
Purpose of Document:	
Primary Audience:	
Secondary Audiences:	
Document Specs (length, format, binding):	
Project Leader:	
Project Staff:	
First Milestone:	
Division of Labor:	
Completion Dates for Jobs:	
Meetings: (date, time, place, agenda):	
Second Milestone:	
Division of Labor:	
Completion Dates for Jobs:	
Meetings: (date, time, place, agenda):	

ASSIGNMENTS FOR 1.2

1. *Peer Reviews* (a) Write up a suggestion for a peer review process that your class can use during this term. (b) Create a Document Review Sheet, a template for responding to the work of your peers.

BOX 1.2   ▼   Principles of Teamwork in College

1. Elect a good leader.

An important decision the team may have to make at the outset is the selection of a team leader. This is the person responsible for seeing to it that the project gets done on time and meets quality standards. The team leader does not act alone in planning or carrying out the project. Instead, the leader presides over democratic decision making, ensuring that everyone participates and that differences of opinion are aired and compromises forged. A good leader does not push his or her views on the team. The leader should be a responsible person, the kind of student who almost never misses class or meetings and always gets work done on time. The leader must be assertive enough to keep on top of things— for instance, by keeping the discussion at a meeting focused on the agenda or by tracking down an errant team member who has missed two meetings in a row.

2. Put talent to work.

Once your team has selected a project, team members should discuss their strengths and weaknesses as participants in the project. Doing so will help in assigning roles. If someone is a good stylist, that person should be the one who overwrites the final text. If someone likes to chat with strangers, that person should do the interviewing. If someone is good at library research, that person should lead the research effort. In student groups, sometimes, a member will claim to have no useful talents. At the outset, at least, the leader can assign that person to be an assistant to one or more team members. As much as possible, team members should learn from one another. A person strong at a task can team up with and mentor a person weak at that task.

3. Develop a decision-making procedure.

At meetings, team members must make the key decisions that solve problems and allow work to go forward. Without a decision-making procedure, debates on peripheral issues may dominate, leaving important work undone. The team must adopt a method for keeping to an agenda, while allowing everyone to assert opinions and float ideas. One approach would be to give the leader the authority to cut off immediate discussion of an issue and ask that team members present their views on that topic via e-mail. The team will have to decide what constitutes a quorum for voting on issues. Does a quorum consist of those attending a meeting? Or should all members have the chance to vote? The team will need a method for resolving differences when members are equally divided.

4. Deal with nonparticipating or uncooperative members.

The team should decide on policies for handling members who don't show up at meetings, don't turn in work, or cause strife. Possible penalties: a letter of reprimand, with a copy to the instructor; a poor end-of-project performance evaluation; expulsion from the group. The team must follow those policies with firm resolve.

2. *Student Evaluations for Group Projects* Only the members of your group will know what contributions each member made to your completed project. Create a table for the evaluation of individual contributions to a group project.

1.3 >——— Big Project Ideas

Below are twenty-six ideas for extensive writing assignments, which we are calling Big Projects. They can be undertaken individually or in teams. As noted, this textbook also suggests many smaller writing assignments in each chapter.

Your instructor may want you to come up with your own Big Project, or your own version of one of the projects described below. If so, here's an interesting approach from Tim Giles, of Georgia Southern University, which he posted on the ATTW-L. We reprint it here with his permission:

> First, everyone in the class writes a proposal [for a project] and submits it to the class listserv. Then, everyone reads everyone else's proposal. Next, we decide which are the best four or five out of a class of twenty. The writers of the proposals cited as the best become group leaders. The other students then apply for jobs with the group [that they want to work in], and the group leader picks no more than four other students to work with her/him. A progress report on the project as well as a final report and an oral presentation are required as group efforts.

As a general principle, design your Big Project for a specific, real audience. This may require a "needs analysis" performed at the site where your document would be used. At the site, you would make observations, carry out interviews, and possibly administer questionnaires to determine what your potential readers already know and what they need to learn.

If possible, you should find a way to turn over your final text to that real audience, in addition to submitting a copy to your instructor. Your course work becomes real technical writing when it becomes useful to someone.

The Big Project suggestions are categorized as follows:

1. Instructions
2. Guides
3. Technical Editing
4. Technical Proposals
5. Public Relations and Marketing Documents
6. Freelance Work
7. Research Reports

At the end of each suggested project is a list of chapters and chapter sections of particular relevance to the writing problem in question.

The following chapters and chapter sections are relevant to *all* writing tasks and are therefore not listed at the end of the project descriptions: Chapters 2 and 3 (for background on the fictional company used to contextualize technical writing in this book), Chapter 4 (on rhetoric), Chapter 5 (on style), and section 13.4 (on progress reports). You should start reading these chapters and section 13.4(5) immediately after selecting your Big Project. In addition, read the particular chapters and sections relevant to your project that are listed at the end of the project description.

▲ 1. Instructions

Outside Documentation Create a piece of instructional documentation that can be used by an office or organization outside your school. You might choose an office at a local company, or a local non-profit organization such as a public library or senior center. Consider writing a beginner's guide or an advanced guide for software to be used at the chosen location. Or you might create a beginner's guide to using a new piece of office equipment, or an introduction to the World Wide Web for senior citizens, or a booklet for tenth-graders at a local school on how to use a spreadsheet to create tables. Go to the site and explore the organizational context to learn about your audience and how your audience would use your documentation. **Chapters 7, 9, 10, 11**

In-House Documentation Do the project described above, but tailor it to a campus office or facility. Consider the equipment in an exercise room, a set of library computer indexes, a science lab machine, or a scientific procedure (such as handling and caring for lab animals). Again, you would be writing a set of instructions, along with some background information for beginners. Print your documentation in the form of a small booklet. **Chapters 7, 9, 10, 11**

Instructional Brochure Here are three ideas for brochures: (a) Create a four- or six-panel, illustrated, idiot-proof brochure on how to fix a flat tire on a car belonging to a close friend or relative. Think of someone who would benefit from having such a document in the glove compartment. Test your first draft of the documentation on your audience, and then revise. (b) Do the previous project, but for a household repair or maintenance job. Again, imagine a person you know who would benefit from having this brochure, write for that person, and then ask that person to try out your instructions while you watch. Then revise. (c) Create an extensive square-page (5″ × 5″), accordion-fold brochure describing and celebrating the program in your major. Your audience would be prospective students and their parents. Include a panel that provides information on registering as a student and declaring a major at your school. Consider each panel an individual "work of art," but also make sure that major design features (like borders, color schemes, and fonts) are consistent throughout and that the panels form a logical sequence leading to a desirable grand effect. **Chapters 7, 12, sections 10.2, 10.3**

▲ *2. Guides*

Frightened-Beginner's Guide Write a short pamphlet that helps newcomers take on a challenge that frightens many beginners: statistics, sailing, public speaking, rappelling. Draw on your own experience. Remember that while part of your purpose is to provide comprehensible instructions, another part is to ameliorate fears and phobias, including perhaps fear of failure or fear of bodily harm. **Chapters 7, 10**

Guide for First-Year Students Write a "street smart" underground guide for first-year students that helps them avoid all the mistakes you (and others you know about) made early on in college. Research important procedures, such as loan applications and grade appeals. Talk about housing, parking strategies, social life, campus restaurants and snack bars, exercise facilities and athletic opportunities, good study habits, getting around in the libraries, course and professor selection, academic support programs, and anything else of practical value. **Chapters 7, 10, 11, section 9.3**

For One Gender Only Write the guide described above, but specialize it for female students. Or for male students.

Course Guide Write a guide, in booklet form, that describes the composition sequence at your university. This booklet would be used as a supplementary text in composition courses. Specifically, it would introduce the English department, explain the composition program (placement, requirements, awards, philosophy, and rationale), give advice on how to do well in composition courses, and provide model student papers. Assume an audience of first-year students.

Or write a similar guide to some other course—again, for possible use as a text. **Sections 9.3, 9.4**

Tour Guide Write a tour guide for your campus and for the town or city where your school is located. Your audience would be visiting parents or conference attendees. Create a route with interesting stop-off places for a two-hour tour. Include a lunch stop. Note bathroom facilities. Draw a map (or use a photograph) with numbered places of interest, and for each one, write a piece of text describing the place of interest. **Chapter 10, sections 7.1, 7.2, 7.6, 9.3, 11.3**

Restaurant and Hotel Guide (Plus T-Shirt or Hat) Write a restaurant and hotel guide for sports fans who have come to your school to see a game. Get an estimate from a local printer on how much it would cost to print your guide, and then put a price on the cover that would bring in a small profit.

In your guide, advertise a T-shirt or hat that you have designed and plan to sell. Display the design. **Chapter 12, sections 7.1, 7.2, 7.5, 7.6, 9.3**

Guide to the Internet Write a student guide to the Internet for social science students, or humanities students, or education students, or science students. (Your instructor may wish you to focus on a particular major, such as English or elementary education.) Include a start-up section for beginners, an annotated bibliography of useful sites, and a poster or fanfold reference sheet. **Chapter 10, sections 9.3, 9.4, 11.2**

Law Guide for Technical and Business Writers Write a useful guide for technical and business writers on copyright law, trademark law, patent law, trade secret law, and other legal issues. Some starting points: Miller and Davis (1990), Pinkerton (1990), and Strate and Swerdlow (1987). **Sections 2.6, 9.3**

Citation Guide Write a guide to citing and documenting print and electronic sources in which you contrast such styles as Modern Language Association (MLA), American Psychological Association (APA), Chicago, Council of Biology Editors (CBE), and any other standards you wish to include. Your audience would be college students who have to switch from one style to another as they write for professors in different departments. You may wish to employ a format like those used in the laminated course guides sold in college bookstores. Or you may wish to create a big poster for word processing labs. **Chapters 10, 11, 12, section 9.4**

Style Guide Write a style guide for your technical writing class. Include the formats for various kinds of assignments as well as the terminology your instructor plans to use (which your instructor would provide).

Or write a style guide for an instructor for another course, such as a guide for writing lab reports or art criticism papers. This would be a document that the instructor gives out to students at the beginning of the term. **Chapters 9, 10, sections 2.4, 8.3**

Correctness Guide Write a sentence-correctness guide for technical writing students. Make use of handbooks, dictionaries, and usage guides. Start with a careful needs analysis. **Chapters 5, 9, 10**

▲ 3. Technical Editing

Style Revise a substantial school or business document, or a substantial part of that document, applying principles of clarity. Select a document that needs such revision. Your instructor may have a few in mind. **Chapters 5, 11**

Simplified English Revise a complex school document into simplified English, using Charles Ogden's (1968) *Basic English* for tips on vocabulary and grammar. Your instructor may provide you with a document that would benefit from being revised in this manner. You can use technical terms not found in Ogden's 850-word dictionary (available on the Web), but define those terms in a glossary and draw only from the 850 in creating your definitions. **Chapter 5**

▲ 4. Technical Proposals

Proposal for a New Lab Write a proposal for a new lab for your school. You may choose a science lab, a computer lab, or any other kind of workshop classroom with machines, tools, supplies, storage, and so forth. Do a needs analysis and any other research necessary to design and equip the facility. Make your proposal convincing. As discussed in Chapter 13, internal proposals usually follow a problem-solution organizational pattern, in which a "need" constitutes the "problem." Address your proposal to the appropriate administrator (find out who that would be). **Chapters 6, 7, sections 13.3, 13.4**

Answer a Student Wish Conduct a survey to find out what students would like to have at your school but don't. Or something they would like to have more of, such as parking spaces. To expand on this example, survey students to find out where they would like to see more parking. Then find space near that location, design the parking lot, and write an internal proposal using a problem-solution format (see Chapter 13). In your report, include the estimated costs along with persuasive arguments for going ahead with this project.

Write this proposal for whatever student wish you choose to attempt to fulfill. Address it to the appropriate administrator (find out who that would be). Or create a multimedia presentation of your report. **Chapter 7, sections 6.3, 13.1**

Proposal in Response to an RFP Consider this scenario: Your office workers need new telephones (or computer desks or computers or printers—some piece of office equipment). Examine catalogs or go to office supply stores and learn about the features associated with different versions of this product. Write a request for proposals (RFP) calling for specific features. Then write a formal proposal in response to the RFP. Use the format for the technical specifications section that appears in Box 8.2. **Chapter 8**

▲ 5. Public Relations and Marketing Documents

Create a Web Site On paper—or, if possible, online—create a multimedia homepage and linked pages for a campus program or organization, such as the writing center, the math tutoring lab, the stat lab, the German Club, the Student Union, the Pheta Data Mu sorority, the Intramural Rugby League, or the Division II Champion Basketball Team. Include images and text, internal "jumps" to pages you've created, and external links to other sites. Also do a needs analysis in which you interview the appropriate people to determine content. In your interviews, encourage the respondents to speak about purpose and audience.

Or create a Web site for your technical writing class. Consider yourself in competition with others or with other groups. The best site may be used next semester as the instructor's official site for this course. **Sections 9.5, 12.1, 12.4**

Create a Presentation Do the previous project; however, this time, using presentation software, create a slide show that showcases a facility or organization on your campus. Include text, still photographs, music, and video. Apply the principles of page design taught in Chapter 12. Make a presentation to your technical writing class. **Sections 6.3, 12.1**

▲ 6. Freelance Work

Job Search Documents With permission from your school's administration, raise money for the Technical Writing Fund by starting a job-application writing service for students. For a small fee (perhaps $5.00), help clients produce several types of resume, as well as cover letters and post-interview letters. In your final report to your instructor, include information on clients, samples of documents you created, and an accounting of your earnings (which will be turned over to the fund). Conclude by making recommendations on how the money could be spent to enhance technical writing instruction at your school. **Chapter 14, sections 11.2, 13.1**

Pens for Hire (for Free) Advertise in the school newspaper and elsewhere that your group will carry out a writing task for any office on campus for free. Get hired and do the job. (Note: Your instructor may have arranged for such jobs prior to the beginning of the semester.) Write a report on your experiences: the kind of writing you did and the writing problems you had to solve and how you solved them. In an appendix, include copies of some or all of your writings. Your instructor may ask you to make an oral report to the class on what you learned. **Section 13.4**

On-Campus Internship Volunteer your services as a professional technical writer for two hours a week in an office at your university—at no charge. Half way through your internship, write a progress report. Then, at the end, write a final report on your experiences: the kind of writing you did and the writing problems you had to solve and how you solved them. In an appendix, include copies of some or all of your writings. Your instructor may ask you to make an oral report to the class on what you learned. **Section 13.4**

▲ *7. Research Reports*

Description of a Local Writing Department Do an on-site study of a documentation department (or publications or public relations department) in a local company or organization. Describe the department's structure (including an organizational chart), the educational and experiential backgrounds of the employees, the kind of writing the department does for both external and internal audiences (with samples), the department's methods of producing documents (collaborative writing process, outsourcing, hardware and software tools, style guide), and the problems the department faces in doing its work. Include employees' ethical, legal, and quality concerns.

Make this document part of a collection that can be used in technical writing courses at your school. Use a format or template already established, or create one. Your instructor may also want you to prepare an online version. **Sections 9.3, 9.4, 9.5, 13.1**

Profile of a Local Technical Writer Do the previous project, but focus on a single professional writer. Make it clear where in the organizational structure this person resides, how the person works collaboratively with others, and what the person's individual responsibilities are. Discuss how the person learned to do the tasks required for the job. When interviewing this person, follow the guidelines in Box 3.3. **Sections 9.3, 9.4, 9.5, 13.1**

1.4 >——— A Writing Process for Big Projects

Once you have created your group (if your class is working in groups) and have selected a project, follow a writing process like the one described below. Some of the steps may not apply to your project, and you may have to do some things not listed. Or you may want to do some of the activities listed below in a slightly different order. The writing process presented here is meant to be suggestive, so you may have to refine it to meet the circumstances of your project.

Planning

1. Learn the product or system or topic you will be addressing in your document.

2. Analyze your audience. As part of that analysis, visit the site where your document will be used, and do a needs analysis: Through interviews, observations, or tests determine what your audience needs to learn. Audience need depends on both the audience's initial state of competence and their projected purpose in using the document, so find out those two things. Suppose, for example, you are writing a guide for a new word processing program. In terms of *initial state of knowledge,* if employees at a company are already doing word processing, you will not need to introduce them to basic concepts. In terms of their *use of the product,* employees who write sales letters will need to learn the mass-mailing features of the new program, but not the auto-indexing function. Do an analysis of multiple audiences, if appropriate.

3. Plan your document structure and appearance. Develop a table of contents and a plan for front and back matter and for the cover and binding. Decide on page layouts and fonts. Determine the types of graphics you will use, the size of the document, and the approximate cost to reproduce. Doing this kind of planning early means that all writers in a group project will be using the same page layouts and the same fonts and font sizes; they will also have a sense of how big each section will be.

4. Devise a plan for carrying out the project. Divide up the labor. Create a timetable for finishing the project.
5. Submit a progress report on your planning decisions and planning documents.

First Draft

6. Do research and gather required documents.
7. Write the first draft.
8. Do a "usability walk-through," trying out each part of the documentation yourself.
9. Do a usability test, preferably with users at the target site.
10. Submit a progress report on the effectiveness of the first draft.

Final Draft

11. Revise on the basis of your testing.
12. Submit a second draft to your instructor or to peers for a critique.
13. Revise on the basis of the critique.
14. Go through the quality checklist below, and note any needed improvements.
15. Make the quality improvements.
16. Edit and proofread.
17. Submit copies of the final draft to each group member and to your instructor.

1.5 >——— A Quality Checklist for Big Projects

You might want to run through this checklist at various stages in the development of your document. On group projects, the labor can be divided up, each team member assessing the document in terms of a portion of these criteria.

Be critical. Nit pick.

Before you turn in your project, attend to any checks in the No column. Ultimately, all entries on the checklist should be marked either Yes or N/A (not applicable).

Yes   N/A   No

☐ ☐ ☐   The document is attractive on the outside.
Comment:

☐ ☐ ☐   The document is easy to read on the inside (uncluttered, large enough fonts).
Comment:

Yes   N/A   No

☐ ☐ ☐   The page design is attractive.
Comment:

☐ ☐ ☐   Necessary front and back matter have been included.
Comment:

☐ ☐ ☐   The document meets all planned specifications for design and layout.
Comment:

☐ ☐ ☐   The table of contents or main menu represents a logical grouping.
Comment:

☐ ☐ ☐   Titles and subheadings clearly identify content.
Comment:

☐ ☐ ☐   Online screens are attractive.
Comment:

☐ ☐ ☐   Online screens are easy to understand.
Comment:

☐ ☐ ☐   Online screens provide useful links.
Comment:

☐ ☐ ☐   Links clearly indicate where they are taking the reader.
Comment:

☐ ☐ ☐   The writing is free of typographical and other sentence errors.
Comment:

☐ ☐ ☐   The writing is clear.
Comment:

☐ ☐ ☐   The text is accurate.
Comment:

☐ ☐ ☐   Necessary warnings appear prominently.
Comment:

Yes   N/A   No

☐ ☐ ☐   Helpful visuals have been included.
Comment:

☐ ☐ ☐   All visuals are justified.
Comment:

☐ ☐ ☐   Instructions have been tested and work well.
Comment:

☐ ☐ ☐   All audiences have been addressed.
Comment:

☐ ☐ ☐   The text is task-oriented and takes the user's perspective.
Comment:

☐ ☐ ☐   Information is easy to find.
Comment:

Technical Writing on the Job

Most professional technical writers are employed by companies, government agencies, or other types of organizations. This chapter looks at how the work of technical writers fits into the structure and purposes of an organization.

The chapter begins by discussing the variety of possible contexts for technical writing. It then narrows the focus to technical writing in a high-tech company. This book uses a fictional telecommunications company as a setting for many of the lessons, and that company is described in detail.

The chapter ends with an examination of ethical, legal, and quality issues of concern to technical writers working in a corporate environment.

2.1 > Possibilities for Technical Writers

Almost every profession uses technical writers. A technical writer might work for a pharmaceutical company writing applications for drug approval to be submitted to the U.S. Food and Drug Administration. A technical writer might work for the Federal Aviation Administration preparing "safety regulations and related documentation to ensure that aircraft are properly operated and maintained" (Barclay & Pinelli, 1998, p. 50). A technical writer might work for a computer firm writing software manuals for end-users. A technical writer might be employed by a gourmet food store to maintain the company's Web site, designing attractive pages, writing precise descriptions of the products, and making sure that customers can navigate the site easily.

How do technical writers end up in these jobs? Many follow a career path in which they first train and work in their field as scientists, engineers, technicians, or other kinds of specialists. They become full-time writers when they rise to the managerial level or when their organization needs someone capable of taking on major writing projects. Others train as technical writers and then learn, on the job, the specific scientific or technical content they will write about.

For more about technical writing in different professions, see Jean A. Lutz and C. Gilbert Storms's (1998) collection of reports from professionals, *The Practice of Technical and Scientific Communication.*

Within an organization, we also find a great deal of variation in the work of technical writers. Their purpose in writing might be to inform, instruct, persuade, or sell. Their audience may be technical experts, informed nonexperts, or complete novices. Professional technical writers may have a variety of responsibilities, including these:

- editing and proofreading the writing of others
- preparing figures and tables for the work of others, as well as for their own documents
- updating documentation after a product upgrade
- designing document layouts
- developing sets of manuals for new products
- writing policy statements
- writing short sets of instructions
- writing detailed descriptions of machines or processes
- working on proposals and bids for contracts
- creating marketing materials
- designing and maintaining Web pages
- creating online documentation.

It is common, in fact, for someone with the job title of "technical writer" to participate in every one of those activities.

ASSIGNMENTS FOR 2.1

1. *Imagine Jobs* As noted in Chapter 1, George Hayoe (1999) defined technical writing as "the transfer of specialized information from subject matter experts to those who need to use it." This section has offered several specific examples of that work, examples rooted in our culture. Think of two other contemporary jobs that might require the skills of a professional technical writer. Briefly describe those jobs in writing, and share your descriptions with the class.

2. *Imagine Other Activities* Look over the bulleted list of activities that technical writers engage in. What other activities can you imagine a professional writer doing for an organization? Contribute two ideas to a class discussion. Your instructor may want you to write them down to turn in as homework.

3. *Report on a Job Description* Find and read a technical writer's description of his or her job. Such descriptions frequently appear in journals like *TechComm* and *Technical Communication*. Or you might pick a chapter in Lutz and Storms (1998). Write a brief summary to turn in to your instructor. Be prepared to make a short oral report to your class.

2.2 >———— A Company Context

To present a realistic picture of the organizational context within which technical writing takes place, we have created a fictional telecommunications company for this textbook—**Pittsburgh Telemax, Inc.** The company provides the setting for many of the lessons in the book. This artifice permits us to get around the endless variation in types of technical writing by limiting our view to a single, but very common, focus: writing about electronic hardware systems and software applications.

We will ask you to create your own company as well, one related to your personal interests or technical knowledge. The creation of that company is the first assignment at the end of this section. Although the creation of a fictional company is not necessary for effective use of this textbook, some of the assignments throughout the book call upon those who have created their own company to write documents for it.

▲ *1. Pittsburgh Telemax*

Pittsburgh Telemax is a fictional, privately held telecommunications company located in Pittsburgh, Pennsylvania (Figure 2.1 shows a company organizational chart). Its primary products are sophisticated point-to-point, and multi-point, multimedia teleconferencing systems and local area networks. These are sold to corporate, government, and educational institutions. In point-to-point teleconferencing, one party calls another and the two confer, using video along with other contemporary multimedia such as VCR and 3-D projection. In multi-point teleconferencing, more than two users participate in a teleconference by calling into a Multipoint Control Unit, which Telemax has designed.

Although Pittsburgh Telemax is reasonably profitable, the company faces strong competition. Its strategy is to hire outstanding employees and to stay ahead of the competition by maintaining a technological edge. This means putting a strong focus on engineering, as well as marketing.

The organizational chart (Figure 2.1) provides our first look at how a high-tech company works, and at how technical writing fits in. Note the

FIGURE 2.1 ▶ Organizational Chart for Pittsburgh Telemax

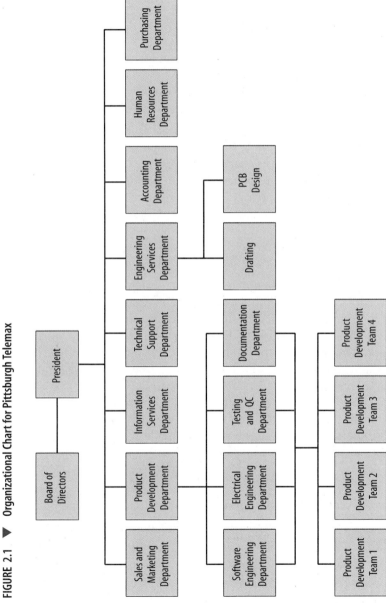

location of the Documentation Department, the home of the technical writing staff.

The rest of this section describes professional personnel and departments, following the chart from top to bottom and from left to right. These professionals are supported by an office manager and eight assistants who perform clerical and secretarial work for all departments.

▲ 2. Board of Directors

The Board of Directors of Pittsburgh Telemax consists of a number of well-seasoned executives and professionals from various fields: a lawyer, a retired CEO, a retired electrical engineer, a retired software engineer, a marketing consultant, and a retired college president.

The Board meets every quarter to review the company's performance and to determine future policy. It also drafts and updates three policy statements: one that applies to the next quarter, one that applies to the next year, and one that applies to the next three years.

▲ 3. President

The president of Pittsburgh Telemax, Howard Stone, oversees the high-level daily operations of the company and makes key decisions. There are no vice-presidents, so the president works directly with top-level department managers, meeting with each of them at least once during the week. When he is able, the president visits with other employees. He takes the time to ask them about their work and to find out first hand about any grievances.

The president uses these meetings and contacts to keep on top of the company's day-to-day business and to evaluate operations in terms of both short- and long-range business plans.

▲ 4. Sales and Marketing Department

Besides general sales and marketing, this department is responsible for:

▌ identifying new markets and new applications for existing products

▌ determining what changes and improvements are required in existing products to maintain market share

▌ selling and maintaining service contracts

▌ evaluating and maintaining customer satisfaction

▌ public relations.

Because of the diverse nature of its work, the Sales and Marketing Department interfaces regularly with other departments. For example, if the Sales and Marketing Department manager, Beverly Yoshida, has found that a customer is unhappy with a product, she may arrange a teleconference between the customer and the Technical Support Department specialist, and possibly a technical writer, to determine if the product is inadequate or defective, or if the product has been improperly installed, or if the documentation is being misunderstood.

Working with the technical writers, Sales and Marketing Department personnel develop sales presentations and marketing materials. Yoshida's staff and the technical writers compose the text. Using desktop publishing and computer art tools, her staff also designs, lays out, and produces "camera-ready copy" of marketing materials. Camera-ready copy is high-quality copy ready for photographic printing.

▲ 5. Product Development Department

The Product Development Department is responsible for creating new products and improving existing products (bringing out new versions). The department consists of a senior manager and four project managers who function as "team leaders" for the production teams.

The project managers meet with one another regularly to share information. For example, if one product development team has developed a new software routine, the leader of that team describes the new routine to the other project managers. A different project manager may find the routine useful just as it is, or with minor modifications. Managers are also responsible for keeping up-to-date on new technologies that might be useful to Pittsburgh Telemax and for sharing those technologies with their staff.

Production teams draw personnel from the following departments to carry out their work.

Software Engineering Department A product development team typically includes someone who writes the embedded software that runs in a plug-in module, someone who writes the software that allows various components to communicate with each other, and someone who writes the software that displays the user interface on a computer screen.

On a shared server (a computer to which the software engineers will have access), the department manager makes available the source code for all software and creates a library of generic software routines accessible to all programmers. The manager maintains a database that describes every routine in the library in detail. As new software versions are developed, the manager records the changes from previous versions.

Electrical Engineering Department   The Electrical Engineering Department consists of a manager and a number of electrical engineers (sometimes informally called "hardware" engineers). The electrical engineers, hired on the basis of specialized skills, are distributed among product development teams according to where their skills are needed. A single electrical engineer may contribute to the work of more than one team.

Testing and Quality Control (QC) Department   The Testing and QC Department consists of a manager and two test engineers. The test engineers are assigned to one or more of the various product development teams. Their job is to place stress on each new product or new version of a product, to make sure that it functions properly. If the product fails under stress, the test engineer works with the project manager and team engineers to determine the cause of the problem.

It is the job of the Testing and QC Department manager to design stress tests for all new products, to coordinate the actual testing, to record results, and to maintain information on corrective measures taken.

This department tests only products, not documentation. The technical writers and others test the effectiveness of instructional texts.

Documentation Department   The Documentation Department consists of a manager, Marge Mendoza, and a staff of technical writers, Louis Frapp and Wendy Smith. The Documentation Department creates and publishes documents that describe the products developed by Pittsburgh Telemax. Mendoza assigns members of the staff to product development teams. A single writer may work for more than one team. Mendoza works with team leaders in determining the types of documents required for each product, and then oversees the production of those documents.

The Documentation Department manager must keep abreast of industry standards in order to maintain the company's documentation standards. Right now she is exploring the possibility of shifting the Telemax approach to a "minimalist" documentation format (discussed in Chapter 9), as a number of companies have done in recent years. Mendoza is responsible for protecting company secrets while providing sufficient information to make published documents usable.

The Documentation Department also works closely with the Sales and Marketing Department in the production of marketing materials.

▲ *6. Information Services Department*

The Information Services Department consists of one person, a manager, who is responsible for maintaining the company's local area network, Internet access, and Web site. The manager modifies online documentation and advertising as that material is revised and updated by the Documentation Department and the Sales and Marketing Department.

▲ *7. Technical Support Department*

The Technical Support Department consists of a manager and two technicians. This department installs systems for customers and solves problems for them on site. One technician also operates phone support and Web site support systems.

▲ *8. Engineering Services Department*

The Engineering Services Department consists of a manager and two assistants, one a specialist in AutoCAD drafting and one a specialist in printed circuit board (PCB) design. This department supports the software and electrical engineers.

The Engineering Services Department manager coordinates the support services and catalogues all AutoCAD drawings and PCB layouts. An expert in government regulations for telecommunications, the Engineering Services Department manager guides engineers and technical writers in complying with those regulations.

▲ *9. Accounting Department*

The Accounting Department consists of a controller and an assistant accountant. This department makes a budget each year based on last year's record and then adjusts that budget as the new year progresses. It performs actual bookkeeping and attends to payroll.

Of interest to technical writers is the cost accounting function, whereby the accountants predict the cost of projects and maintain up-to-date records of actual costs as they occur. A major documentation project may cost Telemax $30,000 to complete. The Accounting Department knows the costs and makes projections for feasibility studies and proposals.

▲ 10. Human Resources Department

The Human Resources Department consists of one person, a manager. This department oversees the hiring of new employees, including the advertising of job openings and the arranging of interviews. It also negotiates with financial service companies to provide health insurance, savings plans, pension plans, and other benefits. The manager represents the employees in disputes with these providers.

▲ 11. Purchasing Department

The Purchasing Department consists of a manager and an assistant. This department determines what items need to be purchased; finds the best supplier; writes RFPs (requests for proposals), often with the help of engineers and a technical writer; helps analyze submitted proposals; places orders; and maintains inventory.

This department also maintains the company's general parts list (GPL), which includes numbers and parts lists for developed assemblies, purchased assemblies, and technical documentation.

ASSIGNMENTS FOR 2.2

1. *Create Your Own Company* On an individual, group, or whole-class level, whichever your instructor prefers, create a fictional company that you will use as a context for some of the writing assignments in this course. Your instructor will tell you how much detail to put into your creation. At the very least, invent a name and a product line, and list any services offered. In other words, describe what your company does to make money. Choose a product or service you know a lot about. Here are some examples to get your mind cooking.

    (a) **AutoKitchen:** Makes food preparation machines (electric choppers, blenders, beaters, meat grinders, cheese graters, etc.). Customers include both home cooks and restaurants. Sells through catalogues and kitchen stores. Provides instructional documentation in both print and online multimedia. Does repair service.

    (b) **Greg's Garden:** Raises seedlings and packages seeds for various trees, bushes, grasses, and flowers used in landscaping. Sells its products via printed, mass-mailed catalogues and through its Web site. Customers include both professional landscapers and homeowners. Provides instructional documentation in both print and online multimedia for each of its products in regard to appropriate use, planting, and maintenance.

(c) **Backyard Booze:** Sells kits for homemade beer, wine, liqueurs, and brandies. Also carries a line of alcohol-related products such as mugs, wine openers, and T-shirts with beer logos. Sells through its own speciality shops as well as through print and Web catalogues to amateur home brewers. Provides instructional documentation for its kits in both print and online multimedia.

(d) **ComputerPlay Products:** Makes a simple programming language, simple graphics program, and educational programs for elementary school children to run on Macintosh and Windows environments. Sells direct to schools through its catalogue and to parents through retail software stores. Provides instructional documentation in both print and online multimedia.

(e) **TestTaker:** Makes test preparation materials and training manuals for the SAT, the GRE, the LSAT, and other exams. Makes online practice tests available to customers and conducts a lot of its sales through its Web site.

2. *Letterhead* Create a letterhead and logo for your company. In preparation, examine letterheads and logos used by your school and by local companies. Your instructor may have left some examples on reserve in the school library.

3. *Organizational Chart* Create an organizational chart for your fictional company.

2.3 >——— The Technical Writers

At the moment, Pittsburgh Telemax employs a three-person technical writing team headed by Marge Mendoza. The other technical writers are Louis Frapp and Wendy Smith. Smith has just graduated from college and has no experience as a technical writer.

To enrich the context, here is a short description of the three individuals who will model the work of technical writers:

▌ *Marge Mendoza* At age 47, Mendoza holds the title of "Documentation Department manager" (DDM). (As noted, the Documentation Department houses the technical writing team.) She has been with the company for fifteen years, almost since its founding. Her initial academic credentials consisted of a B.A. in English, with a business minor, from a New York City college. She then got a night-school

M.B.A. at a local Pittsburgh institution during her first five years at Telemax.

▌ *Louis Frapp* Frapp has been with Telemax for five years and holds the title of "senior technical writer." Supported by a Booker T. Washington scholarship, he earned a B.A. in technical communications from an exclusive university renowned for its engineering programs. In addition to his assignments, Frapp has carried out a number of projects at Telemax on his own time; the largest of these has involved the development of standards documents for technical writers and others, which he publishes in the *Telemax Style Guide.* He writes fast in a clear, staccato style. He is fussy about grammar and about the careful, consistent use of terminology.

▌ *Wendy Smith* When the two junior technical writers left Telemax within a month of one another, the company decided to replace them with one writer, as a cost-saving move. Wendy Smith, a 22-year-old graduate of a small private college, got the job. She has a B.A. in English with a minor in computer science. Smith is fascinated by computers, an interest that will serve her well in her new career. She is a good writer—she won the composition award as a freshman—but the only course she took in technical writing focused on freshman composition issues and general business writing. Smith will have to learn technical writing on the job, with the help of Frapp, who will guide her through her apprenticeship. She composes slowly and thoughtfully, her style tending toward the figurative and elegant. Obviously, she will have to change the way she writes.

ASSIGNMENT FOR 2.3

1. *Technical Writer Job Description* Find a job ad for a technical writing position. Look in your local big-city newspaper or search the Web for ads in major newspapers around the country (e.g., **www.nytimes.com**, **www.miamiherald.com**, and **www.latimes.com**). Chapter 14 specifies other sites for job ads. Try to find an ad that provides a list of duties. In class, create a master list of duties from all the ads brought in. Examine the salaries offered. At the time of this writing, the national average is in the low $30s for starting salary and the low $50s for writers with ten years experience. Also note the terminology used: "technical writer," "technical communicator," "information product engineer." Be prepared to discuss your findings in class. Paste or tape your ad to a piece of paper with your name on it so that you can turn it in to your instructor.

2.4 〉—— Communicating In-House

A new employee must learn how to communicate in writing within the organization. This section looks at two types of in-house communication at Pittsburgh Telemax, memos and e-mail, and concludes by examining the means by which employees take notes for themselves.

▲ 1. Memos

Telemax requires employees to use the American Management Association (AMA) style for printed memos, illustrated in Box 2.1. Note that the heading in this memo is double spaced, while the text of the body is single spaced, with a blank line between paragraphs. The **Re:** line provides a full description of the contents so that someone searching for the memo months later, or even years later, could find it easily by examining the **Re:** lines of memos on file.

Some memos require a response. In that case, the memo writer checks the slot next to **Comment** at the bottom of the memo (again, as in Box 2.1). The receiver writes a response, photocopies the memo with the handwritten response for his or her own files, and then returns the original memo through interoffice mail.

Telemax employees are required to keep copies of all their communications.

▲ 2. E-mail

Electronic mail at Telemax operates through desktop computers connected to small powerful computers called network file servers, forming a local area network (LAN). The LAN is connected though a network hub to other LANs and to the main server, a minicomputer that stores e-mail messages and provides Internet access. The whole system is called an intranet (Figure 2.2).

The Information Services Department manager, Stuart Delaney, registers Wendy on her first day at work to a local server named Lulu. He shows Wendy how to log on using a password of her own invention.

Delaney gives Wendy a short lecture on e-mail communications at Telemax, making the following points.

Privacy Each employee is allotted personal space on the departmental server, but that space is not private. Managers at Telemax are free to roam around in employees' e-mail files, just as they are free to examine printed

BOX 2.1 ▼   Memo Format at Pittsburgh Telemax

Ⓟittsburgh Telemax

To: Marge Mendoza

CC: Howard Stone, President; Sheila Fritz, Marketing

From: Beverly Yoshida *BY*

Date: March 30, 2000

Re: Presentation at Pumpkinville State College

I'd like you to accompany Sheila to the presentation at Pumpkinville. She needs to get caught up on the DL 1000 system, so
please help her with the slide show, too. Let's make this sale.

On Friday at the Week Summary Meeting, can you two show us
what you'll present at Pumpkinville?

 _X_ Comment:

> *Sheila and I will make a presentation at the Week Summary
> Meeting this Friday. —MM*

---

memos stored in central file cabinets. Delaney warns Wendy to keep her
e-mail and Internet communications businesslike. No gossiping, wise-
cracking, or joke telling.

Context Because of the instantaneousness of the e-mail transmission,
office workers often use e-mail to carry on informal discussions of work
issues throughout the day, sometimes in rapid repartee fashion. The messages often have the feel of conversation:

> Great idea. Let's do it.

This informality works as long as the conversation is ongoing and
immediate. But a message like the one above, sent several days after the
"great idea" had been suggested, might befuddle the receiver. What great
idea?

FIGURE 2.2 ▼ Two LANs Within the Telemax Intranet

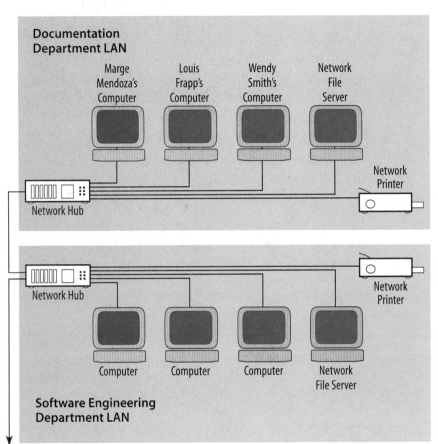

To Other LANs

It is best to provide a complete context for any e-mail message that may not be read within a few hours. Here's an expansion of the above example:

> I like your idea of hiring a professional indexer for the Playtronix documentation. Let's do it.

E-mail Style The conversational character of e-mail communications has also led to a tradition of informal style in the case of short, routine electronic messages:

> Sure, I can meet at 1:00 today to discuss the indexing. Where? How about East conference Room

The writer of the above message uses sentence fragments, drops the article in front of *East,* doesn't bother to correct the inconsistent capitalization in *East conference Room,* and omits the question mark after the final interrogative.

Delaney tells Wendy, "There's nothing wrong with that kind of informality, when the purpose of your short message is to quickly get across one or two pieces of information in order to get work done. However, a long memo filled with uncorrected typographical errors would be a struggle to read."

Delaney urges Wendy to shift into a more careful kind of writing when composing long or formal messages. For those texts, he tells her to take enough time to plan, revise, and edit so that her electronic prose has the same professional look, clear and errorless phrasing, and coherent content that she would want in any of her important business documents.

Delaney remarks: "The brief report you e-mail to your immediate supervisor may get printed, distributed to high-level executives, and discussed around a conference table. You don't want the most important people in the company puzzling over a casual, sloppy, contextless report with your name on it."

▲ *3. Log Book*

At the beginning of the calendar year, Telemax gives each technical and managerial employee an attractive log book with the Telemax trademark, the employee's name, and the year printed in gold on the cover. Employees use the log book to keep notes on daily activities and to keep track of scheduled meetings and deadlines.

During meetings, employees take notes in their log books. After a meeting, it is common for an employee to sit in private for a few minutes to record further notes and impressions on what occurred in the meeting, and perhaps some ideas for action or a list of things to do.

Employees usually consult their log books the first thing in the morning to take note of scheduled meetings. They also examine them just before leaving the office at the end of the day to get a look at tomorrow's schedule and to determine if they need to bring any work home with them.

ASSIGNMENTS FOR 2.4

1. *Write A Memo* Demonstrate your command of memo format by writing a two-paragraph memo to your instructor discussing (a) your concerns about the Big Project you are engaged in; or (b) your work experience,

especially in regard to writing on the job and use of computers; or (c) any other subject your instructor indicates.

2. *Create A File System* As a student taking a technical writing course, follow the Telemax rule about keeping copies of all communications. Create a small file cabinet (a cardboard box will do) with folders containing hard copies of every planning document (outlines, notes from group meetings), every draft and final copy of assignments, and every message you send and receive. Your instructor may wish to examine your files at various times during the semester.

3. *Tips and Tricks* Explore the e-mail system at your school. Bring to class a tip or trick that not everyone knows and be prepared to share it with your classmates. Write down your tip or trick so that you can turn it in to your instructor.

4. *Message Clean-Up* Tired at the end of a long day, you wrote the following sloppy, error-ridden, rambling, contextless e-mail message to your boss, Belinda Rios. Fortunately, you had the presence of mind to read it over and see the need for improving the text before sending it. Write a revision, using your imagination to fill in missing information needed to make the message explicit.

   Well, BR, I don't know if you'll get this before you leave the office today, in which case youl'l get it tomorrow. I can't work with Rumford on the newsletter thing, he doesn't understand the idea we talked about and teh need for standardizing the format. Thats waht comes of working with a marketing type instead of a texh writer. Not that Rummy is not good at his job, this just isn't his line of work. I'll think of someone. If you have any ideas on that, of courrse. Well, the clock's at 5:15 and my spouse is awaiting. Gotta go. Tommorrow!

5. *Keep A Log Book* This semester, keep a log book yourself. Buy one at a store or create one of your own design (you can just staple together some blank pages and write dates at the top of each page). Your instructor may ask you to turn in your log book occasionally, or to report to the class on the kinds of entries you have been making.

2.5 >—— Ethical Concerns for Technical Writers

Numerous types of ethical problems arise in a business or organizational context, but their roots are similar. As Carolyn Rude (1994) puts it:

> Problems in . . . ethics arise because the right, good, and fair often conflict with personal advantage—profit, advancement, convenience, or expediency. (p. 171)

Rude goes on to make a key point about ethics in the work environment:

> The best motive for ethical conduct is . . . the commitment one makes as a professional person to the well-being of the profession and its members as well as to people who are affected by the actions of the profession. (p. 171)

This section looks at several important issues in the ethics of technical writing and how they arise out of the organizational context.

▲ 1. Professional Codes of Ethics

Almost every profession has at least one professional organization, and many of those organizations develop and publish their own code of ethics. The Society for Technical Communication (STC) has a code of ethics for technical writers (Box 2.2). The Documentation Department at Pittsburgh Telemax has adopted this document as its ethical guide.

Note that the ethical code for the STC reflects Rude's emphasis on commitment to the well-being of the profession and those the profession serves.

▲ 2. Misleading Puffery

For technical writers, ethical problems sometimes arise when they are working on marketing materials. Pittsburgh Telemax's Sales and Marketing Department subscribes to the Better Business Bureau's "Basic Principles" for ethics in advertising (available at the BBB's Web site: **www.bbb.org**). However, commitment to principles is only the first step to ethical behavior. The application of such principles can be problematic.

The designers and writers of advertisements, sales letters, and brochures are under strong pressure to make money for the company. To achieve that goal, marketing personnel employ a standard practice in advertising called "puffery." Puffery claims include the following:

▌ superlative statements of pride in the company or its products and services ("50 years of excellence")

▌ positive statements about the subjective qualities of a product ("makes your skin feel like silk")

▌ hyperbole; exaggerations understood as such ("to die for").

Puffery, per se, is not unethical or illegal. However, the BBB code objects to puffery claims when they "tend to mislead." This can be a gray area. As a technical writer, you may find yourself in conflict with

BOX 2.2 ▼ **The STC Ethical Principles for Technical Communicators**

As technical communicators, we observe the following ethical principles in our professional activities.

Legality

We observe the laws and regulations governing our profession. We meet the terms of contracts we undertake. We ensure that all terms are consistent with laws and regulations locally and globally, as applicable, and with STC ethical principles.

Honesty

We seek to promote the public good in our activities. To the best of our ability, we provide truthful and accurate communications. We also dedicate ourselves to conciseness, clarity, coherence, and creativity, striving to meet the needs of those who use our products and services. We alert our clients and employers when we believe that material is ambiguous. Before using another person's work, we obtain permission. We attribute authorship of material and ideas only to those who make an original and substantive contribution. We do not perform work outside our job scope during hours compensated by clients or employers, except with their permission; nor do we use their facilities, equipment, or supplies without their approval. When we advertise our services, we do so truthfully.

Confidentiality

We respect the confidentiality of our clients, employers, and professional organizations. We disclose business-sensitive information only with their consent or when legally required to do so. We obtain releases from clients and employers before including any business-sensitive materials in our portfolios or commercial demonstrations or before using such materials for another client or employer.

Quality

We endeavor to produce excellence in our communication products. We negotiate realistic agreements with clients and employers on schedules, budgets, and deliverables during project planning. Then we strive to fulfill our obligations in a timely, responsible manner.

Fairness

We respect cultural variety and other aspects of diversity in our clients, employers, development teams, and audiences. We serve the business interests of our clients and employers as long as they are consistent with the public good. Whenever possible, we avoid conflicts of interest in fulfilling our professional responsibilities and activities. If we discern a conflict of interest, we disclose it to those concerned and obtain their approval before proceeding.

Professionalism

We evaluate communication products and services constructively and tactfully, and seek definitive assessments of our own professional performance. We advance technical communication through our integrity and excellence in performing each task we undertake. Additionally, we assist other persons in our profession through mentoring, networking, and instruction. We also pursue professional self-improvement, especially through courses and conferences.

Source: Reprinted with permission from *Technical Communication,* the Journal of the Society for Technical Communication, Arlington, VA.

Note: Adopted by the STC Board of Directors September 1998.

marketing personnel over whether or not a particular statement or illustration is misleading. A familiar example is the photograph on the cover of a cookbook that subtly suggests you will be able to create that beautiful dish—if only you buy the book. Is that legitimate or misleading puffery? Answers to questions like this can depend on whether you are using a "Reasonable Person" standard or an "Ignorant Person" standard (Clement, 1987). In other words, are you writing for the average reader or the least knowledgeable reader?

▲ 3. Misleading Statements of Fact

Even accurate statements of fact can be misleading if they are expressed in vague or ponderous language—language perhaps deliberately designed to hide unpleasant truths. Notice in Box 2.2 that the STC includes "clarity" as a factor in "truthful and accurate communications."

J. E. Porter (1987, p. 187) provides an example of ponderous prose that hides a clause in an insurance policy. The policy is advertised as offering "one million dollar lifetime protection"; however, it turns out that *lifetime* does not mean that the insurance will be in place for the lifetime of the customer but that the insurance will be in place for the lifetime of the policy, which the company can cancel at any time. Here is how the procedure for annual renewal of the insurance policy is explained in the company's literature:

> This Certificate [the policy] is effective as of the date shown on the Identification Card and is renewable automatically, according to the mode of payment designated, by the payment of fees by or for the Member [the customer] and the acceptance thereof by The Corporation [the insurance company] subject to such membership fees and coverage provisions in effect on the date of any such renewal.

Using similar words, Porter revises the passage to make it clear and ethical:

> This Certificate is effective as of the date shown on the Identification Card. It is renewable automatically (according to the mode of payment designated) *only under the following conditions:*
>
> 1. the payment of fees by or for the Member; and
> 2. the acceptance of those fees by The Corporation. The Corporation reserves the right to refuse acceptance, or to cancel membership, by giving written notice thirty (30) days prior to the Annual Renewal Date.

▲ *4. Time Pressures*

Technical writers are sometimes under great time pressure to get their work done (Clement, 1987; Lanyi, 1994). That pressure can lead to unethical expediencies, such as

- assuming that a set of steps will produce the desired result
- borrowing sections from other company documents without checking the fit
- leaving out useful information
- rushing or skipping editing or proofreading.

Behaviors such as those in the above list, which betray the writer's obligation to the reader, are unethical.

▲ *5. Cultural Sensitivity*

Technical writers must be sensitive to "cultural variety" within their readership, as the STC code points out. This means avoiding expressions or statements that may be perceived as insulting to various groups (for a thorough discussion, see Murdick, 1999, pp. 62–82). It is best to avoid unnecessary references to race, ethnicity, religion, age, or gender (almost all such references are unnecessary), as well as assumptions about the characteristics of groups (for example, that Asians are good at math, that women are sensitive, that men are physically strong).

Writers involved in international communications should, of course, study cultural differences. But even in this domain, writers need be cautious about the generalizations that arise in cultural profiles. It may be true that business executives from a particular country prefer a handshake to a contract, but an individual executive from that country may not. In terms of writing, cultural information may be more useful for telling a writer what to avoid than what to do. For example, a document that uses an image of the palm side of a hand to indicate "stop" will inadvertently insult a large group of readers in the Eastern Mediterranean region, for whom that gesture is obscene.

See Axtel (1993) and Murdick (1999) for discussions of international communications.

▲ *6. Gender-Exclusionary Language*

Not too long ago, it was the universal habit of writers of English to use masculine pronouns to refer to groups of mixed gender:

1) When criticism comes from above, a good manager will take the blame for his subordinate.

But nowadays a sentence like the one above is inappropriate because it seems to assume that managers are always male. Since English doesn't have a gender-neutral singular pronoun to refer to people, a number of solutions have been devised to address this problem. Usually the best solution is to pluralize the noun so that a plural, gender-neutral pronoun—_they, them,_ or _their_—can be used in place of _he, him,_ or _his._ This approach also eliminates the need for the awkward _he or she, him or her,_ and _his or her._ Here is sentence (1) revised to avoid gender-exclusionary language:

> 2) When criticism comes from above, good managers will take the blame for their subordinates.

Another effective method is to replace pronouns with articles or nouns:

> 3) When criticism comes from above, a good manager will take the blame for a subordinate, even if the subordinate acted without authority.

Certain familiar nouns, because they contain the German root for person (_man_), also seem to exclude females: _chairman, foreman._ Replace them with synonyms: _chair, supervisor._ It is not possible to ignore all words that contain the German root _man._ We can't get rid of _woman,_ for instance. Restrict your concern to situations in which exclusion has been a problem.

Don't concern yourself with words based on the Latin root _man_ meaning "hand": _manicure, manual, manifest, manipulation._

ASSIGNMENTS FOR 2.5

1. _A Code of Ethics_ Write a code of ethics for students taking a technical writing course.

2. _Advertisement_ (a) Find an advertisement and evaluate its puffery and statements of fact for ethical legitimacy. Be prepared to discuss your findings in class. (b) Rewrite the ad, making it scrupulously honest.

3. _Policy_ Find an insurance policy, apartment rental contract, or some other official document, and analyze it for clarity and honesty. (Office supply stores sell standard forms; alternatively, your instructor may have left some on reserve in your school library.) Be prepared to discuss your findings in class. Revise some of the sections in the document to make them clearer to an "Ignorant Person."

2.6 >——— Legal Concerns for Technical Writers

As in the case of ethics, legal concerns for technical writers vary considerably, according to the kinds of products and services that are being documented and according to the kinds of work that technical writers are assigned within an organization or take on as independent contractors. We will look at two broad areas that are relevant to many situations: respect for intellectual property rights and responsibility for product safety.

▲ 1. Respecting Intellectual Property Rights

Technical writers must be careful to respect the legal intellectual property rights of others as those rights apply to copyright, trademarks, trade secrets, and software ownership. Technical writers should know the basics of copyright law in order to protect their own and their organization's rights and to avoid violating the rights of others. The *Chicago Manual of Style* (1993) offers the beginning technical writer a usable, complete summary of copyright law. D. R. Johnson (1999) provides a brief but practical summary of what is protected, along with a set of Web sites for specific issues. Of particular interest are the 1998 Internet guidelines signed into law by President Clinton (**law.copyright.gov/325.htm**).

Copyright Protection Copyright refers to ownership of "the original expression contained in a work" (*Chicago Manual of Style,* 1993, p. 126). *Original,* however, is a very broad term here, and may include something as mundane as the ordering in a presentation of public domain information. The law differs for works published before and after 1977. Most relevant to technical writing is the fact that copyright law protects works created after 1977, even in manuscript form, for fifty years after the death of the author. Registration of such works with the Copyright Office "offers legal advantages (evidence and awards) in case of an infringement" (Rude, 1994, p. 173), but it is not mandatory. Any work created by anyone—even a student's essay—automatically has copyright protection, whether published or not. No copyright notice has been required since March 1, 1989.

Fair Use The vague notion of "fair use" governs whether you can quote (or paraphrase; no distinction is made in the law) a passage or set of passages without obtaining permission from the copyright holder. The purpose to which you put your text would be taken into consideration in any legal proceeding. Those copying text for nonprofit educational purposes are given more leeway than those creating a text to be sold or used in a commercial enterprise, such as computer documentation distributed with a product.

Permission is required for whole works. Otherwise, in regard to parts of a work, the proportion of the text being reproduced is relevant. Publishers sometimes use the "500 words" rule of thumb for the maximum size of quotations usable without permission, but actually it is more a matter of the relative size of the reproduced section to the whole, as the *Chicago Manual of Style* (1993) points out: "to quote five hundred words from an essay of five thousand is likely to be more serious than from a work of fifty thousand" (p. 146).

Also important is the effect of the reproduction on the original work. If you steal the heart out of a work, and thereby make it less valuable in the marketplace, you may be violating the copyright holder's rights.

In all cases, writers must give credit to texts that they quote or paraphrase from, usually through a system of formal documentation.

Works Made for Hire When someone hires someone else to write something, the texts are called "works made for hire" and the employer is the "author" in legal terms and owns the texts. Pittsburgh Telemax holds the copyright for all the writings done by the Documentation Department, as well as for any work done by independent consultants.

Trademarks Trademarks include names, titles, slogans, and logos. They are protected by law after they have been registered with the U.S. Patent and Trademark Office (PTO). The applicant must demonstrate that the trademark meets a standard of originality. When writers use someone's trademark-protected words or symbols, they should capitalize them: "thin as Kleenex." Companies can alert readers that something is a trademark by putting the trademark symbol® after it, meaning PTO registered, or ™, meaning that the company is claiming trademark status, prior to or without PTO registration.

Trade Secrets Technical writers, like other employees, are responsible for protecting the trade secrets of the organizations they work for. Trade secrets are protected by law only "if the owner takes necessary steps to preserve the secrecy" (Rude, 1994, p. 175). When changing jobs, you may be breaking the law if you divulge information about your former employer's products, especially if you have signed a nondisclosure agreement with the original employer. Telemax requires all employees to sign such an agreement upon being hired.

Software Finally, technical writers must never use pirated versions of software. In doing so, they would put their company at risk of a costly lawsuit. Writers should also be cautious when using clip art. Some clip art is sold or distributed for personal, nonprofit use only.

▲ *2. Maintaining Product Safety*

Technical writers have a clear duty to help maintain product safety. A company may be liable for damages if its product is defective. Here is a definition of *defective* from legal experts Marilyn Bedford and F. Cole Stearns:

> A product is legally defective if it has any of the following:
> • a manufacturing defect
> • a design defect
> • inadequate warnings
> • inadequate instructions. (1987, p. 127)

Note that the technical writer plays a key role in the last two bulleted criteria. Both adequate warnings and clear instructions are necessary for product safety. Bedford and Stearns comment:

> Warnings and instructions are often the most neglected aspect of a product, yet legally the most risky in terms of potential liability. An unsophisticated jury relates to signs and instructions, or the lack thereof, with more ease than to principles involving the manufacture or design of products. (p. 128)

Technical writers themselves are not likely to be sued, but they can play a role in protecting their company in two ways:

❚ by properly incorporating warnings into their texts

❚ by writing clear instructions.

Companies are responsible for safety during both proper uses of their products and improper uses that could be anticipated. These include misuses by people other than intended users. A device that could cause an electric shock, if situated on a table close to where people pass by who do not use the device, should display a warning to those passing by.

The American National Standard Institute (ANSI), an organization made up of representatives from a range of industries, has established a set of standard policies and signs for warnings. (See their Web pages on warnings: **www.hazcomsys.com/domes.html.**) Within the ANSI system, warnings should always have at least these four components:

❚ an alert symbol, typically an exclamation mark within a triangle, indicating that a cautionary message follows (so that the reader does not skip this section)

▌ a signal word, such as DANGER or CAUTION

▌ a pictograph (a picture showing the danger or how to avoid it)

▌ a color code.

The ANSI system delineates five levels of warning:

▌ DANGER means that you *will* be harmed or harm others if you don't avoid the hazard.

▌ WARNING means that you *could* be harmed or harm others if you don't avoid the hazard.

▌ CAUTION means that you may suffer or cause minor injury if you don't avoid the hazard.

▌ NOTICE means that you may harm the product if you act improperly.

▌ IMPORTANT means that you may damage your own work, or lose efficiency, if you don't follow the advice in the message.

The pictograph may consist of a unique image suitable for the situation, such as an image of a coiled snake on a trail sign alerting hikers to watch out for poisonous vipers. Or it may consist of a standard image such as flames for fire, skull and crossbones for poison, or a lightening bolt for electrical shock.

Color codes exist for the three highest-level warnings:

▌ DANGER—Black on a red background

▌ WARNING—Black on an orange background

▌ CAUTION—Black on a yellow background.

Warnings should be placed close to the danger area, or just before the instructional step in which the danger arises. They should be prominent. In texts, the alert symbol and the signal word usually appear in the margin.

The content of the message should explain:

▌ the nature of the danger

▌ the consequences of not avoiding it

▌ the steps necessary to avoid it.

Instructions that contain warnings should be written for the least knowledgeable, least proficient user. As David Clement (1987) puts it: "Write with the knowledge that if it is possible to screw up, at least a few people will do so" (p. 152).

For more on ANSI standards, see Kemnitz (1991); for more on effective warnings, see Parsons, Seminara, and Wogalter (1999).

ASSIGNMENTS FOR 2.6

1. *Copyright* Study copyright law as it pertains to reproducing handouts for classes like your technical writing class. Write an informal report to your instructor and classmates summarizing their rights and responsibilities in distributing copies of copyrighted materials.

2. *Study Warnings* (a) Study warning signs that show up on your campus. Write an informal report on their effectiveness, using the guidelines in section 2.6. (b) Do (a), but apply it to warnings in instructional writings found on your campus.

3. *Write Warnings* (a) Following the guidelines in section 2.6, create a warning sign for a dangerous device (either a sign for a wall or a plate to be attached to the device itself). (b) In a paragraph of text, describe the operation of a dangerous device, including placement of a warning message at an appropriate location.

2.7 >—— A Theory of Quality

Many ethical and legal problems can be avoided if a company commits itself to high quality in its products and services. Indeed, there has been a worldwide movement within corporations toward formalizing such goals, as seen in the approaches known as Total Quality Management (TQM) and International Standards Organization (ISO) 9000. In that spirit, the *Telemax Style Guide* includes a section describing the company's theory of quality. The quality section serves as a formal statement of goals for both product development and documentation. We quote here from the *Style Guide*:

Characteristics of High-Quality Products

From the company's perspective, a high-quality product

▮ meets the planned specifications

▮ shows no errors or defects

▮ has an attractive appearance.

From the customer's perspective, a high-quality product

▮ is acquired at a reasonable price

▮ contains the requested features and performs the required tasks

▮ is easily learned

▮ performs smoothly and quickly

▮ performs reliably, without breakdowns or hang-ups

▮ performs safely

▮ has an adequate product life. In other words, it doesn't quickly deteriorate; it's expandable; and it undergoes regular updates or new versions to keep it from becoming outdated.

Characteristics of High-Quality Documentation

From the company's perspective, high-quality documentation has

▮ reliability (it's accurate)

▮ portability (it uses standard company formats and language; sections can be transferred to other manuals under development)

▮ modularity (one section can be updated without necessitating changes in other sections)

▮ maintainability (it's easily changed to reflect product updates)

▮ functionality (customers are satisfied, so there are few calls to Technical Support).

From the customer's perspective, high-quality documentation

▮ stores easily and lies flat when in use

▮ includes an appropriate set of texts, such as guides for installation, maintenance, repair, start-up, full reference, and quick reference

▮ has an effective table of contents and index

▮ includes all necessary information and no unnecessary text to wade through

▮ explains clearly

▮ includes adequate warnings.

To examine another company's theory of quality, consult Table 2.1, which presents a list of characteristics of good documentation developed by the technical editors at IBM's Santa Teresa Laboratory.

ASSIGNMENTS FOR 2.7 ———————————

1. *TQM/ISO 9000* Using the Web or your school's library, find out about TQM or ISO 9000 international standards and make a report, oral or written, to your class on the role of writing in these programs to advance quality.

2. *A Theory of Quality for a Fictional Company* Create a theory of quality for your own fictional company. Your theory should make sense in terms of your company's products and services.

TABLE 2.1 ▼ Santa Teresa Laboratory's Theory of Quality

What is quality technical information?

Based on comments from users and experience in writing and editing technical information, we have found that quality technical information has these characteristics:

Accuracy	Freedom from mistakes or errors; adherence to fact or truth
Clarity	Freedom from ambiguity of obscurity
Completeness	The inclusion of all necessary parts—and only those parts
Concreteness	Freedom from abstraction; the inclusion of appropriate examples, scenarios, similes, and analogies
Organization	A coherent arrangement of parts that makes sense to the user
Retrievability	Presentation of information in a way that enables users to find specific items quickly and easily
Style	Correctness and appropriateness of writing conventions and choices in words and phrases
Task orientation	A focus on helping users complete the tasks associated with a product in relation to their jobs
Visual effectiveness	Attractiveness and enhanced meaning of information through use of layout, illustrations, color, type, icons, and other graphic devices

Source: From *Developing Quality Technical Information* by Gretchen Hargis. Reprinted with permission of Prentice-Hall, Inc.

3. *Use a Theory of Quality for Planning* Consider how the Telemax or the IBM theory of quality could be used in your planning process for your Big Project (see the twenty-six ideas for extensive writing assignments in section 1.3 near the beginning of this book). For example, how can you be sure that your documentation will have "reliability"? Write a statement to your instructor indicating how you will apply a theory of quality to the development of your Big Project or some other text.

Collaborative Writing

Technical writers approach their work differently from someone writing an essay or a business letter. For one thing, most technical writing is a collaborative effort. This chapter provides an overview of a collaborative writing process for large writing projects. It then shows how a technical writer, working semi-independently, might go about writing a brief set of instructions.

3.1 >—— A Writing Process for Long Documents

Frapp encourages Wendy to take home a copy of the *Telemax Style Guide* and asks her to read, as soon as possible, the section covering the process by which documentation is developed at Telemax. Frapp tells her, "Technical writers generally work as part of a team. This section will give you a general sense of your role in that team effort."

Here is the excerpt that Wendy will read:

THE DOCUMENT DEVELOPMENT CYCLE

This section describes the process Telemax uses in developing documentation for a product in its general product line—that is, one that will be sold to many customers. Telemax also creates products for specific customers in response to requests for proposals (RFPs). That process begins differently from the one described below. Our RFP process is described in a later section on business documents. —L.F.

A Product Is Born

1. *Department managers identify a market niche related to the company's general product line.* Ideas come from varied sources: journals, trade magazines, conversations with customers, trade shows, Web searches, shop talk at weekend parties, personal frustration with a product.

2. *Managers conduct a preliminary feasibility study.* One or two business managers consider the general demand for the new product, the approximate costs of development and production, and the potential profit margins.

3. *Managers conduct a formal feasibility study.* If the results of the preliminary study look good, a small team of managers will develop a formal feasibility study. A number of departments contribute: The marketing department ana-

lyzes potential demand for the product, software and electrical engineers predict development time and the number and types of components that will have to be developed or purchased, and the purchasing department estimates the cost of components that need to be purchased. Then, on the basis of information gathered, the managers consider the company's ability to design, produce, and market the product. They also consider the degree to which any of the development tasks must be outsourced and whether it would be feasible to form a partnership with another company to develop the product. Finally, they summarize the potential benefits and risks of going forward with the project.

4. *The feasibility study is presented to a meeting of department managers.* The president may also attend this meeting, mainly as an observer. The managers debate the merits of the proposal, and they determine whether the feasibility study is complete or needs more work. If they decide to go forward with the project, the Product Development Department manager appoints a project manager (the team leader who will supervise the work of the product development team) and schedules a kick-off meeting.

Assignments Are Made

5. *A project kick-off meeting is held.* In a company like Pittsburgh Telemax, the product usually involves both software and electronic components, so managers from both the Software Engineering and Electrical Engineering Departments attend. The Documentation Department manager (at this time, Marge Mendoza) also attends. At this meeting, the senior Product Development Department manager describes the product and its components. The group then assembles a development team. They assign individual engineers on the basis of experience and availability, and they determine who among themselves will function as the project manager. At this point, the Documentation Department manager notes who is assigned to each product component. She also assigns a technical writer to the project team.

6. *The project manager assigns engineering tasks and develops a Gantt chart (a kind of flow chart used for task management).*

7. *The Documentation Department manager (hereafter, DDM) writes a formal memo to the appropriate technical writers about the nature of each engineering task, naming the engineer assigned to each task.* The technical writer, or writers, assigned to the project will learn the details about the product by interviewing the appropriate engineers. In fact, the writers may spend as much time gathering information as they do writing.

8. *The DDM adds the new documentation project to the document database.* The document database includes critical information about each document, such as the title, principal author, part numbers, format, and soft-copy location on the computer system.

9. *The DDM appoints a technical writer to be the primary author for the documentation.* This person will also be a part of the production team. If the project is fairly small, this person may be the only writer. If the project is extensive, the whole technical writing staff, including the DDM, might participate.

The Documentation Is Planned

10. *The DDM schedules a documentation kick-off meeting.* The DDM invites the project manager and the technical writer assigned to the project. The project manager may bring along a number of engineers as well, if their input would be helpful. The DDM may also invite the Engineering Services Department manager if government tests and approvals are required.

11. *At the documentation kick-off meeting, the participants determine the overall documentation requirements.* The number and nature of the product's components, as well as their relationship with one another, largely determine what types of documents and how many documents must be developed. The number of audiences also affects the number of documents. (There may be a need for a separate user guide, installation guide, and technical reference manual.) The Engineering Services Department manager points out any documentation features that must be present to meet government testing requirements or regulations. For example, if the product is to be sold overseas, it must include power cords that conform to the local power-supply sockets. The documentation must state that a different power cord cannot be substituted. Or if the product contains a potentially dangerous electronic device, such as a transformer or a large capacitor, the documentation must warn the user not to open the outer case.

12. *The DDM meets with the marketing manager.* At this meeting, the physical format for the documentation is determined. This includes page size, binding method, and boxing method.

13. *The DDM and the assigned technical writer develop preliminary document outlines based on a rhetorical analysis of the likely users and on what is known about the products so far.* After working together at one or more meetings on the outlines, the technical writer makes hard copies of the outlines and submits them to the DDM for review. If they look weak to the DDM, she asks the technical writer to continue working on them. Otherwise, she attaches sign-off sheets, marks each copy as the first draft, and distributes copies to the project manager and the marketing manager. These recipients mark up the outlines, initial the sign-off sheets, and return the outlines to the DDM.

14. *The DDM meets with the project manager and the marketing manager to resolve conflicting comments.*

15. *The assigned technical writer revises the document outlines on the basis of the consensus reached in step 14.*

16. *The DDM reviews and redistributes the revised outlines.* She directs the technical writer to make the necessary changes. When the outlines satisfy her, she submits them to the project manager and the marketing manager for another review. If further revisions are required, the outlines are recycled until everyone is satisfied. Planning is very important in large projects, and the initial outlines must constitute a close prediction of what the final copy will contain.

The Documentation Layout Is Designed

17. *The DDM creates the required computer files for the documentation project based on standard templates.* The templates are selected from existing company

page-layout and book-design formats, thus ensuring a continuation of the "company style" in documentation. The DDM duplicates these formats into a set of files for the new documentation.

18. *If part numbers are required, the DDM meets with the Engineering Services Department manager to determine the part numbers.* The DDM enters any part numbers into the company's inventory system and the document database.

The Writing Begins

19. *The DDM develops Gantt charts to schedule the writing part of the project.*

20. *The DDM meets with the project manager to set up meetings between engineers and the technical writer.* The technical writer begins interviewing engineers, who by this time may be well along on the project. At this stage, the writer begins to offer ideas that affect the shape of the computer interface. For the customer, *the interface is the product,* and the Documentation Department at Telemax wants that interface to be user friendly. As technical writer Alice Landy has put it, "[T]he writer who spends an hour convincing an engineer to change a feature, improve a menu, or clarify an error message, has done more toward earning that day's pay than the writer who spends four hours grimly documenting the poor design" (1994, p. 162).

21. *On the basis of outlines and interviews, the writer develops first drafts of the documentation content.*

The Document Cycling Process Begins

22. *The writer submits the first drafts to the DDM.* The DDM who updates the document database as required, attaches a document sign-off form [Box 3.1], and distributes the first drafts to the appropriate engineers for review.

23. *The engineers review the first drafts, mark up the copy with informative criticisms and corrections, initial the attached sign-off sheets, and promptly return the drafts to the DDM.* At least that is what is supposed to happen. In the imperfect world of the professional workplace, not all activities run smoothly or on time. Engineers are busy and have their own priorities. Often the DDM must tactfully goad engineers to return drafts, and the engineers' marginal comments may be sparse, perfunctory, or cryptic.

24. *The DDM files the sign-off sheets and returns the marked-up first drafts to the technical writer.* The DDM updates the document database as required, a continual process. All drafts of all documents are stored in the electronic database, and hard copies are stored in file folders.

25. *The technical writer makes the required revisions to develop the second drafts.*

26. *Upon receiving the second drafts, the DDM attaches second-draft sign-off sheets and redistributes the documents to the engineers for review.*

27. *The engineers review the second drafts, mark them up, initial the second-draft sign-off sheets, and return them to the DDM.* The document cycling continues through as many drafts as required, until everyone is satisfied.

BOX 3.1 ▼   Document Sign-Off Form

Please review the attached document for completeness, accuracy, and clarity. Mark any comments or corrections directly in the document using red or blue ink, and <u>bookmark the altered pages with a post-it note extending outside the page to the right.</u>

After you have finished reviewing the document, enter your initials and the date in the appropriate blocks to the right of your name. *Accept* means the document is acceptable without any revisions. *Accept with revisions* means the document is acceptable if your comments are incorporated into it. *Further review required* means that your comments must be included and you must review the document again before approving it.

After you review the document, return it to the Documentation Department manager. The document will be revised as required. If you accepted the document, it will be forwarded to the next reviewer. If you indicated that further review is required, the document will be returned to you.

The attached document should be approved in the following sequence: engineers, project manager, proofreader, Documentation Department manager, Engineering Services manager, and Division manager. The engineers have primary responsibility for verifying the technical accuracy of the document.

The review process must be completed by: _____

Title:			
Principal author:			
Document author:			

	Accept	Accept with revisions	Further review required
Engineer:			
Engineer:			
Project manager:			
Proofreader:			
Proofreader:			
Documentation Department manager:			
Engineering Services manager:			
Division manager:			

Charge number: _____

Final Copies Are Prepared

28. *After the engineers are satisfied with the documentation, the technical writer develops manuscript copies and computer files of the final drafts and submits them to the DDM.*

29. *The DDM attaches the document sign-off sheets to manuscript versions of the final copies and submits them for approval to the project manager, the Engineering Services Department manager, and the marketing manager.* The DDM initials the sign-off sheet when the review process has been completed and all required approvals have been acquired.

The Documentation Is Tested

30. *Members of the Documentation Department, usually with the help of personnel in the Sales and Marketing Department, conduct a usability test.* They recruit individuals to try out the documentation under close observation.

31. *The technical writer revises the documentation on the basis of the usability test results.*

32. *Another technical writer, possibly Mendoza, and a member of the Sales and Marketing Department edit and proofread the final manuscript, making necessary corrections.*

The Documentation Is Printed

33. *The DDM produces the print files that are required for production.*

34. *The DDM meets with the project manager, the Sales and Marketing Department manager, and the Purchasing Department manager to determine how many final copies should be printed.*

35. *The Purchasing Department manager writes an RFP to get bids from vendors for reproduction.* The manager then selects a vendor, applies for a purchase order number, and supplies the print files to the selected vendor.

36. *Upon receipt of the printed copies of the documentation, the DDM meets with the Engineering Services Department manager and the Purchasing Department manager to update the company's inventory system.*

Maintenance Is Ensured

37. *The DDM selects a technical writer—usually, but not always, the primary author—to maintain the document files.* This person will be responsible for updating the documentation with every new version of the product. (Sometimes a new employee will be assigned to an updating job as a means of orienting the employee to writing formats and company products.)

Marketing Begins

38. *The assigned technical writer meets with the marketing manager to begin work on sales literature and, if appropriate, the development of computer presentation text and visuals.* The technical writer may travel with a salesperson to help make presentations and to explain the product.

Quality Is Addressed

39. *The DDM, the assigned technical writer, and members of the Sales and Marketing Department who participated in the usability testing meet to analyze and assess the process they just went through.* They look for ways to improve the documentation development process.

ASSIGNMENT FOR 3.1

1. *Collaborative Project Description*   Collaborative efforts usually involve a division of labor, with different individuals working concurrently on different aspects of the project. They also usually include meetings to share data or to evaluate progress. Although some jobs are done concurrently, some have to be completed before others are begun. Later in this book you will learn how to plan concurrent activities using management tools such as Gantt charts. For now, however, describe in a set of numbered statements a group project in which you have participated. Make clear what your role was in the process, and what you were doing while others were working on their part of the project. Examples: (a) a group oral report for a class; (b) a piece of collaborative writing you contributed to; (c) a volunteer project, such a cleaning up a public park; (d) a sports activity, such as an organized softball practice.

3.2 >—— The Document Database

The steps in the above-mentioned documentation development cycle refer several times to the document database, which the DDM develops during the course of the project and which a technical writer will maintain as a routine assignment. A computerized database is simply an organized collection of information; it can include both text and numerical data, as well as formulas to manipulate numerical entries. Databases put different information into different tables and then, within each table, into different slots, called "fields," so that specific pieces of information can be displayed on command by calling up the fields. At Pittsburgh Telemax, the database for a documentation project would include at least two tables, one for word processing documents and one for graphics files. Box 3.2 shows the fields that Telemax uses for these two kinds of files.

Telemax employees are able to use standard relational database operations to analyze the state of technical documentation. For example, they are able to determine the release dates for all documents pertaining to a particular project. Or they can filter out for display all documents written by a particular person that were released before a particular date.

BOX 3.2 ▼ Document Database Fields

The explanations in parenthesis do not appear in the real files.

Word Processing Files
Document title:
Version number:
Draft number (if not a final document):
Release date (if published):
Primary author:
Subject-matter experts (engineers who reviewed the document):
Location (full path):
Primary product dependency (the primary product described in the document):
Secondary product dependencies (other products mentioned in the document):
BOM number (Bill of Materials or part number):
Distribution (general, limited, internal):
Miscellaneous (a memo field for additional information):

Graphics Files
Program (Corel Draw, Adobe Illustrator):
Vector graphic (yes/no):
Bitmap format (BMP, GIF, JPL):
Location:
Primary product dependency:
Secondary product dependency:
Miscellaneous:

ASSIGNMENT FOR 3.2

1. *Design Document Database* Design a document database for the assignments in your technical writing course. For example, you might begin by classifying documents into three folders: homework, drafts, and final copies. If you have access to database software, use it to create your files. Otherwise, use your word processing program. Maintain a developing record of your work throughout the course. Your instructor may ask you to submit this record at the end of the term.

3.3 ❯—— An Object-Oriented Writing Process

Telemax uses an object-oriented writing process. "Objects" are pieces of text that are likely to be reused, with appropriate modification for the new context. They are stored on a computer disk in an "object library."

Objects may be visuals or passages of writing. The object librarian (at Telemax, that would be Mendoza) may designate whole chapters, subsections, or paragraphs as objects. Even an important, complicated sentence might be stored as an object in the object library.

When technical writers use an object-oriented writing process, they partially write the new text and partly assemble it from objects taken from the library. The key to providing access to objects is to store them in a hierarchical arrangement of files understandable to everyone using the library. For example, Mendoza has stored persuasive arguments about the quality of Telemax's products under the descending file names **PERSUASIVE / Products / quality**, so that one would find such objects by opening the **PERSUASIVE** folder, then within that the **Products** folder, and then within that the **quality** folder, where one would find a set of file names for specific objects (particular passages presenting specific arguments).

Compared to texts created from scratch, object-oriented texts are quicker to write, they contain fewer factual and proofreading errors, and they exhibit more polished phrasing.

ASSIGNMENT FOR 3.3

1. *Create An Object* Create a passage of writing that could be added to an object library (a) for your fictional company, or (b) for a Big Project you have begun for this course. When submitting this text object to your instructor, indicate at the top of the page a file path that shows how the object fits into a hierarchical library file structure.

3.4 ⟩── Research

Technical writers are generally translators of information, rather than creators of new information. They take information and ideas from subject matter experts (SMEs) and convey them to those who need to use them. Their research, therefore, tends to take the form of finding out what needs to be transformed into a documentation package.

▲ 1. Routine Preparatory Research

To prepare for writing on their subject, technical writers at companies like Pittsburgh Telemax routinely undertake research activities such as:

1. Attend "design review meetings" at which engineers discuss—and debate—design elements of the product.

2. Read the "design specification document," the engineers' first outline of the product.

3. Create a rough outline for the documentation and then fill in as many parts as possible. This is done on the basis of steps 1 and 2 above, and by studying earlier documents on earlier versions of the product, if there are any.

4. Interview engineers, focusing on the parts of the outline not yet filled in.

5. Try out prototypes of the product, if possible with an engineer present to answer questions.

6. Ensure continuity in publications by seeking out other company documents and computer files to study templates.

Writers may also do an on-site needs analysis to find out what end-users don't know about the product and what they need to know to perform key tasks.

Technical writers spend a lot of time interviewing SMEs and end-users. Any time they interview someone outside their own organization, they follow a process like the one shown in Box 3.3.

▲ 2. Survey Research for Needs Analysis and Product Evaluation

Technical writers sometimes use written questionnaires to determine customer needs in regard to documentation for new products and to obtain customer evaluations of existing manuals. Here are some general guidelines for written questionnaires:

▌ Keep the questionnaire short, one or two pages.

▌ Begin with a statement explaining the purpose of the questionnaire and thanking the respondent for participating.

▌ Use the same type of question throughout, or at least vary the type of question as little as possible. (Box 3.4 violates this rule in order to illustrate the various types of questions available to you.)

▌ Use closed questions to obtain information you want to quantify. (A closed question is one that offers the respondent a set of answers to choose from.)

▌ Use open questions to get in-depth responses on complex issues. (Open questions require the respondent to invent an answer.)

▌ Avoid phrasing that is ambiguous, convoluted, or biased:

Confusing: Does this product not seem overly complex? ___Yes ___No

Revision: Rate the complexity of this product:
___Too complex   ___Complex but usable   ___Easy to use

BOX 3.3　▼　Guidelines for Interviewing

1. **Call ahead and make an appointment.**
   Never just show up. It is often a good idea to ask a supervisor at the site to select an appropriate person for you to interview. You can sometimes induce people to meet with you by taking them out to lunch.

2. **Prepare a set of questions.**
   For each area you are interested in, prepare broad open questions. These you might send ahead to the SME or customer to be interviewed. Also prepare specific follow-up questions that you may use.

3. **Dress well, show up on time, and act friendly but professional.**

4. **Begin by explaining what you hope to learn and what you will do with the information.**
   A person who understands your purposes will be more likely to provide relevant and useful statements.

5. **Ask for permission to tape record the interview.**
   You might do this at an early stage, before the interview takes place. If you can't tape record the interview, you will have to take good notes of the key points, noting the exact phrasing for quotations and for things like numerical data. Even if you do tape record the interview, take notes of important points; those notes will help you create an initial outline for your text.

6. **Let the respondent do the talking.**
   Be friendly, but don't become chatty. When a moment of silence occurs, wait to see if the respondent will fill it before asking your next question.

7. **Keep the interview on track.**
   If the respondent rambles, bring the discussion back to your interests by restating, in different words, your original (unanswered) question.

8. **Make sure you understand.**
   If you are not sure what the respondent said or meant, say so and ask for a clarification. You might restate the respondent's answer in your own words and ask if your understanding is correct.

9. **Thank the respondent, and ask whether you can call if you need anything clarified later.**

10. **Write up your report on the interview as soon as possible, while it is still fresh in your memory.**

11. **Send a thank-you note to those you interviewed.**

BOX 3.4 ▼   Types of Survey Questions

CLOSED QUESTIONS

1. You have completed four tasks following the instructions in the quick start guide. Order those instructions by quality, with 1 indicating the best set and 4 indicating the least effective:

   ____ Task 1   ____ Task 2   ____ Task 3   ____ Task 4

   > **Rank-order question**

2. You have used the reference manual to find instructions for several basic processes. Circle a number from 1 to 11 to indicate the speed with which you are able to find in the manual the instructions for completing a typical process, such as page numbering.

   > **Lickert scale**

1	2	3	4	5	6	7	8	9	10	11
very quickly					acceptable					very slowly

3. Put a check mark next to each of the tasks that you found to be well documented.

   ____ Task 1   ____ Task 2   ____ Task 3   ____ Task 4

   > **Check answers**

4. Do you believe the quick start guide you just tested is adequate for its intended purpose?

   ____ Yes   ____ No   ____ Can't tell/Comment:

   > **Yes/No Either/Or**

5. Your age: _____   Gender: _____

   Latest job title: _____

   > **Fill-in-the-blank demographic question**

OPEN QUESTION

6. Which characteristics of the documentation that you tested did you like the most, and which characteristics did you dislike the most. Why?

   > **Open question: No choice of answers; participants left to create their own answers.**

▌ Don't require feats of memory. Instead, try providing ranges to choose from.

Hard to answer: How many times did you compliment one of your staff writers last year? _____

Revision: How many times did you compliment one of your staff writers last year?

_____ Every day   _____ 2–4 times a week
_____ Once a week   _____ Once a month

▌ Leave demographic information for the end. Begin with an interesting question to draw the respondent into the survey.

Technical writers are not expected to have the expertise necessary for survey research that involves mailing questionnaires to a large population. For that kind of research, organizations usually use their marketing departments or hire outside consultants.

However, a technical writer may become involved in devising a questionnaire intended for a small population for which it would be easy to survey every member, eliminating the need for complex sampling. An example of such a population would be all the employees in a company who use a particular piece of documentation.

Box 3.5 shows a questionnaire designed for a needs analysis. This information would be used at Pittsburgh Telemax for creating a "Rhetorical Analysis Sheet," a device designed to focus the writer's attention on audience needs (see Box 4.1 in Chapter 4). Box 3.6 shows the kind of product evaluation form that Pittsburgh Telemax leaves with its customers when it installs its products.

▲ *3. Library Research*

Professional technical writers and others doing technical writing may have to conduct library research.

To take an uncomplicated example, suppose your manager returns from a professional conference talking about "minimalist documentation" or "ISO 9000 standards" or some other subject you know little about. Your manager asks you for a memo presenting your views on the matter. On your way home from work that day, you head for the nearest academic library or big-city public library to peruse journals, books, and reference books. A journal like *Technical Communication* will have articles on minimalist documentation (see section 9.6 in this book for a discussion of the minimalist approach). The library will have books on International Standards Organization (ISO) standards, an approach to business that includes extensive documenting of goals, policies, processes, and outcomes.

BOX 3.5 ▼ **Needs Analysis Questionnaire**

We will use the data from this survey to plan our user manuals. By filling in this questionnaire, you will be helping us to write better user manuals for you and others. Thank you for your time. Please send completed questionnaires to:

Pittsburgh Telemax, Suite 4, 8000 Boulevard of the Allies, Pittsburgh, PA 15219

1. Name of the product you are buying from us (include version number): _____

2. Have you used an earlier version of this product? ____ Yes   ____ No

3. How familiar are you with products of this nature?
   ____ Very familiar   ____ Some experience
   ____ Almost no experience   ____ Completely unfamiliar

4. What is your attitude toward using high-tech products in general?
   ____ Enthusiastic   ____ Interested   ____ Indifferent   ____ Worried

5. What is your attitude toward using this product?
   ____ Enthusiastic   ____ Interested   ____ Indifferent
   ____ Prefer present technology   ____ Worried

6. What is your attitude toward using manuals to learn a new product?
   ____ Very positive   ____ Positive   ____ Negative   ____ Very negative

7. What work do you do that requires use of this product? _____
   _____

8. What functions of this product will you mainly use? _____
   _____

9. What functions of this product will you occasionally use?_____
   _____

10. What is your job title?_____
   _____

E-mail additional comments to MMendoza@Pittsburghtelemax.com

3 Collaborative Writing

Using Reference Works Important reference works for technical writers (and students of technical writing) include handbooks, dictionaries, histories of technology, and books on how science and technology work. The most up-to-date of these will be shelved in the reference section of the library. C. D. Hunt's *Information Sources in Science and Technology* serves as a guide to such reference books.

The following two encyclopedias provide excellent introductions to technologies:

■ Van Nostrond's 2-volume *Scientific Encyclopedia*
■ the *McGraw-Hill Encyclopedia of Science and Technology.*

BOX 3.6 ▼ **Documentation Evaluation Questionnaire**

We wish to know how well our user manuals are serving our customers. Your partici-pation in this survey will help us supply you with the best possible documentation for future product releases. Thank you for helping us improve our service. Please mail your completed questionnaire to

Pittsburgh Telemax, Suite 4, 8000 Boulevard of the Allies, Pittsburgh, PA 15219

1. **Document Identification**   All information requested here can be found on the title page of the manual.

   Name of the manual that you are using: _____

   Release date: _____

2. **Quality Assessment**   Rate each characteristic of the manual from 1 to 5, using this scale:

   5 = Excellent   4 = Good   3 = Functional   2 = Troublesome   1 = Unacceptable

   ____ *Accessibility* Were you able to find information easily?

   ____ *Clarity* Were you able to understand the information and directions easily?

   ____ *Efficiency* Did the manual tell you only what you wanted to know and no more?

   ____ *Completeness* Did the manual supply you with all necessary information?

   ____ *Accuracy*   Were the information and directions accurate?

   ____ *Visual support* Were the visuals helpful?

3. **Discussion**   On the back of this sheet, please provide explanatory comments on any characteristic that you rated 2 or 1. Indicate how the manual could be changed for the better.

   E-mail additional comments to MMendoza@Pittsburghtelemax.com

On a more specialized level, you can find specific books of abstracts focusing on government publications or books for a particular major field: biology, chemistry, computers, electronics, energy, minerals, pollu-tion, and so forth. A reference librarian is the best source for finding the specific reference books needed for your research.

Finding General Books and Articles Finding books on a particular subject is fairly easy in the contemporary library. The electronic indexes will allow you to perform title, author, and key-word searches of the books in your school and probably also the books in nearby public libraries; in addition, they make possible such searches in *Books in Print.* To find recent publications, sometimes with reviews, search for books on any of the online book stores, such as Amazon (**www.amazon.com**) and Barnes & Noble (**www.bn.com**).

You can also search for journal articles on the library's electronic indexes. The online *Applied Science and Technology Abstracts* is particularly useful for such searches.

Once you have found one article that deals with your subject, you can search for earlier articles by looking at the bibliography at the end of the first article. You can find more recently published articles on your subject by finding articles that cite your first article. Libraries have citation indexes for this purpose.

You can also pick out several important journals that may carry articles on your subject and thumb through their tables of contents. Or you can examine a relevant "contents journal," a journal that presents the tables of contents of a large number of journals within a discipline.

Evaluating Sources It is important to evaluate carefully the source of the information you find. A report on a study that appears in an academic journal in psychology, such as the *Journal of Counseling Psychology,* will be more reliable than a report in a popular magazine like *Psychology Today.* A quick way to distinguish between a popular magazine and an academic journal is to note that a magazine can be purchased at a newsstand or bookstore whereas a journal is available for purchase only by subscription.

Students should check with their professors about what kinds of sources are permissible for their research projects. Here are four levels of periodicals, listed from the least formal and reliable to the most formal and reliable:

advocacy magazines and tracts
(*American Rifle and Pistol; Manufacturing News*)
newspapers and popular magazines
(*New York Times; Newsweek; Science Digest*)
non-refereed academic journals
(STC's *Intercom; School Board; Pennsylvania Scholar*)
refereed academic journals
(*Journal of Business and Technical Communication*).

Advocacy publications take a strong one-sided view on a subject. For example, a magazine with a name like *American Rifle and Pistol* is not the place to look for an even-handed treatment of the gun control issue. Instead, such a publication will provide, most forcefully, the arguments of those who oppose gun control. Try to imagine the standpoint of each publication you examine. Essayists who write for advocacy publications, regardless of which side they take on an issue, may draw information from "right thinking" but unreliable sources without bothering to check for accuracy.

Newspapers and popular magazines also usually have a slight bias. Even when trying to be evenhanded, writers for these publications don't always look deeply enough into subjects to get the story right. If you find an important fact in one of these sources, try to confirm it elsewhere. Consider any interpretation of facts or events suspect until you have found substantial information to confirm it or have seen alternative interpretations to compare it to.

Non-refereed journals have characteristics of both magazines and scholarly publications. They treat serious subjects, but the contents of the articles have been checked for accuracy or intelligence only by the journal's staff, who generally don't have time to do much checking. Use these journals as starting points.

Refereed journals should provide reliable information. Before an article is published in this kind of journal, it is sent out to several readers (referees) who are experts in the field and in the specific subject that the article is examining. A list of the names of these readers will appear at the beginning of the journal, before the table of contents, so by finding this list you can determine that the journal is refereed. The readers will make a recommendation to the editors as to whether the article is worthy of publication, and if so, with what revisions. In addition, the editors themselves, also chosen for their prominence and expertise, will carefully examine any article before selecting it for publication. It's hard to get anything phony or unsubstantiated past such gatekeepers.

Authors writing for refereed journals must meet a high standard in writing about their subject. They must know their subject thoroughly, and they must know how to talk about it honestly and accurately. They follow rhetorical and stylistic traditions that embody carefulness and caution in the statements made and the conclusions drawn. For example, a Florida newspaper editor, arguing that schools start too early inasmuch as teens are on a different sleep-wake cycle than adults, backed up his point by saying that "studies have proven it." No scholar writing for a refereed journal would make such a statement. The scholar would, first of all, name the studies and, then, would say something like "these studies support the contention that. . . ." In the careful rhetoric of the scholar, scientific studies never "prove" something, since they are open to replication and possibly different results.

▲ *4. Internet Research*

Today most Internet research is carried out through the World Wide Web. (See the inside back cover of this book for some sites of interest to technical writers and technical writing students.) Anyone doing technical writing should own a good text on using the Internet for writing, such as Nick Carbone's *Writing Online: A Student's Guide to the Internet and World Wide Web,* 3rd ed. (Houghton Mifflin) or Tara Talishain and Jill Nystrom's *Official Netscape Guide to Internet Research,* 2nd ed. (Netscape Press).

The Reliability Problem The reliability of Web sources poses a particular problem, since anyone can publish on the Web. Except within some online journals, Web texts are not monitored by experts. The Web is largely unregulated, and contributors may post inaccurate information.

It's a good idea, therefore, to know something about the source of any Internet text you use as a basis for your own writing. When examining a Web page, look for a button that will take you to a homepage, where the name (and nature) of the organization will likely appear. Be especially cautious of sites that are nonorganizational—that is, personal sites. They often have a tilde (~) in their name. When individuals offer their views on the Web, they may play light and loose with the facts. Be suspicious of phrases like "research shows that . . ." when there are no references to specific studies, and don't credit any statistics offered unless the specific source is also named and it is a source you can believe in, such as a federal agency.

It is not always possible to find scholarly studies on your subject on the Web. During your Web search, the only relevant information that you find may consist of the opinions of experts and the general lore that accumulates around professional work. Accept that for what it is, and present it accordingly in your own writings.

Here is a simple, seven-step procedure for conducting a Web search.

1. Create a research question.

> Example: Under what circumstances is starting a business at home a good option for women with children?

2. Develop key words and phrases that approach the subject from various angles.

working at home	home-based business
working mothers	entrepreneurs
mail order	businesswomen

3. Create a notebook for keeping a record of each search. Do not rely on bookmarks, since that approach would overload your bookmark collection. Use bookmarks only for sites that you return to frequently. Instead, keep a notebook and write down the sequence of each foray. For example, the search recorded below shows each step the student took, first, to find a search engine that searched for subjects of interest to women and then, using that engine, to arrive at a useful site with essays on her topic. The arrows indicate each jump to a new site or page. This student used double quotes around phrases she typed and single quotes around choices or links she selected at each page. She began at the AltaVista search box, where she typed in the words "search engine women." This search took her to a list of hits, from which she selected 'Women in Trades.' That search engine offered some selections on its homepage, one of them 'WIT' which led nowhere useful, so she hit the Back button. Her next choice was 'Wanto online.' In the end, her search brought her to **Womenconnect.com**, which had a search box, into which she typed "home business" and found a useful site.

> #1 AltaVista search box: "search engine women" → 'Women in Trades'→ 'WIT' → 'Back' → 'Wanto Online' → 'Related Sites' → 'Women Working: Outlook to 2005' → Womenconnect.com → "home business" → http://search.womenconnect.com/Display/TextSearch/ Process.htm (this site is right on target; many articles, including some focused on women's problems and others on legal issues)

Note that the last entry includes a summary of what was found and its quality or usefulness to the project. It also includes the uniform resource locator (URL) for the final page. With this record, the student can return to the final page at any time or to earlier stages in the search in order to select other links along the way. The student has numbered the search (#1). If she prints a page from the search, she will put the search number at the top, so that later, when studying the printed text, if she wants to return to the search path to explore related sites, she can easily find the directions in her search notes.

When doing any kind of extensive research, you should categorize information as soon as possible; in other words, create major subheadings for the report. Then invent a code for each category (each subheading) so that you can easily mark notes as to which sections of your developing text they are relevant to. In our model problem above, the writer might create categories like these:

> Difficulties: Legal (LD), Financial (FD), Psychological (PD)
> Benefits: Family (FB), Earnings (EB), Satisfaction (SB)

When a note or a printed article deals with, let's say, legal difficulties and earnings benefits, the student can mark the printed text **LD** and **EB**.

Then, when it's time to write the section on legal difficulties involved in running a home business, she can bring together all her notes and pages marked **LD**.

4. Start by using topic-specific search engines and databases. Topic-specific engines limit their scope to one domain, such as women's sites or education sites. You can find such engines by using broad-searching Web engines like AltaVista (**www.altavista.com**) and Dogpile (**www.dogpile.com**). Entering this phrase—search engine women—in the AltaVista search box yields these promising limited-search engines:

Womens Info

Women in Trades

A Dogpile search for **search engine women** produces this possibility:

Femina

As a first step in your actual search, try out your key words and phrases using topic-specific search engines. Remember to keep a record of the sequences of links that you follow and of what you find at the end. Many such searches will result in dead-ends. Don't get discouraged.

Don't get distracted, either. The Web is an entertaining place and it is easy to succumb to the lure of interesting sites unrelated to your research project.

5. Search using general search engines that provide subject listings. Engines like Yahoo (**www.yahoo.com**), Infoseek (**infoseek.go.com**), Lycos (**www.lycos.com**), Webcrawler (**www.webcrawler.com**), Beaucoup (**www.beaucoup.com**), and Dreamscape (**www.dreamscape.com.frankvad/search.html**) provide subject headings that limit your search. For our model search problem, Yahoo, for example, yields these likely categories to search under:

Women in business

Best of the Web (small-business research sites)

6. Search using engines that broadly cover the Web, such as AltaVista. When using engines like AltaVista, you'll find that it sometimes pays to write out whole questions in the search box. For example, the question *Should women with children work at home?* produces this interesting prospect:

WAHM.com The Newsletter and Online Magazine for Work at Home Moms

7. Fine-tune your search. If all your hits are only tangentially related to your subject, consider using the Boolean search option found on engines like AltaVista (click on Advanced Search). Under AltaVista's Advanced

Search, click on Help for a short tutorial. Infoseek (**www.infoseek.com**) also provides a nice tutorial for its Boolean search procedures.

In brief, using OR between key words in a Boolean search results in a search for either of the two key words: **mother** OR **mom**. Using AND will produce only those hits in which both the key words are found: **home** AND **business**. Using NOT will eliminate hits that have particular words that are interfering with your search: **women** AND **business** AND NOT **shopping**. Finally, the asterisk functions as a wild card within key words, meaning that where the asterisk appears all characters are accepted. A search for **wom*n** will find texts with both **women** and **woman** in them.

Some search engines offer other options, such as searching for words in titles only. Examine each search engine homepage carefully to see what it offers.

In choosing a search engine, don't be overly impressed by metacrawlers—search engines that activate a large collection of other engines like AltaVista and Yahoo. Metacrawlers actually take only a small percentage of the hits that those other engines find. Use metacrawlers, but also use powerful instruments like AltaVista and Yahoo. For two (quite different) rankings of search engines, see SearchIQ at **www. searchiq.com** and the Berkeley library tutorial on Web searching at **www. lib.berkeley.edu/TeachingLib/Guides/Internet/FindInfo.html**. For more printed information about search engines, see Archee (2000).

▲ 4. Documenting Sources for Library and Internet Research

When you draw unique information, ideas, or phrasing from another person's work, you should indicate to your reader the source of your borrowing. This is called *documenting sources*. The only exception to the need to document occurs when you are borrowing from in-house texts that are the property of the organization.

Documentation usually occurs in two parts: (a) parenthetical notes in the text, signaling that borrowing is taking place, and (b) a corresponding bibliographical note at the end of the text that provides all necessary information for finding the borrowed source. Here is an example of in-text parenthetical documentation using the style preferred by the American Psychological Association (APA):

> Abernathy (1998) notes that "many start-up companies go out of business because they cannot keep up with orders" (p. 89).

In the above sentence, we find the author's name, the year of the publication, and the page number on which the quotation occurs. This is enough information to find the appropriate entry in the bibliography, which will look like this:

Abernathy, L. (1998). Why start-ups fail. *Small Business Newsletter,* 7(2), 34–40.

Professional organizations in the humanities, the social sciences, and the physical sciences have developed conventions for documentation. Companies and other organizations often don't care which method you use, as long as the documentation is systematic and clear.

Following are some popular style choices for technical writing:

▮ American Psychological Association (APA) style; see the *Publication Manual of the American Psychological Association*

▮ Chicago style; see the *Chicago Manual of Style*

▮ American Management Association (AMA) style, published annually in its January issue

▮ Council of Biology Editors (CBE) style; see *Scientific Style and Format: The CBE Manual for Authors, Editors, and Publishers* (note that the CBE has recently changed its name to the Council of Science Editors)

▮ Modern Language Association (MLA) style; see the *MLA Handbook for Writers of Research Papers.*

You can find the above texts in any academic library. Nowadays, standard English handbooks include information on several different styles. A first-year composition handbook will likely provide you with all the details of documentation that you need.

The Web provides good models of parenthetical notes and bibliographical entries for documenting both print and online sources. Search for these using obvious key words, such as **APA citations.**

▲ *5. On-Site Observation and In-House Testing*

Technical writers research the effectiveness of documentation not only through surveys and interviews, as discussed above, but also through on-site observation of customers who are using the documentation and through in-house testing of the documentation. Formal observation and testing are discussed in detail in Chapter 10.

ASSIGNMENTS FOR 3.4

1. *Create a Questionnaire* Create a questionnaire that could be used as part of a needs analysis for a product or service, or that could be used to evaluate a product.

2. *Evaluate a Textbook for a Course* Create a questionnaire that could be used to evaluate a textbook for a course. Administer the questionnaire, and write a memo report to the class on the results.

3. *Interview an SME* Assume that your instructor is writing a book entitled *How They Do It: How People and Devices Do Everyday Things in the World Around You.* You have been asked to make a contribution to this developing text. Find someone who has technical knowledge of a subject that you don't have, such as an auto mechanic who understands the contribution of computers to the efficiency of the modern car engine, or a purchasing agent who knows how to get the best deal on products, or a pizza-parlor worker who knows how to twirl pizza dough into a circle. Determine and write down a purpose for interviewing this person—that is, what you want to know in preparation for a one-page chapter intended for a general adult audience. Following the interviewing advice in Box 3.3, interview your SME, and then write the one-page book chapter.

4. *Evaluate Your Library's Resources* Evaluate your library's technical writing resources in one or more of the following ways (your instructor may wish to divide the labor among groups or individuals). (a) Find out which technical writing journals your library subscribes to and describe each journal. Begin by creating a template so that the descriptions are formatted alike and contain the same information. Indicate whether the content is scholarly or practical or both. Include the span of years for which your library has volumes. (b) Find the locations of technical writing books in your library. Write a memo describing the different types. Are most of them textbooks (meant for students taking a course) or trade books (meant for people who want to learn how to do something on their own)? On the basis of their tables of contents, determine what subjects the textbooks cover. And keeping in mind that trade books usually focus on one subject, such as technical editing or the use of visuals, find out what individual subjects are addressed by the technical writing trade books in your library.

5. *Analyze a Reference Book* In your library's reference section, find one of the reference books listed in this section or another reference book related to technical writing. Analyze the book's content and write a brief informative memo-report on that content to your class.

6. *Learn a New Technology* Use a technical encyclopedia to learn about a new technology. In a memo addressed to your instructor, explain the technology. Name your source at the end of the memo.

7. *Analyze a Web Source* Explore one of the Web sources that appear on the inside back cover of this book. Through that source, find an informational or educational source that interests you and write a brief memo-report on it to your class.

8. *Document Sources* Obtain a handbook that shows how to document sources. Then (a) summarize an article in the journal *Technical Communication.* Quote the author several times, using parenthetical notes and a single-entry bibliography for the article. (b) Choose a subject related to your Big Project or some other assignment in a course you are taking. Use your library's computer indexes to create a "working bibliography" —that is, a list of works you might consult in researching this subject. Include at least one book, one article, and one online source. Use proper bibliographical format following one of the conventional styles, such as APA.

3.5 >—— The Resource Room

Many organizations have small, focused libraries within their buildings. The Documentation Department at Pittsburgh Telemax, for example, has its own library, or "resource room," as the employees call it.

The Documentation Resource Room at Telemax is a rectangular room with a counter running along one of the long sides, with book shelves above and cupboards below. Filing cabinets and a coffee-klatch area line the opposite side. A conference table takes up the middle space. The room is connected to Mendoza's office, but it also has a door to the hallway so that it can be accessed without disturbing Mendoza.

Frapp introduces Wendy to the resources:

▮ trade books on various types of technical and business writing (manual writing, proposal writing, and so forth), written by professional technical writers

▮ books on English grammar and usage

▮ other reference books, including texts describing national and international standards for conveying technical information, and texts on Internet resources for technical writers

▮ journals featuring technical and business writing, going back ten years, including *Technical Communication, IEEE Transactions on Technical Communication,* and *The Editorial Eye*

▮ copies of all documentation written at Telemax, except certain "classified" manuals describing products developed for government national security agencies, which are kept elsewhere in a safe

▮ copies of the *Telemax Style Guide,* a work in progress.

ASSIGNMENT FOR 3.5

1. *Your Own Resource Room* (a) If no resource room for technical writing exists on your campus, create one as a whole-class project. Perhaps your writing center will give you a shelf on a bookcase and a drawer in a file cabinet for this purpose. Plan a method for adding materials to the resource room, and then add those materials during the semester. (b) If a resource room for technical writing already exists, write a memo describing what is already there and explaining your plan for adding materials during the semester. Then add those materials as opportunity arises, keeping track of your contributions. Your instructor may want you to report on these contributions at some point in the term.

3.6 ⟩—— A Writing Process for Short Instructions

We have presented an overview of a writing process for long documents, and parts of that process are taken up in more detail in Part III. To conclude this chapter, we now look at how technical writers typically develop short documents, using "short instructions" as a concrete example. Short instructions may stand alone, or they may be a part of a long manual. For convenience, we will assume in this section that the instructions stand alone as an independent document.

The technical writing process for short instructions combines individual work with collaborative activities. It calls for considerable planning and a procedure for testing the effectiveness of the text before the text is considered acceptable.

▲ 1. Planning the Project

Technical writers often engage in project planning. They plan how they will write a document before they plan the document's content. Their plan typically encompasses the whole process of document creation, from research through publication.

For example, suppose students at your school are having difficulty using the new photocopier in one of the libraries. The instructions that came with the machine are badly written. As a technical writing intern, you have been assigned the task of creating a new set of instructions. In a short time, you can create a plan like the one shown in Box 3.7. A writing plan helps you work smoothly through a project without forgetting important steps. It also allows you to gauge your progress at that moment when your supervisor asks, "How's it coming along?"

Technical writers sometimes use flow charts to plan writing projects. As Figure 3.1 demonstrates, it is conventional to use boxes to indicate steps and diamonds to indicate yes-no questions. Lines with arrows show the flow of activity.

BOX 3.7 ▼ Writing Plan for a Short Set of Instructions

Prepare

1. Learn the basics of the photocopying machine myself.

2. Perform an audience analysis and needs analysis: Determine who will use the copier for what purposes and how sophisticated the users are with such machines.

3. Examine the existing directions to determine if they can be revised, or if I will need to start from scratch.

Write

4. If old instructions are revisable, make the necessary changes and jump to step 7.

5. If complete revision is necessary, review my organization's style guide on writing short instructions.

6. Draft the new instructions.

Test and Revise

7. Conduct a usability test:

    a) Gather together one or two primary users from the site and observe them as they read the existing directions: Where do they go wrong?

    b) Interview the users: What do they say is confusing?

8. Revise, test again, and if necessary revise again.

Finish Up

9. Edit and proofread.

10. Get approval from my supervisor to print the new instructions.

FIGURE 3.1 ▼   Flow Chart for a Writing Plan

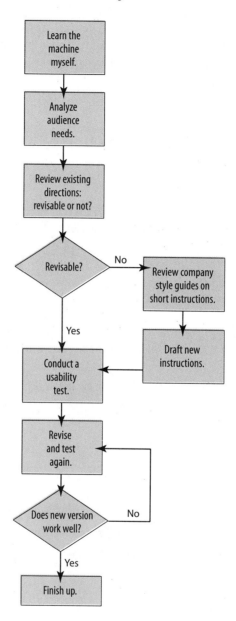

▲ 2. Planning the Content and Format

The best way to plan content for a short, in-house set of instructions is to begin with a needs analysis. Devices like photocopiers often come with options that users don't need. So you would interview likely users to determine which features they want to use. You would then create a rough outline of the features that will be documented. You might begin with the easiest and most common functions, progressing to the most difficult and least common ones.

In planning content, you would also examine organizational documents on standards for the kind of document being created. These standards would address both content and format.

Short instructions often use visuals, which are part of the content and should be planned along with the text and format. Visuals are taken up in detail in Chapter 7, but for now take a look at Figure 3.2, which shows how the use of a visual can greatly clarify even a simple set of instructions. Visuals are often planned through the use of "storyboards." Table 3.1 shows the three-column storyboard that writers at Pittsburgh Telemax use for incorporating visuals into the planning process.

▲ 3. Drafting

This is the one part of the technical writing process during which the writer works alone. Even here, however, the writing is a social act in that

Table 3.1 ▼ Storyboard for Planning Visuals

Text Organization	Visuals to Be Included	Type of Visual
PART I		
1.1 Exterior of machine	1.1 Front and side views	1.1 Photographs
1.2 Interior of machine	1.2 Simplified display of interior	1.2 Line drawing
1.3 Functions of machine	1.3 None	1.3 None
1.4 Models and costs	1.4 Chart showing model numbers and prices	1.4 Line drawing of table
1.5 Availability	1.5 List of dates	1.5 Boxed insert
PART II		
2.1 Dealing with technical problems	2.1 None	2.1 None
2.2 Dealing with human problems	2.2 People conferring at a conference table	2.2 Infographic

FIGURE 3.2 ▼ Using Visuals to Clarify Short Instructions

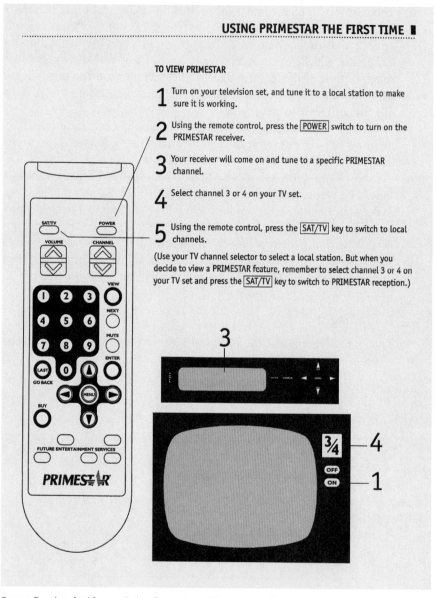

USING PRIMESTAR THE FIRST TIME ■

TO VIEW PRIMESTAR

1 Turn on your television set, and tune it to a local station to make sure it is working.

2 Using the remote control, press the POWER switch to turn on the PRIMESTAR receiver.

3 Your receiver will come on and tune to a specific PRIMESTAR channel.

4 Select channel 3 or 4 on your TV set.

5 Using the remote control, press the SAT/TV key to switch to local channels.

(Use your TV channel selector to select a local station. But when you decide to view a PRIMESTAR feature, remember to select channel 3 or 4 on your TV set and press the SAT/TV key to switch to PRIMESTAR reception.)

Source: Reprinted with permission from General Instrument Corporation.

the writer is guided by standards established by the organization. Box 3.8 shows a set of guidelines used by Pittsburgh Telemax for the writing of short instructions, and Box 3.9 shows the final product for a set of short instructions that follow those guidelines.

Table 3.2 shows another approach to short instructions, the one that Telemax uses for its in-house e-mail guide. This approach involves the "table" or "minimalist" design.

BOX 3.8 ▼ Guidelines for Short Instructions

Consult the audience analysis.

Determine if any safety warnings will be required.

Determine if visuals will be necessary.

Use this logical order for parts of the text:

1. Introduction to the process, including definition of terms,
2. Tools and materials required,
3. Steps. *Consider including the following information:*
   a. What the step accomplishes,
   b. Initial status of the operation (e.g., what the user sees on the computer screen),
   c. Action: what the user is to do,
   d. Consequence: what happens if all goes well (e.g., what the user sees on the computer screen),
   e. Troubleshooting: what to do if things go wrong.

IMPORTANT:

- Place warnings ahead of the step in which the danger or potential problem arises. Make warnings prominent.
- Always number steps.
- If the process requires more than 6 or 7 steps, break it up into sections with subheadings. The subheadings tell the users what they will do next. The numbered steps tell them how to do it.
- Avoid confusion by following the *Telemax Style Guide* for word choice, especially the rule of consistency in word choice. For example, Telemax requires writers to use the term *computer screen* to refer to displays and *computer monitor* to refer to the hardware. By following that guideline, you will avoid using *screen* on one occasion and *monitor* on another to refer to screen displays.

BOX 3.9 ▼ Model of Short Instructions

Pumpkinville College Library
How to Photocopy

To photocopy articles or pages from books, you must obtain and use a Copy-Card. Our photocopying machines do not take cash.

NOTICE: It is the responsibility of each person using the photocopiers in this library to abide by U.S. copyright laws. For a handout on those laws, see the reference librarian.

Create an Account on Your CopyCard.
1. Get a CopyCard at the reference desk. It costs 60 cents.
2. Put your CopyCard in the slot in the Charge Box next to any copier.
    • The card should be face up with the magnetic strip to the left.
3. Put as many one dollar bills or five dollar bills in the money slot as you wish. This amount will be credited to your account.
    • The bills go in face up, as shown in the picture.

Use Your CopyCard to Photocopy.
1. Turn on a photocopier.
    • The power button is located on the right side, near the front.
2. Wait one minute for the machine to warm up.
    • When the machine is ready, the green Ready button will light up.
3. Position your text on the glass plate.
    • For regular printing, place the top of the text toward the back of the machine.
    • For landscape printing, place the top of the text toward the left edge of the glass plate.
4. Set parameters.
    • The default prints to real size.
    • To print enlarged or reduced size, press the appropriate button in the Size box.
    • For multiple copies, hit the Number of Copies button and then enter a number on the number pad.
5. Hit the blue Go button.

Problems?
If your machine does not work properly, get help at the reference desk.

TABLE 3.2 ▼ Layout for E-mail Instructions

Operation	What You See	What You Enter
Log On	1. NAME:	1. [Your username]
	2. PASSWORD:	2. [Your password]
	3. [Daily announcements from management] HIT C TO CONTINUE	3. C
Read Mail	1. $:	1. mail
	2. Mail:	2. dir
	3. [A list of new messages]	3. [A message number or the Enter key]

Chapter 6 describes the tools of the modern technical writer. Those writing tools help the company and the technical writers standardize documents. In writing your set of instructions for the school photocopier, you might take advantage of advanced features of word processing programs and desktop publishing programs, such as templates and auto-numbering, as well as the ability of these programs to incorporate graphics. A desktop publishing program makes multiple-columned text, as in Table 3.2, easy to prepare.

▲ 4. Testing and Revising

Technical writers test their instructions whenever possible. This process is called "usability testing." When writing long, complex manuals, they also obtain reviews by engineers and others before revising; however, that may not be necessary for short instructions.

Usability testing, discussed in detail in Chapter 10, can be an elaborate procedure, but you could test a set of short, in-house instructions simply by asking two or three likely users to try out the directions while you watch. You would be careful to select at least one "least proficient" user for testing; in the case of the school photocopier, for example, you would find a student who professes to be awkward with machines. You would then revise on the basis of the errors and moments of confusion exhibited by the users. You could also informally interview the users to obtain more information about their understanding of your directions.

After revising, you might retest the instructions with one or two users who have not yet tried them out, and then revise again if necessary.

▲ 5. Carrying Out the Production Process

The production process refers to those steps that occur after the text is written. They include editing and proofreading. When working alone on a short project, you might get someone else to read over your text to see if you missed any errors or left in any inconsistencies. As a last step, you would take the text to your supervisor and get permission to print and distribute it.

The production process is much more complicated for long documents, such as the sets of manuals that Telemax produces for its telecommunications systems. Part III of this book looks at planning, writing, and production issues as they arise within the context of producing long documents.

ASSIGNMENTS FOR 3.6

1. *Analyze Instructions* Write a memo to your instructor indicating how the model of short instructions in Box 3.9 illustrates the guidelines that appear in Box 3.8.

2. *Write Documentation* Write a short set of instructions for some process at your school, such as the log-on procedure for your computer network, basic e-mail operations, drop-add, using the library's computers to find a book by subject search, or using one of the machines in the exercise room. Follow as many of the steps discussed in section 3.6 as your instructor wishes.

3. *A Medical or Dental Procedure* Imagine that you are a doctor, a veterinarian, or a dentist who has prescribed a procedure for a patient (or pet) to carry out at home, such as a procedure for attending to a sprained ankle or a hurt paw, or a procedure for recovery from gum surgery, or a process of elaborate teeth cleaning. Draw on your own experience. Write a short set of instructions for this procedure.

4. *Sports and Hobbies* Drawing from your own expertise in a sport or hobby, write a short set of instructions for a complex skill, such as the service motion in tennis, the fly-casting motion in stream fishing, a flourish in guitar playing, or the use of negative space in drawing.

5. *Around the House* Write a short set of instructions for a home activity you are familiar with, such as making fluffy pancakes, painting a room, changing a washer in a kitchen faucet, or transplanting a bush.

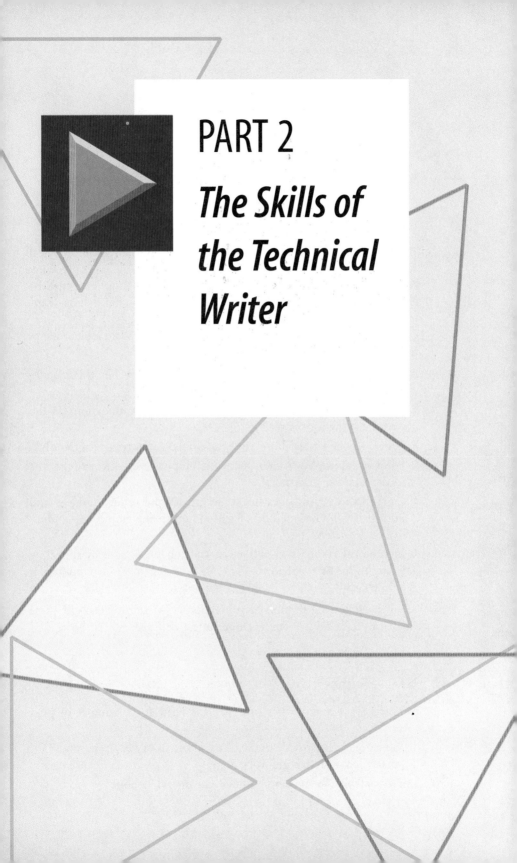

PART 2

The Skills of the Technical Writer

Rhetoric

This chapter examines general rhetorical principles for good technical writing. Rhetoric refers to how a writer approaches the task of writing; it reflects the writer's goals and the means by which those goals will be achieved. Rhetoric includes style, but we will be discussing style as a separate issue in the next chapter.

If you were to analyze the rhetoric of a text, you would look at issues like these:

▌ **Purpose** Is the writer trying to educate? Show how? Persuade? Arouse? Becalm?

▌ **Audience** Who is this written for? What accommodations is the writer making for the reader?

▌ **Tone** Has the writer chosen to be invisible? Authoritative? Friendly?

▌ **Point of View** Whose perspective is emphasized—the writer's, the reader's, or the company's?

▌ **Organization** How does the writer group and order the ideas and information? What method of reasoning is being employed—inductive or deductive?

▌ **Methods of Persuasion** Is the writer trying to persuade by appealing to emotions? By appealing to logic? By referring to her own reputation or authority?

In the following numbered subsections, we examine each of these rhetorical elements as it applies to technical writing.

4.1 >—— Purpose

Technical writers and other professionals write for a number of purposes:

1. **To inform** To provide the reader with necessary information to make decisions and get work done.
2. **To instruct** To show how something should be done.

3. **To persuade** To convince the reader to take a particular course of action (e.g., to select their company's product over a competitor's).

4. **To request** To ask for favors or information.

5. **To document decisions** To make a written record of who said what to whom, when, and where.

6. **To assign work** To tell other employees what to do.

7. **To report on work** To show the results of a study, or the status of work in progress, or the outcome of a job. To document a writer's contribution to a project.

8. **To sell a product** To advertise. To create proposals.

9. **To promote the company** To project an attractive image for the organization.

10. **To fulfill social obligations** To congratulate and commiserate. To maintain good relations with fellow employees and those outside the organization.

Writers often have multiple purposes. They must inform, for example, in order to carry out almost every other purpose. Persuasion figures into many purposes. Writers must juggle these purposes with decisions about content, while keeping an eye on the needs of the audience. Given this complexity, it is easy to lose sight of one's purpose. Beginning writers sometimes produce texts that read well but work against what they are trying to achieve through the document.

Writers have global as well as local purposes. A global purpose applies to the whole text; a local purpose determines what the writer is trying to achieve in the immediate section, or paragraph, or sentence. It is important to stay focused on both global and local purposes. For example, writers undermine their global purpose when they

▌ adopt an inappropriate tone

▌ ignore a crucial segment of their audience

▌ fail to include blocks of information necessary for a full treatment of the subject.

Writers undermine their local purpose when they

▌ elaborate on subjects they think are inherently interesting or important when such development isn't required

▌ show off their technical knowledge to an audience that needs non-technical explanations

▌ allow arbitrary topics, rather than purpose, to control the direction of their sentences (an example on the next page illustrates this problem).

4 Rhetoric

At Telemax, the DDM, Marge Mendoza, requires writers to fill out a Rhetorical Analysis Sheet before planning a new document or planning a major revision of an old document (Box 4.1). Note that the "R-A Sheet" (as the Telemax writers call it) begins with a statement of global purpose. Mendoza believes that writers will stay more focused on their global purpose during the crucial planning stage if they state that purpose in writing. A typical entry for that part of the R-A Sheet looks like this:

> Since this system is being purchased by a federal agency, the manuals must meet government standards for documentation (e.g., a full installation manual, even though we will be installing). Since the government has systems experts available, the manuals should provide all information required for complete understanding, maintenance, and use of the product. We want users to be able to get along without technical support once we have installed.

The two general purposes expressed in the above paragraph—meeting government regulations and making users as independent of technical support as possible—are typical global purposes for a company like Telemax. Other organizations will have different frequently occurring global purposes, such as educating beginners in the use of a new kind of product, or, in the case of a charitable organization, convincing the public of the worthiness of its causes.

On the local level, writers must remain alert to their immediate purposes. Experienced writers continually pause in their composing to ask themselves this central question: *Given what I have said so far, what do I need to say next to accomplish my immediate purpose?*

This is not to say that writers stop and mouth those words to themselves; but on some semiconscious level, they do continually assess what they've done and plan the next move in terms of purpose. If you review your text frequently and remind yourself of your purpose, you will avoid the kind of rambling that occurs when a writer allows an undisciplined stream of consciousness to guide development. In the example below, a writer is attempting to convince the reader that the index that comes with a manual makes the manual easy to use. Note how the writer starts to lose track of that local purpose:

> The index will help you find answers to your questions. We list over 3,000 entries. In keeping with our policy of "only the best," we outsource our indexing to highly competent professional indexers. While other companies are cutting corners to save money, we are investing in quality.

The strength of the index is relevant to the purpose, but the writer shifts from selling the product on a particular basis to praising the company in general. The original point may be lost.

BOX 4.1 ▼ **Rhetorical Analysis Sheet**

Document name _____ Document number _____
Author of this analysis _____ Date _____

Purpose of Document: _____
_____
_____

Audience Demographics
Age range _____   Gender of most readers: ____M   ____F   ____Mixed
General level of education (check more than one if there's a range):
_____h.s.   _____training post-h.s.   _____college   _____advanced degree

Audience Analysis
Identity of primary (P) audience for this documentation: _____
_____

Identity of least proficient (LP) audience for this documentation: _____
_____

How audience will use the product:
(P) _____
(LP) _____

Audience experience with this or similar products:
(P) _____
(LP) _____

Audience attitude toward product (interested, hostile, afraid, etc.):
(P) _____
(LP) _____

Problems you foresee in communicating with readers:

(P) _____
_____
(LP) _____
_____

4 Rhetoric

ASSIGNMENTS FOR 4.1

1. *Analyze a Sales Letter* Purpose in sales letters is usually transparent. Find
   a sales letter (search your junk mail), and analyze its global and local purposes. What is the letter trying to do overall and in each segment? Write
   an analysis for your instructor in memo form. Include a copy of the letter.

2. *Analyze Your Text* Do assignment 4.1(1), but this time use one of your own writings. Do any of the passages undermine, or stray from, your global or local purposes?

4.2 >———Audience

The audience for a text, in the simplest terms, is the reader. In the traditional understanding of audience, the reader is a single real person (or group of people), known to the writer and possessing identifiable characteristics. During the planning stage of writing, you might analyze the readers in terms of those characteristics:

- **What is their degree of knowledge of the subject?** How much will you have to explain?

- **What is their purpose in reading?** What do the readers need to know in order to perform a task or make a decision?

- **What is their predisposition toward the issues or subject matter?** Are you addressing a group that agrees with your views or disagrees? Are the readers looking forward to working with your product, or are they dreading it?

- **What are their personal characteristics?** How will their age, gender, educational level, and ethnic or regional identity affect your approach?

The issue of audience begins to get complicated when we realize that a single document may have more than one type of audience. As Mathes and Stevenson (1991, pp. 42–47) have pointed out, your in-house proposal or report may have all of these types of audiences:

- a primary audience who will act on your text by making decisions

- a secondary audience who will play an implementation role after the decisions have been made

- an immediate or nominal audience who first receives your message for reasons of organizational structure or protocol and then passes it on to the primary and secondary audiences.

Furthermore, your in-house text may address issues relevant to

- audiences in your own department
- audiences in related departments
- audiences distant in the organization.

Each of those audiences will have its own purposes in reading and its own requirements for information (Table 4.1). How can a writer handle mixed

TABLE 4.1 ▼ Audiences for Technical Writing

Reader	Purpose in Reading	Example	Content Requirements
End user	To learn how to use a product or service	A secretary learning to use a spreadsheet	This novice user needs basic information and little or no technical or theoretical information. Assume the reader is apprehensive and error-prone.
Operator	To learn how to operate a machine or carry out a service	A commercial artist learning how to use a new camera	This specialist user needs a small amount of theoretical information and a lot of mechanical and process description.
Technician	To do installation, maintenance, and repair	A systems technician using an alarm table to fix a network problem	This technical expert needs theory of operation as well as technical information presented in how-to format.
Engineer	To understand design features	An electrical engineer learning the structure of a new component purchased from another company	This design expert needs both theoretical and technical information.
Financial manager	To make cost-benefit decisions	A president deciding whether or not to develop a new product line	This financial expert needs just enough theoretical and technical informtion to understand the competitive value of the product and its approximate production costs.
Marketing manager	To make sales decisions	A sales manager developing an ad campaign for a new product	This marketing expert needs enough technical information about the product to be able to laud its virtues and compare it to the competition.
Regulator	To certify that products and processes are based on written standards	An ISO 9000 inspector evaluating a product-testing process	This informed generalist or field specialist needs enough technical information to be able to evaluate processes and products for quality and safety.

4 Rhetoric

audiences? The formats for proposals and reports compartmentalize information into separate sections of interest to different readers. A long report, for example, begins with an executive summary to be read by the top decision makers, and the rest of the report may include separate sections of interest to engineers, operators, and marketing personnel.

External documents—those going outside the organization—also have to address different audiences. Pittsburgh Telemax, as we will see, usually provides separate manuals for each type of reader. In addition, Mendoza, as mentioned earlier, requires writers to do an R-A Sheet as part of the planning process for documentation for end-users (Box 4.1). The large middle section of the R-A Sheet concerns two audiences: primary users and least proficient users.

Adding to the complexity of multiple audiences, modern theories of audience have raised questions about how well writers can actually know their audiences (Ede, 1984; Ede & Lundsford, 1984; Kirsch & Roen, 1990; Kroll, 1984). Technical writers often address people they don't know personally. Furthermore, even the writer's understanding of a "known" audience actually consists of a "fictional version" of that audience in the writer's imagination. We don't really know anyone's views perfectly, we don't really understand exactly what our readers know and don't know about a subject, and we cannot anticipate precisely what they will need to know to get their work done. This doesn't mean that competent writers give up on audience consideration. Rather, they make the best educated estimates they can, sometimes doing research to improve those estimates.

Writers occasionally approach the problem of audience by invoking a role for their audience to play and then inviting their readers to adopt that role and become that fictional audience. For example, if you were trying to persuade your company's president that the company should contribute to a charitable fund to protect the environment, you might begin your pitch by saying:

> As a community leader who appreciates the importance of a clean environment, not only for our business but for our society, you might wish to consider. . . .

In this way, you would invoke the sort of audience who would be attracted to your cause.

Despite the complexity of audience, good technical writers ponder the effects of their words on their imagined readers. This continual reflection is an important part of the writing process for competent writers.

ASSIGNMENTS FOR 4.2

1. *Write an Analysis* Write a traditional audience analysis (specifying the readers' knowledge of the subject, purpose in reading, predisposition, and personal characteristics) for a guide to correctness written for your technical writing class.

2. *R-A Sheet* Write an R-A Sheet for a guide to using the computer indexes in your school library.

3. *Different Audiences* Imagine that two of your hometown friends, Mike and Sally, are coming to visit you on campus. You've arranged for them to meet you outside your technical writing classroom at the end of the period. Mike attended your school for a year, five years ago, and has a rough sense of the campus layout. Sally has never set foot on campus. Explore the idea of multiple audiences by writing two sets of directions, one for Mike and one for Sally. Start at the point where they would enter the campus and end at the door to your technical writing class. Be prepared to comment in class about how the directions differ and why.

4.3 >——Tone

Tone is the sound your writing makes. Your prose may come across as angry, calm, enthusiastic, authoritative, or neutral. The tone communicates your feelings and attitudes toward your subject, toward your purpose in writing, and toward your audience. Telemax has specific tone guidelines for its documents:

▌ Manuals should sound neutral, the author invisible.

▌ Quick-start guides should come across as friendly and informal (but avoid humor).

▌ Most business documents should sound authoritative; we know what we're talking about.

▌ Promotional material should use an authoritative or enthusiastic tone, as appropriate.

An important aspect of tone is level of formality. A very formal tone can convey displeasure if used with someone you know well. Suppose, for example, you have an assistant, Sarah Smith, a young woman you play tennis with and have over to your house for big family dinners. The two of you call each other by your first names. Now, compare these two versions of the same message:

Informal

Sarah, I really need that section on installing the video software, which was due a week ago. Hey, this is the third reminder. If you're having trouble getting information from the engineers, or having any other kind of problem, let me know immediately so I can expedite. Thanks.

Formal

Ms. Smith, you have not yet submitted your section on installing the video software, which was due a week ago. I have reminded you twice since the due date. Inform me if you need any assistance. Thank you.

If Sarah Smith received the second version she would probably conclude that you were quite angry with her.

On the other hand, a formal tone can be respectful if your reader is an important person whom you do not know intimately, while an informal tone used with such a person could be insulting. Suppose you are writing a cover memo for a progress report on the documentation for a major project. Your memo is addressed to the project manager, but like any such report, it may be read far up the line of authority in your company. This kind of informality would be inappropriate:

Margaret, you're gonna love this report. Get ready for some great news on the documentation front!

In this case the appropriate tone is one of respectful formality:

Attached is a detailed progress report on the documentation for the Patterson Company project. As you will see, the documentation is shaping up well, and we expect to be finished ahead of schedule.

In short, you should vary the level of formality according to your relationship to your reader and the effect you wish to convey.

ASSIGNMENTS FOR 4.3

1. *Analyze Tone* Examine the letters to the editor in the past issue or two of your school newspaper. Identify and describe as many different tones as you can find, along with a sample sentence for each. Prepare a memo report to your instructor, who may also ask you to report to the class.

2. *Use Different Tones* Using a friendly tone in order to put your reader at ease, write a short set directions for use of a product sold by your fictional company (or choose a simple product such as a cassette tape recorder or a

simple process such as erasing a computer diskette). Then rewrite the directions using a neutral tone, making yourself as unnoticeable (as "invisible") as possible to the reader.

4.4 ⟩—— Point of View

In a grammatical sense, point of view refers to "person": first person, second person, third person. When we use the first-person point of view, we refer to ourselves using the pronouns **I, me, we, us,** or **our(s)**. The previous sentence is written in the first-person-plural point of view ("When we use . . ."). The first-person point of view, especially the singular **I**, is considered somewhat informal. The author as a person has become part of the text, instead of being an invisible force behind the words. Note that the second of these two sentences, written in the first-person point of view, has a more personal, less formal tone:

(1) The client received the necessary assistance.

(2) I assisted the client as necessary.

The second-person point of view, which uses **you** or **your(s)**, is also considered slightly informal. However, technical writers regularly use the "command" form for directions: "Do this, do that." In such statements, the **you** is deleted but implied: "(You) do this, (you) do that."

The most formal point of view is the third-person point of view, which makes no reference to the writer or the reader. In this perspective, the subject of the sentence, if singular, takes the form of a singular noun or the pronoun **he, she,** or **it**. If the pronoun subject is plural, the subject appears as a plural noun or as the pronoun **they**. Here are some examples of the third-person point of view:

(3) The client received the necessary assistance.

(4) He received the necessary assistance.

(5) Technical writers provide the necessary assistance.

(6) They provide the necessary assistance.

We have just discussed point of view as a grammatical concept. As a rhetorical concept, point of view refers to the perspective taken by the writer. Does the writer focus on his or her own interests? If so, the writer would use the first-person point of view frequently. Most business and technical documents, however, take the perspective of the reader or client. This is called the "you-perspective." By using the you-perspective, the writer shows the readers why they should be interested in, or accepting of, the ideas being presented—what's in it for them. The you-perspective often uses the second-person point of view, with the pronoun *you* frequently showing up as the subject of sentences.

Finally, it is possible to join the I-perspective and the you-perspective into the we-perspective, which reflects the mutual interests of writer and reader. In the we-perspective, the pronoun *we* often turns up as the grammatical subject of sentences.

Below are three versions of the same text, each taking a different perspective. An office manager, in an internal proposal for remodeling, tries to convince a district manager to OK the purchase of an expensive brand of wallpaper:

I-Perspective:
I saw a room papered in the Professional Perl wallpaper, and although this paper is expensive, I think that this color and style would be best for our offices in the Brandon Building. I like the quiet tone and conservative look that it provides. It makes me feel relaxed, yet ready to concentrate on work.

You-Perspective:
Though expensive, the Professional Perl wallpaper has the quiet, conservative, professional style that you prefer. You will feel comfortable bringing clients into offices decorated with this wallpaper.

We-Perspective:
As the office manager at the Brandon Building, I share your goal of creating a more productive workplace. We can do that partly by creating a more professional atmosphere. The Professional Perl wallpaper, though expensive, will contribute to our effort to make the offices at Brandon appear quiet, conservative, and professional.

ASSIGNMENTS FOR 4.4

1. *Perspectives* Which of the three perspectives illustrated at the end of section 4.4 is the most persuasive? Be prepared to defend your judgment in class.

2. *Take-Home Exam* Write three versions of an appeal to an instructor for a take-home exam instead of an in-class test, using the I-perspective, the you-perspective, and the we-perspective.

3. *Convince the Boss* Do assignment 4.4(2), but direct your effort to convincing your boss at your fictional company that you should be allowed to work at home two days a week instead of coming into the office on those days.

4.5 >——— Content

Certain types of documents have conventional or required content. For example, a manual for a computer network will have a systems maintenance section, which in turn will almost certainly have subsections on theory of operation, procedures for routine maintenance, procedures for corrective maintenance, and troubleshooting decision tables. However, even in the most conventional texts, technical writers always make some of the decisions about content—what should go into a text and what should be left out. That decision is guided by the purpose and audience the document will serve. If the document is a reference manual, for instance, then the writer will probably choose to include all parameters and options for all parts of the system, as well as some conceptual information.

By contrast, for a task-oriented document (one that helps end-users carry out their work), the writer may provide the *least* amount of information necessary to help the reader perform the task. Researchers have found that avoiding unnecessary information makes instructional writing more effective.

Determining what is necessary or unnecessary can be difficult. In Chapter 2, section 2.5 introduced the concept of "least knowledgeable" user, and section 2.6 talked about the "Ignorant Person" standard. Both of these concepts suggest that writers should write for the least capable reader. That principle makes sense, but it also tempts writers to include unnecessary information, especially conceptual or background information. End-users performing a task usually don't need to be told anything except how to do the task. They usually already know why they are doing the task, and they usually don't need to know how the system works—only how to make it perform as desired. When considering whether to include background or conceptual information in task-oriented documents, ask yourself how this information will help the reader perform the task. If it won't, you should probably leave it out.

ASSIGNMENTS FOR 4.5 —————————————————————

1. *Analyze Text for Conventional Content* Select a text you are familiar with (for example, an introductory psychology textbook, a sales letter, a recipe, a resume) and, by looking at two examples of this kind of writing, determine where their contents overlap; that is, determine what conventional content is found in both samples. Be prepared to report on your findings in class.

4 Rhetoric

2. ***Critique Instructions for Photocopying*** Examine the instructions for photocopying in Box 3.9 in Chapter 3. Do those instructions contain any information not related to performing the task? Should that information have been removed from the document? Present your critique to your instructor in a memo and be prepared to defend it in class.

3. ***Remove Unnecessary Information*** Revise the following text twice, removing unnecessary information. For the first revision, assume an audience of elementary school children. For the second revision, assume an adult audience.

How to Load Staples in the Mark IV Stapler

The Mark IV Stapler is an efficient instrument that is sturdy and reliable, as well as easy to use. Its operations do not require experience or technical ability. To load staples:

1. Open the stapler by holding the base in one hand and lifting the top with the other. This action will pull back a sliding pressure bar that will eventually push the staples forward during use.

2. Remove a string of standard staples from their box, being careful not break them up. "Standard" staples will be labeled as such on the box.

3. Lay the staples pointed side down in the channel inside the stapler. They should fit nicely.

4. Slowly move the top back into place until you hear a click.

5. Sometimes the first attempt to staple an object does not work effectively, and the first staple must be cleared out of the stapler. Therefore, place a piece of scrap paper onto the shiny plate on the base of the stapler and press down firmly on the top of the stapler to eject the first staple. You are now ready to use the Mark IV Stapler.

4.6 >——— Organization

Organization (sometimes called "arrangement") refers to how information and ideas are grouped and ordered.

▲ *1. Grouping*

Grouping is the art of assembling similar things together. Unfortunately, this process is complicated by the fact that most sets of things can be logically grouped in more than one way. For example, how would you group these elements: chapters, table of contents, index, pages? You could do this:

Group 1   chapters & table of contents
(because the TOC is a list of chapters)

Group 2   pages & index
(because the index refers readers to pages)

Or you could do this:

Group 1   chapters & pages
(they both constitute the main text)

Group 2   table of contents & index (as front matter and back matter, they're both outside the main text)

Or you could do this:

Group 1   chapters, pages, index
(all are page-numbered in Arabic numerals)

Group 2   table of contents
(page-numbered in lower-case Roman numerals)

Decisions about grouping may depend on your purpose in writing. For example, suppose you wanted to present the Santa Teresa Lab's characteristics of quality technical information (see Table 2.1 in Chapter 2) in a way that showed how each characteristic made the documentation *easy* for the reader to handle. Here's the Santa Teresa list: **Accuracy, Clarity, Completeness, Concreteness, Organization, Retrievability, Style, Task orientation,** and **Visual effectiveness**. Given that purpose, you might follow this suggestion from Gretchen Hargis, the primary author of the Santa Teresa list:

▌ Easy to use—task orientation, accuracy, completeness

▌ Easy to understand—clarity, concreteness, and style

▌ Easy to find—organization, retrievability, and visual effectiveness (Hargis, 1998, p. 2).

With that grouping, your text would have three main sections with three subsections in each.

▲ *2. Ordering*

Once you have decided on grouping, you must decide on ordering— which element in the group will be presented first, second, third, and so on. Here you have many options, including these standard approaches:

1. General to specific (also called "deductive" development) (main point followed by supporting detail)

4 Rhetoric

2. Specific to general (also called "inductive" development) (background or supporting detail leading to the main point)

3. Most important to least important

4. Least important to most important (quickly dealing with the unimportant before focusing on the important)

5. Most important audience to least important audience (example: executive summary to operators' appendices)

6. Visual (some possibilities: far to near, around the outside, outside to inside, top to bottom)

7. Chronological (from earliest to latest; or from latest to earliest— reverse-chronological—as found in resumes)

8. Easiest to most difficult

9. Familiar to unfamiliar (old information as a background or setting for new)

10. Necessary to dependent (example: conditions or concepts that must be understood before steps in a process)

11. Shortest to longest

12. Most interesting to least interesting (examples: Sales letters begin with attention grabbers, and surveys leave boring demographic questions until last)

13. Least controversial to most controversial (what we can agree on comes before what we must compromise on)

14. Left to right (because that is how Westerners read texts; other cultures read right to left)

▲ 3. Revealing the Organization

In long texts, technical writers take pains to make their organization clear to the reader. From the outset, a table of contents serves as an initial statement of grouping and order. An initial abstract or summary will inform the reader of the approach taken throughout the document or in a given section. And within the text itself, writers use "signpost" sentences to guide the reader. For example:

> Now that you have seen how to save a file to your hard disk, we will look at the process of saving your file to a 3-1/2 inch floppy disk. Your 3-1/2 inch floppy disk drive is located in your computer bay. It is designated Drive A: by your computer system.
>
> Begin by putting a 3-1/2 inch disk in the disk drive. . . .

In the above example, the first paragraph begins with a signpost indicating the direction the text will now take. The second paragraph begins with a conventional word (*Begin*), indicating that the writer is starting to describe a procedure. Clues like these help readers understand complex texts, or even simple texts that are being read under stressful conditions.

Revealing your organization to your reader should be a continuing local purpose, executed with phrases and sentences like the ones illustrated above. It should also be a global purpose, executed through structures like a table of contents, an initial summary, and a system of headings and subheadings.

Each type of heading should be formatted uniquely. Here are typical specifications for levels of headings in a technical document that uses 12-point Times Roman for its text:

▌ Level 1: Chapter titles (Helvetica font, 24 pt, centered; 6 blank lines below)

▌ Level 2: Section headings (Bold Helvetica font, 14 pt, flush left; 3 blank lines above, 2 below)

▌ Level 3: Subheadings (Italic Times Roman font, 12 pt, flush left; 2 blank lines above, 1 below)

To further reveal the structure of the document, you can decimal-number the headings and subheadings (1.1, 1.2, 1.3, 2.1, and so on).

▲ 4. Repeating Organizational Patterns

Technical writers establish patterns for presenting information and then stick to those patterns. For example, a writer might create this pattern for presenting steps in a process:

Step 1   Statement of what Step 1 accomplishes
Why Step 1 is necessary
Initial conditions necessary to begin Step 1
Actions:
    1.
    2.
How to tell if Step 1 was carried out successfully

Step 2   Statement of what Step 2 accomplishes
Why Step 2 is necessary
Initial conditions necessary to begin Step 2
Actions:
    1.
    2.
How to tell if Step 2 was carried out successfully

When writers follow a strict pattern like the one illustrated above, they are less likely to leave out important information. A familiar pattern of presentation helps readers efficiently absorb new information and correctly follow instructional steps.

ASSIGNMENTS FOR 4.6

1. *Analyze This Textbook* On what bases are the chapters in this textbook grouped and ordered? How else could they be grouped and ordered? Be prepared to discuss your conclusions in class.

2. *Analyze Another Text* (a) Do assignment 4.6(1), but analyze the contents of a text for another course. (b) Create your own grouping for the Santa Teresa list of characteristics of quality technical information. Write a memo to your instructor explaining the logic behind your grouping and ordering.

3. *Evaluate the Organization of Your Text* Evaluate the organization of one of your own writings. What principles did you use? Be prepared to discuss your findings in class.

4. *Use Principles of Ordering* Drawing from the fourteen principles of ordering, write two different one-page statements on the value of a college degree in your particular major, using a different ordering principle for each. Label each text so that your instructor knows which principle you are illustrating. Within a text, you may note the use of more than one principle; in that case, label methods in the margin. The goal for the assignment is to produce two substantially different versions based on different ordering principles.

5. *Order Other Texts* Do assignment 4.6(4), but apply it to one of these: (a) the value of a college degree in general, or the value of pleasure reading, or the value of something else of your own choosing; (b) a description of a lab on campus written for a brochure to be sent to prospective students and their parents; or (c) a welcoming letter from the president of your school to entering freshmen.

6. *Create an Organizational Pattern* Design an organizational pattern (or template) for describing products in a catalogue. Then write two product descriptions following that template. The catalogue can present products either from your fictional company or from a real company. You might visit an electronics or office supply store and get information on two kinds of beepers or cellular phones or fax machines or similar products.

4.7 >—— Methods of Persuasion

Most of the methods of persuasion that we use today can be found in Aristotle's *Rhetoric*, written about 2,300 years ago. Aristotle pointed out three broad categories on which persuasion can be based: the reputation of the speaker, appeal to emotions, and logical argument.

Let's apply those three methods of persuasion to writing external proposals at Pittsburgh Telemax. External proposals are persuasive documents. The writers try to persuade the potential client to select their company over the competition when purchasing a service or a product. Here is the application:

- The writers can persuade on the basis of their company's **reputation**. Telemax writers emphasize that their company is known for producing products at the cutting edge of technology and that Telemax is an established, reliable firm that has been around longer than most other high-tech companies. The writers offer references to satisfied customers who will testify on behalf of the company.

- The writers can persuade on the basis of an appeal to **emotions**. (a) Customers have pride. Telemax frequently sells to universities, which want systems that they can showcase to potential students and other visitors. Telemax makes top-of-the-line products, so the writers say that "owning a Telemax system is like owning a Cadillac."
  (b) Customers worry that a product will soon be out of date. Telemax writers acknowledge that legitimate concern, then show why the company's systems are never out of date.

- The writers can persuade on the basis of **logic**. There are many different approaches under this category, among them these common strategies:

  History. Because Telemax has satisfied customers in the past, it is reasonable to assume that it will do a good job in the future.

  Examples. The writers list Telemax's accomplishments, such as product awards the company has won. They also list prominent customers: the U.S. Senate, the CIA, Princeton University, U.S. Steel.

  Comparison. The writers at Telemax seek out opportunities to compare their company favorably with other companies. Earlier, we saw a Telemax system being associated with the Cadillac automobile, suggesting that Telemax, too, symbolizes high class. Telemax technical writers often make comparisons of data as well (e.g., the speed of their system versus the speed of their competitor's product).

Consequences. Writers can effectively persuade by pointing to the consequences of actions (such as not updating one's system, falling behind).

Definition. Writers can even argue by defining the problem the way they want it to be perceived. *Problem: The prospective client company is stuck having to completely replace its old system because it originally bought an inexpensive system, instead of investing in a high-quality upgradable system like the ones Telemax builds.* Notice that this definition of the problem includes argument from consequences, discussed above. Often two approaches—such as definition and consequences—will overlap.

ASSIGNMENTS FOR 4.7

1. *Analyze a Proposal* Find a real proposal. If you don't have access to one, use a model in a book; alternatively, your instructor may have left one or more examples on reserve in your school's library. In a memo to your instructor, point to instances in which the proposal uses the methods of persuasion discussed in section 4.7. Point out any other methods that you notice.

2. *Analyze a Sales Letter or Brochure* Do assignment 4.7(1), but apply it to a sales letter or brochure.

3. *Write a Persuasive Proposal* You have heard that your computer center is opening another small computer lab for students. Write a short memo proposal addressed to your school's computer center director suggesting that the center purchase a particular kind of computer (or some other piece of equipment or furniture) for its new lab. Leave a big right margin when you print your memo, and in that margin, with a pen, note your methods of persuasion.

4. *Write a Persuasive Memo* Write a persuasive memo addressed to one of your instructors requesting that an upcoming in-class test be changed to a take-home exam. Write a second memo to your technical writing instructor explaining the persuasive appeals you employed. Turn in both memos.

4.8 >—— Rhetoric and Cross-Cultural Communication

The end of the twentieth century has seen a worldwide shift toward democratic governance and open markets, leading to a "global economy." Doing business with foreign companies and foreign entrepreneurs is becoming routine. However, communicating across cultures carries its own set of writing problems.

▲ *1. Cultural Difference*

Experts in international communications have described in broad terms the cultural differences important to communication. On the most general level, the United States, Israel, and the countries of northern Europe, especially the Nordic countries and Germany, use similar rhetorics and ways of doing business, whereas countries in southern Europe, the Mideast, Asia, and Latin America differ, in varying ways, from the first group in regard to a number of important issues such as directness in communication and the importance of ritual.

It is important not to put too much trust in such groupings. If you are going to communicate with someone in Country X, you should research the specific culture of that country—if possible, talking to people who have lived and worked there. The categories and generalizations are best used as a starting point, a guide to what to look for in your research.

People who grow up and work in different cultures do tend to develop different attitudes and behaviors in regard to such matters as these:

▮ **Time** In some cultures, punctuality is important; in others, it is not. Similarly, business ventures are characterized by slow and cautious behavior in some cultures and by quick and daring behavior in others.

▮ **Deals** Some cultures prefer friendship and oral agreements; others, written contracts.

▮ **Decision making** Some cultures allow individual decisions; others require consensus decision making. Some cultures share authority; others operate by a strict hierarchy.

▮ **Formalities** Some cultures place a higher priority on ritual and saving face than do others.

▮ **Directness of communication** Some cultures prefer direct approaches to the main points; others, indirect approaches.

These differences affect the content and rhetoric of an organization's international communications. They can be explored through library research and the Internet. To get a sense of what can be found on the Web, consult the following sites on doing business in India and Mexico:

> **gonow.to/india**
> **www.cs.unb.ca/~alopez-o/busfaq.html#Personal**

Japan provides a good example of a culture that is significantly different from that of the United States in ways relevant to communication (Murdick, 1999). When making a proposal to a Japanese counterpart, for instance, you will be more effective if you approach the subject slowly and inductively instead of being "upfront" and "to the point" (approaches admired in the United States). You should be quiet and patient, not exuberant or pushy. The person you are writing to probably does not have the authority to make a decision without consulting with others, so don't ask for a prompt decision. The Japanese like to move slowly and cautiously; attempts to hurry them won't work. Don't overexplain or try to make your communications "idiot proof." Americans appreciate clarity over every other consideration, but the Japanese prefer an opaque and suggestive style, and may be insulted if you seem to be treating them like children who cannot intuit or deduce your meaning.

Again, these are generalizations. In Japan, as in every other country, you will find individuals and individual companies that do not fit the mold.

▲ 2. Cultural Chauvinism

If you are a U.S. citizen at this time in history, when the United States is the strongest military and economic force in the world, you may feel that it is up to people from *other* cultures to find out how *you* like to communicate, and up to them to imitate the North American style. And you may indeed get away with that arrogant approach. But there are at least two reasons why you would be better off studying and respecting the cultures of the foreigners you deal with.

First, knowledge of the culture will help you avoid misunderstandings that can undermine your own business interests (Axtell, 1993). Second, your international venture is more likely to succeed if the relationship is based on genuine friendship rather than mere necessity. In some countries, businesspeople make deals only with people they know, like, respect, and trust on a personal level.

You can begin to establish a good personal relationship with your foreign partners by learning how to communicate and behave in a manner that they will perceive as respectful.

▲ 3. Cultural Difference at Home

Despite our self-image as a melting pot, and despite the existence of what might be called a "shared culture" and a "common set of business practices" in the United States, many of our locales are dominated by racial or ethnic groups that retain their unique identity and habits, including their ways of communicating and doing business. For instance, Southern California has become the center of a rising middle-class Hispanic-American culture. The *Washington Post* quotes a successful entrepreneur from this milieu:

> A lot of corporate people . . . don't understand that our values are different. We're skeptical of government and large banks. We want personal and familial relationships. Our first call is an introduction call. We do business with handshakes. We don't sue each other. We tend to back away from paperwork. (Cannon, 1997, p. 33)

When published sources on these regional groups are not available, you can sometimes get a start-up profile by studying their homeland cultures. For example, Glen Fisher (1992), in his book *Mindsets*, describes a business mentality found throughout much of Latin America that matches very closely the *Post* article's information on the California subculture. But once again, it makes sense to consult with an actual member of the cultural group in question, or with someone who has experience working with that group, instead of relying on "book knowledge" alone.

ASSIGNMENTS FOR 4.8

1. *Cultural Gaffes* Using library or Internet sources, find a report of a miscommunication gaffe based on cultural difference and summarize it for your instructor. Indicate the lesson this anecdote holds for international communicators.

2. *Cultural Profile* Assume that your company is entering into an agreement with a company in another country and that you have been assigned to handle preliminary discussions, most of which will be done in writing. Develop a cultural profile of this country that includes useful information for communicating with your potential partners. Here are two possibilities. (a) France: One good starting point is Claire Gouttefarde's "American Values in the French Workplace," *Business Horizons* (March/April), 39(2), 60–69. The full text of this article is available online through both InfoTrac and the Business Source CD-Rom. (b) Japan: One good starting point is *The Portable Business Writer* by William Murdick (Houghton Mifflin, 1999).

Technical Writing Style

5

The technical writer tries to achieve immediate and accurate communication. A clear style is crucial to that effort. The subject matter of technical writing is usually complicated enough without burdening the reader with phrasing that delays or interferes with understanding. This chapter presents guidelines for clarity in technical writing. It extends that discussion to international communication and ends with a discussion of company style guides, using the *Telemax Style Guide* as an example.

5.1 >—— Clear Style: Sentence-Level Issues

In this section and the next one, we look at seventeen guidelines for enhancing clarity. These guidelines are presented in two sections instead of one to make classroom discussion, homework, and learning more manageable. Note, however, that the guidelines are numbered consecutively throughout the two sections.

Much more could be said on the subject of clear style than we take up in this chapter, but presenting an overwhelming flood of detailed information would violate one of the principles of clarity and undermine the usefulness of our treatment. The seventeen statements presented in these first two sections provide a challenging introduction for students trying to adjust their style for maximum clarity.

One major feature of a clear style in technical communications is the "visual style" of the presentation. This involves principles of layout and the use of graphics to accompany text. We leave those subjects for later chapters.

▲ 1. Prefer Right Branching to Left Branching or Embedding

Sentences that begin with the subject-verb combination and then add text to the right of the verb are said to be right branching. Left-branching sentences begin with substantial text before the subject. Sentences with embedding have substantial text between the subject and the verb. Below are five model sentences illustrating five patterns, three that are difficult to read followed by two that are easy to read. The model sentences discuss the use of an electronic pen and pad to control camera angles in a distance-learning classroom.

Here are the three difficult-to-read sentences. The first is characterized by extensive left branching:

xxxxxxxxxx SUBJECT VERB xxxxx

(1) Because the pen allows more precise control on the pad, to move both cameras, in most cases, **teachers should use** the pen rather than the mouse.

The second involves extensive embedding:

SUBJECT xxxxxxxxxx VERB xxxxx

(2) **Teachers** wishing to move both cameras, because the pen allows more precise control on the pad, **should use** the pen in most cases rather than the mouse.

The third involves both significant left branching and significant embedding:

xxxxxxxxxx SUBJECT xxxxxxxxxx VERB xxxxx

(3) Because the pen allows more precise control on the pad, **teachers,** to move both cameras, in most cases **should use** the pen rather than the mouse.

Now we come to the easy-to-read sentences. The first is characterized by right branching only:

SUBJECT VERB xxxxxxxxxx

(4) **Teachers should use** the pen rather than the mouse to move both cameras, in most cases, because the pen allows more precise control on the pad.

The other involves insignificant left branching:

xxx SUBJECT VERB xxxxxxxxxx

(5) In most cases, **teachers should use** the pen rather than the mouse to move both cameras because the pen allows more precise control on the pad.

Sentence (5) above brings the sentence modifier *In most cases* to the front. A short left-branching element does not decrease clarity. In fact, it may be necessary to prevent the sentence from ending on a weak phrase, taking away emphasis from the main point. Pattern (5) is better than this version below:

> (6) Teachers should use the pen rather than the mouse to move both cameras because the pen allows more precise control on the pad, in most cases.

We are talking here about preferences and general patterns of style, not strict rules. You may sometimes find it necessary, for example, to use substantial left branching to signal an important condition for an action:

> (7) If the red warning light comes on, shut down the machine.

▲ 2. Keep Subjects and Noun Strings Short

A bloated subject makes for difficult reading, even if the subject comes at the beginning of the sentence and is immediately followed by the verb:

> (1) High-quality text, adequate speed, easy installation, and a price between $250 and $350 were the established criteria.

Take the information in the subject and put it after the verb:

> (2) We established these criteria: high-quality text, adequate speed, easy installation, and a price between $250 and $350.

Long noun strings, which usually show up as subjects, should also be avoided. Don't write:

> (3) The host system access determiner is. . . .

Instead, write:

> (4) Access to the host system is determined by. . . .

▲ 3. Break Up Long Sentences

Varying sentence length increases the pleasantness and, often, the readability of your text. But in technical writing you should avoid the very long sentence that does one or both of these:

■ gives multiple instructions
■ provides an overwhelming amount of information.

For example:

> (1) If your computer freezes, reset the computer and, when the opening screen reappears, use your mouse to select the PowerDrive icon, which looks like a hammer with the letters PD crossing the handle.

That sentence contains multiple instructions, along with detailed information about an icon. One solution to the overly long sentence is to break it up into two or more shorter sentences:

> (2) If your computer freezes, reset the computer. Wait for the opening screen to reappear. Then use your mouse to select the PowerDrive icon, which looks like a hammer with the letters PD crossing the handle.

In the example below, the writer has stuffed too much information into one sentence:

> (3) A progressive dial-out conference is built one party at a time as an operator sequentially calls and joins participants by calling and immediately joining each party in a progressive fashion or by calling each party and putting them on hold until all parties can be joined together in conference simultaneously.

We can make (3) more readable by breaking it up:

> (4) A progressive dial-out conference is built one party at a time by an operator. The operator sequentially calls and joins participants in either of two ways: The operator can call and immediately join each party in a progressive fashion, or the operator can call each party and put them on hold until all parties can be joined together in conference simultaneously.

Let us add a caution here. Shortening sentences can sometimes reduce cohesion and hide relationships between statements. Consider these examples:

> (5) Save your file. Then check spelling. Any global operation, improperly executed, might result in the loss of your file.

> (6) Before checking spelling, save your file, because any global operation, improperly executed, might result in the loss of your file.

In the longer sentence, the reason for saving your file is made explicit.

▲ *4. Prefer a Verbal Style to a Nominal Style*

A *nominal* is any word or structure that functions as a noun. A nominal style is noun-heavy. It uses a lot of nouns derived from verbs through the addition of a suffix: *select → selection, assist → assistance, operate → operation*. A nominal style tends to use weak verbs that carry little meaning. The linking verb *be* is the most common. Learn to recognize *be* in all its forms: *am, is, are, was, were, been, being, be.* (*Be* can also function as an auxiliary verb, but we are not concerned with that situation here.)

There's nothing wrong with using *be* to link nouns and adjectives to the subject:

(1) Those instructions are too long.

However, when a sentence is expressing an action, using *be* is less effective because the action must then be expressed by a nonverb—a noun or an adjective. Compare (2) and (3) below:

(2) The young intern was an assistant to Dr. Jones during the operation.

(3) The young intern assisted Dr. Jones during the operation.

In (2) the action of assisting appears as a derived noun after *was* (*was an assistant*), but in (3) the action is expressed more directly as the verb (*assisted*).

A number of weak verbs merely indicate that something happened but don't name the precise action: *occur, implement, happen.* Here's an example:

(4) Shutting down of the machine should occur in emergencies.

The action—*shut down*—is expressed through a derived "-ing" noun (a "gerund"); the verb *occur* doesn't name the specific action. Compare with this:

(5) Shut down the machine in emergencies.

The verbal style, in contrast to the nominal style, uses strong verbs that name the action. Below is a passage written in each of the two styles.

Nominal style:
(6) At the end of the day, an efficient office worker has her desk in a cleared condition, and she has knowledge of the location of everything.

Verbal style:
(7) At the end of the day, an efficient office worker clears her desk and knows where to find everything.

The nominal style often shows up in the writing of bureaucrats, who apparently feel that it makes them sound intellectual and knowledgeable. Perhaps it does. Research has shown that office workers looking at memos and even English teachers looking at compositions are more impressed by a clunky nominal style than by a tight, fast-paced verbal style. It is arguable, then, that the nominal style works in some situations. However, *it does not work in technical writing.* Technical writers gain nothing by sounding pedantic.

Competent technical writers use a verbal style.

▲ *5. Make the Agent the Subject*

Richard Lanham (1981), in a book on business writing style, titles one of his chapters "Who's Kicking Who?" Lanham argues that writers should put the "kicker" in the subject position and the "kickee" in the object position. The kicker, in grammatical terms, is the "agent," the person or thing doing the action. The kickee is the grammatical "object," the person or thing being acted on.

We saw in the previous section that when the writer uses weak verbs, the action can get lost in a nominal or modifying element. Likewise, the actor, or agent, can get lost if placed somewhere other than in the subject position. In the sentence below, the writer has buried the agent in an initial subordinate element:

(1) With consumers losing interest in our product, a decline in sales occurred.

A *decline* didn't really do anything. The primary kicker is *consumers.* Another agent, or actor, is *sales*—they declined. Let's make *consumers* and *sales* subjects:

(2) Consumers lost interest in our product, and sales dropped.

In the sentence below, the agent, *beginners,* gets buried in a subordinate element occurring in the predicate:

(3) Using the mouse is better for beginners than using keyboard commands.

In a first attempt at revision, let's put the word *beginners* in the subject position and turn the nominalized *Using* into the verb:

(4) Beginners should use the mouse rather than keyboard commands.

Technical writers like to make the reader the agent when feasible. Let's further revise this sentence to make the reader the unspoken subject of a command:

(5) Use the mouse rather than keyboard commands.

That would work if we were addressing an audience of beginners. If addressing an audience of mixed proficiency, we might say:

(6) If you are a beginner, use the mouse rather than keyboard commands.

Sometimes writers leave the agent out of the sentence completely. Lanham offers this example:

(7) If there is significant negative reaction to the taste, then changes in the recipe would be recommended. (p. 16)

Here's Lanham's revision:

(8) If people don't like its taste, we should change it. (p. 17)

We have to be careful when making generalizations about style. A writer's style arises over the course of passages, not just within sentences. What makes for a clear sentence may depend on what has come before. A series of sentences developing the topic of "mouse use" might effectively begin with *Using the mouse* . . ., as in sentence (3) above. At that moment, the writer may be more concerned with maintaining a coherent focus on the topic than with following a rule about agency.

Still, when editing your texts for clarity, continually ask yourself "Who's kicking who?" If you find an agent buried in a subordinate element, consider moving it into the subject position. If you can't find an agent at all, consider putting one in and making it the subject of a strong verb.

▲ 6. Prefer Active Voice to Passive Voice

We have already determined that it is preferable to make the agent (the doer of the action) the subject of the sentence. The active voice allows that; the passive voice does not. For example:

the agent (the one who controls)
Active: *The system administrator* controls access at every level.

the agent (the one who controls)
Passive: Access is controlled at every level by *the system administrator.*

Notice above that the passive voice removes the agent (*administrator*) from the subject position, and replaces it with the object (*access*). Box 5.1 presents a full structural analysis of voice. Sometimes the writer of a passive-voice sentence removes the agent from the whole sentence, as in this example:

(1) Next, the installation program should be run.

Installation sounds technical: Should the user, or a technician, run the program? The reader may be left wondering.

Even when the agent is included in the passive-voice sentence, the statement is often clumsy:

(2) Next, the installation program should be run by the user.

In the active-voice version of this same sentence, the agent becomes the subject:

(3) Next, the user should run the installation program.

BOX 5.1 ▼ A Structural Analysis of Voice

NP = noun phrase

AUX = auxiliary verb (*have, be,* or modal auxilary)

V = main verb

-en = the past-participle form of the verb (verbs usually take an *-ed, -en,* or *-t* inflection in the past participle form, as in *helped, given, spent*)

BE = the verb *be* as a required verb in passive-voice constructions (*be* takes these forms: *am, is, are, was, were, been, being, be*)

( ) = optional (for example, sentences require a V but no AUX, so we put parentheses around AUX) (see below)

Active	Passive
$NP_1 + (AUX) + V + NP_2$	$NP_2 + (AUX) + BE + V^{-en} + (by + NP_1)$

With no auxiliary verb:

Sarah wrote the manual.	The manual was written by Sarah.
Sarah always writes the manual.	The manual is always written by Sarah.

With *have* or *be*:

Sarah has written the manual.	The manual has been written by Sarah.
Sarah is writing the manual.	The manual is being written by Sarah.

With a modal auxiliary (*can, could, will, would, shall, should, may, might, must*):

Sarah should write the manual.	The manual should be written by Sarah.

With a modal auxiliary, *have*, and *be*:

Jeff could have been editing the manual by now.	The manual could have been being edited by now.

Distinguishing features of the passive voice:

The verb *be* followed by a past participle, and the presence or possibility of a *by* phrase.

Or, with the active voice, the writer can make the reader the agent by using the command form, with its implied "you" as the subject:

(4) Next, run the installation program.

The passive voice has its uses. For example, use the passive voice when you don't know (or don't care) who did the action of the verb:

(5) Most high-tech companies in this city were founded in the 1980s.

instead of

(6) Somebody founded most high-tech companies in this city in the 1980s.

You may wish to use the passive voice to refer to things that are generally true:

(7) Real estate is valued for its location.

Or to things that experts generally do:

(8) Accounts are balanced at regular intervals, usually monthly.

Report writers often use the passive voice to avoid a bragging tone:

(9) These goals were achieved by February.

Instead of

(10) I achieved these goals by February.

The passive voice is also used to maintain focus on a particular topic. For example, in the following sentences, the writer wishes to focus on the nature of "projects":

(11) Most work in this organization is accomplished through projects. Projects are carried out by teams, and they usually last more than a month.

When written in the active voice, the focus shifts to employees:

(12) Employees in this organization accomplish most of their work through projects. Employees work in teams and usually spend at least a month on each project.

Employees are the doers, so to focus on them we use the active voice. Since projects don't do anything, we need to use the passive voice to keep our focus on them. Most writers, however, have a tendency to use the passive voice more often than necessary. Learn to recognize the passive voice in your own texts so that you can revise to active voice if appropriate.

▲ 7. Emphasize Parallel Structure

Using parallel structure means phrasing elements in a list in as similar a form as possible. Box 5.2 shows an explanation from the *Telemax Style Guide*. When the parallel structures are long, writers sometimes emphasize the parallelism by repeating words in order to add to the clarity. Note, below, how the parallelism in (1) has been emphasized in (2):

(1) The new policy, though not improving the quality of reports, did, however, result in a decrease in improperly formatted reports, fewer late submissions, and less complaining all around.

BOX 5.2 ▼ Excerpt on Parallelism from the Telemax Style Guide

USE PARALLEL STRUCTURE

Principle: When creating lists, put the elements in the list in as similar a form as possible. The list in this sentence consists of *-ing* words:

> That company prefers packaging, addressing, and loading its packages at its warehouse.

Most Common Problem: A breakdown in parallel structure, which looks like:

> That company prefers packaging, addressing, and to load its packages at the warehouse.

The unbalanced element in the above sentence is *to load*.

Correction: The easiest solution to such a problem is to change the unbalanced element so that it matches, as closely as possible, the structure of the other elements in the list. In the example above, this is easy to do: just change *to load* to *loading*.

Additional problems: Sometimes the unbalanced element cannot easily be changed into the desired form, as in this example:

> The company's performance last year was erratic, confusing, and with lots of ups and downs.
> The company's performance last year was erratic, confusing, and up-and-downish.

Up-and-downish doesn't work. So in this circumstance, remove the awkward element from the list:

> The company's performance last year was erratic and confusing. The stock went up and down.

Spotting the Problem: When editing for balanced structure, look for elements within sentences connected by *and* and *or*. In addition, all vertical lists should be parallel. In the example below, the fourth item is not parallel:

Telemax provides these services:
- Customized product development
- Full product documentation
- Installation and training
- Answers its hotline 24 hours a day

The first three items in the list are noun phrases. Change the last item to a noun phrase:

- A 24-hour-a-day hotline

(2) The new policy, though not improving the quality of reports, did, however, result in a decrease in improperly formatted reports, a decrease in late submissions, and a decrease in complaints all around.

▲ *8. Use Punctuation to Maintain Clarity*

Punctuation enhances clarity by revealing sentence structure. Take this structure, for example:

xxxxx, SUBJECT PREDICATE

The comma after the introductory element, before the subject noun phrase, signals the end of the introductory material and the beginning of the subject. Note how the absence of this comma can lead to misreading:

(1) Below the switch for the camera you will find the switch for the lights.

(2) Below the switch for the camera should be in the off position.

Clarity is improved by the use of the comma after the introductory element:

(3) Below the switch for the camera, you will find the switch for the lights.

(4) Below, the switch for the camera should be in the off position.

Although many professional writers routinely leave out that introductory comma, technical writers make a habit of putting it in. Another optional comma technical writers tend to use for clarity is the comma after the penultimate element in a list (called the "serial comma"). In the example below, the serial comma is the one after Y:

(5) You need to purchase X, Y, and Z.

Leaving the comma out after Y is permitted by most style guidelines, but it can lead to confusion when the elements in a list are complex:

(6) The personnel manual for West End Clothing Outlet communicates policies on a variety of issues, including personal appearance, work habits and attitude, after-work dating of employees and harassing employees.

The comma missing after the first *employees* may lead the reader to at least momentarily read *dating of employees and harassing employees* as a pair, like *work habits and attitude.* The result would be a false impression that *after-work* applies to *harassing.* The following version is clearer:

(7) The personnel manual for West End Clothing Outlet communicates policies on a variety of issues, including personal appearance, work

habits and attitude, after-work dating of employees, and harassing employees.

Semicolons can be substituted for commas to separate elements in a list when one or more of the elements has internal commas. The first example below is less clear than the second:

(8) The Telemax Communicator II system supports a multimedia user directory, a built-in user directory, a set of eight preset configurations, all of which can be accessed and applied to conferences, and a dialed number identification service (DNIS).

(9) The Telemax Communicator II system supports a multimedia user directory; a built-in user directory, a set of eight preset configurations, all of which can be accessed and applied to conferences; and a dialed number identification service (DNIS).

▲ *9. Write Correctly*

By *correctly* we mean consistent with Standard American English: permissible sentence structure; educated use of words; conventional punctuation; standard use of capitalization, italics, and quotation marks; and so forth. Standard American English consists of those practices found in the work of good writers across the country today. Bear in mind those three criteria: confirmed by practice, national, and up-to-date.

Get in the habit of observing those standards as they show up in your reading, and get in the habit of using reference books when in doubt. As you do so, be alert to small differences in standards from one context to another. For example, technical writers write percentages like this: 5%. Authors of literary texts and essays often use a different format: 5 percent.

For a usage dictionary, which will tell you how to correctly use selected words and grammatical constructions, you would be well served by a text that bases its judgments on observation of good writing, such as *Webster's Dictionary of English Usage*. Those that base their judgments on the opinions of "experts" are more likely to promote tastes in usage that are whimsical and out-of-date.

The same criticism can be made of standard English handbooks: that they prohibit certain word uses, punctuation practices, and grammatical constructions that the best professional writers routinely use. However, such books will answer noncontroversial questions about "mechanics". (capitalization, use of italics, use of quotation marks, and so forth), and they will show you how to correctly document sources. Handbooks will also pinpoint places where common "performance errors" (slip-ups), such as subject-verb agreement errors, are likely to occur. Get an English handbook, read through the sections on sentence correctness once, and then keep it handy.

For many college students, learning to write sophisticated sentences, and then learning to write them correctly, is a lengthy undertaking. A study by Richard Haswell (1986) showed sophomores making significantly more errors than freshmen when writing the same kind of text under the same conditions. As these second-year students began to use newly acquired vocabulary and syntax, they opened themselves to more opportunity for error. The junior-year students in the same study exhibited more control over this sophistication, although they still made slightly more errors than the freshmen.

There are no shortcuts to this kind of learning. Most people go through a process in which increased sophistication leads to increased error, a phenomenon that psycholinguist Thomas Bever (1982) calls "regression in the service of development." If you are having particular trouble with grammatical correctness (permissible syntax and appropriate word use), try these two strategies: (1) Use your school's writing center; make it your second home; and (2) take up reading as a hobby; place reading material at your bedside and all over your home so that wherever you alight, there's something to read.

Reading is the best way to learn high-level grammar (Murdick, 1996). Lessons and drills are worthless when it comes to learning the countless limitations on syntax, and the even greater number of semantic restrictions on individual words, that you need to know in order to write correctly. This world of knowledge must be absorbed through extensive contact with written language—what you get from prolific reading.

▲ *10. Prefer Positive to Negative Phrasing*

Positive phrasing is usually more informative and clearer than negative phrasing. Telling someone what not to do may leave that person wondering what *to* do. Double negatives can be especially confusing ("not only should you not . . ."). Take this awkward sentence:

(1) When giving directions, not only should you not use the passive voice but you should also not use the third-person point of view.

That statement becomes much clearer if you tell the reader what to do:

(2) When giving directions, use the active voice and the second-person point of view.

Despite this general rule, warnings often require a negative form for clarity and emphasis, especially when there is no positive action or specific step to be taken:

(3) WARNING: Never remove the case from your monitor!

▲ 11. Be Blunt

According to writing expert Leo Rockas, "[T]he advice 'Be clear' might often be more helpfully put as 'Be blunt'" (1992, p. 210). Instead of the indirect instruction in (1), write the direct command in (2):

(1) Removing the case on your monitor is inadvisable.

(2) Don't remove the case on your monitor.

Instead of

(3) We do not have the means to serve as a financing agency, nor do we have a payment structure allowing delays for those of our customers who lack full funding at the time of installation.

write

(4) Full payment is due upon installation. We don't finance or give credit.

ASSIGNMENTS FOR 5.1

Note: Most of the sentences to be revised in these assignments come from published texts or company documents. To protect privacy, they are presented anonymously.

1. *Right Branching and Long Subjects* Rewrite these sentences to increase right branching and to eliminate long subjects.

   a. Knowledge of an athlete's genetic endowment for muscle fiber type distribution obviously would provide a tremendous advantage, particularly in terms of developing precise training recommendations.

   b. The concept of the filament of a three-dimensional spiral wave considerably simplifies the description of the wave pattern.

   c. It has been in addressing problems of precision and conceptual sophistication in the writing of reasonably mature upper-classmen, of American and foreign graduate students, and occasionally of university scientists who have sought assistance in preparation of manuscripts for publication, that I have utilized sentence combining.

2. **Long Sentences** Break up these sentences into two or more sentences to make the texts more readable. Make any other changes that would add to clarity.

   a. It has been in addressing problems of precision and conceptual sophistication in the writing of reasonably mature upper classmen, of American and foreign graduate students, and occasionally of university scientists who have sought assistance in preparation of manuscripts for publication, that I have utilized sentence combining.

   b. A concern over possible post office closings has also been based upon the fact that the postal service has been losing money and that the postal service is searching for economies as reflected in the Budget Resolution passed by the United States Senate which calls for certain reductions in postal subsidies.

   c. Manufacturer has reserved the right to change the price to Dealer of new motor vehicles without notice, and if such cash delivered price is increased by Dealer, Purchaser may, if dissatisfied therewith, cancel this Order, in which event if a used motor vehicle has been traded in as part of the consideration for such new motor vehicle, such used motor vehicle shall be returned to Purchaser upon payment of a reasonable charge for storage and repairs (if any) or, if such used motor vehicle has been previously sold by Dealer, the amount received therefor, less a selling commission of 15% and any expense incurred in storing, insuring, conditioning or advertising said used motor vehicle for sale, shall be returned to Purchaser.

3. **Verbal Style with Agent in Subject Position** Revise these sentences to a more verbal style. Figure out who's kicking who and what the main action is; then put the kicker in the subject position and the action in the verb.

   a. There were evaluations of all policies by the manager.

   b. The installation of your system by our professional crew will reach completion within one week of purchase.

   c. The resignation of the supervisor was a prompt event once his understanding of his loss of respect became clear to him.

4. **Voice** Revise these sentences as necessary, changing passive voice to active voice wherever it is reasonable to do so. Invent agents if necessary.

   a. The report you received this morning was finished two weeks ago, but got delayed by Henderson, who thought that some of the data should be rechecked.

   b. All reports are to be written in Microsoft Word so that they can be easily edited and proofread by the technical writing staff.

c. The proposal is being returned to you so that it can be revised before being sent to the prospective client.

d. The sales effort was completed successfully—our Communicator II will be purchased statewide!

Examine the first paragraph in section 5.1. Why do the authors of this book use passive voice starting with the second sentence? Write the paragraph entirely in the active voice and then entirely in the passive voice. Are either of these versions better? Be prepared to justify your answer.

5. *Parallel Structure and Punctuation* Make these sentences clearer by using optional punctuation and by emphasizing parallel structure.

a. The Blast feature of the Communicator III allows the chairman to dial into the MCU and enter a passcode and the preset numbers associated with the passcode will automatically be blast dialed.

b. As can be seen in the consolidated balance sheet of May 31, 1998 our report includes a record of operations, stockholders' equity and changes in financial position.

c. Given Telemax's high performance multimedia conferencing platform the Communicator IV is ideal for specialized applications requiring limited port capacity such as distance education, as we have seen, telemedicine, both home based and hospital based, telebanking, and kiosk Automatic Call Distribution (ACD).

6. *Correctness* Use a handbook or usage dictionary to determine:

a. punctuation of the phrase *such as*

b. uses of the colon

c. subject-verb agreement when the subject is "The Document Department manager or her two technical writers. . . ."

d. the difference between *lie* and *lay* and between *historical* and *historic.*

In a memo to your instructor, summarize one of these articles on correctness:

a. Leonard, D. J. (1990). Language in change: Academics' and executives' perceptions of usage errors. *Journal of Business Communication*, 27, 137–158.

b. Haswell, R. H. (1988). Error and change in college student writing. *Written Communication*, 5, 479–499.

c. Hairston, M. (1981). Not all errors are created equal: Nonacademic readers in the professions respond to lapses in usage. *College English*, 43, 794–806.

7. *Positive Phrasing and Bluntness* Revise these sentences to make them more positive and direct in their phrasing.

   a. It not only would not be a good idea to not save your document before performing a global operation on it, such as a spell check, it would not be advisable to write and not save at regular short intervals in an environment in which brownouts are not infrequent.

   b. The development of competence in this software usually requires an extended learning curve.

   c. The present version of Pro Scribbler, although perfectly usable, is not without minor problems due to unanticipatable performance anomalies under certain conditions.

5.2 >——Clear Style: Word-Level Issues

We now turn to enhancing clarity at the word level.

▲ 1. Prefer Nouns to Pronouns

Although pronouns are said to be useful for achieving cohesion because they connect one part of the text to an earlier part (the thing they refer to), that same interdependence can cause trouble when the reference, or "antecedent," is unclear. Consider this sentence:

> (1) Use the pen to momentarily move the camera focus at the local site from the students to the white board. This will provide students at the remote site with a quick glance at how the local class has solved the problem.

Does *This* at the beginning of the second sentence refer to using the pen or moving the focus? Because you're not sure, the intended emphasis is lost. Revise to:

> (2) Use the pen to momentarily move the camera focus at the local site from the students to the white board. This simple pen action will provide students at the remote site with a quick glance at how the local class has solved the problem.

Or revise to:

> (3) Use the pen to momentarily move the camera focus at the local site from the students to the white board. This shift in focus will provide students at the remote site with a quick glance at how the local class has solved the problem.

Avoid *they* to mean authorities, operators, salespeople, and so on, when there is no antecedent:

(4) At a small retail store, they will charge you twice as much.

Revise to:

(5) A small retail store will charge you twice as much.

Some beginning writers tend to use a noun once and, thereafter, time and again, a pronoun to refer to it. Professional technical writers are more apt to use a pattern in which they repeat the noun two or three times, then use a pronoun, then go back to using the noun again. Compare (6) and (7) below:

(6) The Japanese prefer an indirect rhetorical approach in which they approach the main point slowly, sometimes only suggesting or hinting at the intended message. (Americans, of course, like to start with a clear statement of the main point.) They are educated in a school system that expects students to figure things out for themselves, and they expect readers to get the point without being told everything explicitly. They consider direct questioning about the obvious to be childish. (American students are told that there's no such thing as a "dumb question.") They view direct expression of the obvious as condescending.

(7) The Japanese prefer an indirect rhetorical approach in which the writer approaches the main point slowly, sometimes only suggesting or hinting at the intended message. (Americans, of course, like to start with a clear statement of the main point.) The Japanese are educated in a school system that expects students to figure things out for themselves, and they expect readers to get the point without being told everything explicitly. The Japanese consider direct questioning about the obvious to be childish. (American students are told that there's no such thing as a "dumb question.") The Japanese view direct expression of the obvious as condescending.

Professional writers always switch to a pronoun when the repetition of a noun sounds unpleasant. For technical writing, push your text to that level, then retreat. In other words, keep using the noun until the repetition sounds bad; then substitute a pronoun.

▲ 2. Prefer Simple Vocabulary

Readability research has shown that increases in the sophistication of vocabulary make reading more difficult (Fry, 1988). This is true even when the reader knows the meanings of the "big" words. Common words are easier for the brain to process. Compare these two statements:

(1) The Preface delineates the differences in company infrastructure as proposed in the 1998 and the 1999 strategic plans.

(2) The Preface shows the differences in company organization as proposed in the 1998 and the 1999 strategic plans.

No doubt you can read both, but the second is easier to comprehend. Of course, one has to be careful that the simpler version doesn't lose anything in the revision. There will be instances, for example, when the term *infrastructure* implies something not captured by the term *organization*. Nevertheless, technical writers should scan their texts for sophisticated vocabulary, editing to a simpler vocabulary when possible. A simpler vocabulary does not mean that the writing is less sophisticated. As Edward Fry points out, "best-selling novels are written at an eighth-grade level according to readability formulas" (1988, p. 87).

Also, be alert to the fact that commonly occurring words can become difficult when used idiomatically or in a technical sense. Take this sentence, for example:

(3) The Kucera and Francis word frequency list is based on over a million words of running text sampled from fifteen different kinds of writing.

The term *running text* indicates that Kucera and Francis did not randomly select words from a book or article but, rather, took long passages or selected the whole text as the source for words. Both *running* and *text* are simple words, but put together as a technical term they may baffle a reader. More safely, though less economically, we could have said this:

(3) The Kucera and Francis word frequency list is based on over a million words drawn from fifteen different kinds of writing, using long passages or whole texts.

On the other hand, you can confuse experts by avoiding technical terminology that they know and expect. Accountants, for example, might wonder what you meant if you were to write "We check on the accuracy of our accounts every month." Are you saying that you "balance" the accounts?

▲ 3. Use Consistent Terms

In a creative writing class, you may be taught to employ "elegant variation," the use of synonyms to avoid a tiresome repetition of words. In technical writing, however, you should continue to use the same technical term to refer to any one thing. Changing terms may cause the reader to wonder if you are talking about something new. Avoid this:

> (1) Note that the <u>monitor</u> now displays several <u>options</u> for directing calls. You can choose any <u>selection</u> on this new <u>screen</u> by clicking on it with your mouse arrow.

Instead, write this:

> (2) Note that the <u>screen</u> now displays several <u>options</u> for directing calls. You can choose any <u>option</u> on this new <u>screen</u> by clicking on it with your mouse arrow.

"Controlled language" is language specified by an organization for use in its texts. Every company has its own terminology that it uses to refer to itself, its products, its product components, and its services. A beginning technical writer like Wendy Smith needs to learn this terminology quickly and must use it consistently. Pittsburgh Telemax, for example, has rules about the use of its name. *Telemax*, to refer to the company, is permissible for internal documents, but documents that go outside the company must always use the full name *Pittsburgh Telemax* (and in addresses, *Pittsburgh Telemax, Inc.*). An exception occurs when *Telemax* is part of a product name: *Telemax Communicator II*. The company has specific terms for each product component, and those terms must be used, even in documents that may be read by nontechnical audiences.

Most words in English have multiple meanings. However, controlled terms are used in only one way; that is, each term is permitted only one meaning within company texts. For example, in software documentation for the Windows platform, you will often find the term *activate* used to mean "select" or "make active" a particular window that is already open but inactive. However, Telemax writers never use *activate* in that way. Instead, the writers use *activate* to refer to what happens to a conference call when it is transferred to the bridge for the purpose of making connections. The call is "activated."

Since *activate* is not available to Telemax writers for any other meaning, the writers use the phrase "*click on* the window" to mean "select or activate the window."

Important: Do not extend the concept of one-meaning-only to nontechnical language. Most words have two or more standard meanings, and all of those meanings are acceptable. Don Bush, an important authority on technical writing, has criticized the *Microsoft Manual of Style for Technical Publications* (a text that he admits has many good qualities) for insisting that words like *since* and *while* be used only as adverbs of time and never as expressions meaning "because" and "although," and for banning useful expressions like *activate* (Bush, 1999, p. 38). Almost any word can be ambiguous in some imaginable context. Determine whether your use of a word is truly ambiguous by examining it in its context, not by following contrived rules that ignore what good writers do.

▲ 4. Define Abbreviations, Acronyms, and Technical Terminology

A member of the military, criticizing the use of abbreviations and acronyms in the armed services, posted this statement for the U.S. government's plain-English Web discussion group:

> So, to take this a step further, if I want to suggest a change in how to imput time to make it more friendly, I would have to submit the proper SCR to the IPT, who will then run it up the flagpole with the RM folks and CSIM. If it gets the nod there, of course, CSIM and RM will have to submit the proper DA form to modify the reg; which requires input from MP ITTS, WARSIM, PM CATT and the Loggies; of course any permenant change will have to have the blessing of the CG, the OMA and budget wienies, as well as the PMs for TWGGS, JANUS, and C4I!

The author of that statement comments that in "every briefing I have attended which had people outside my command attend, you could tell that half of what was presented was not understood by the majority of people."

There's nothing wrong with insiders using abbreviations and acronyms to communicate among themselves, but whenever a text is going to be read by someone outside the circle, each abbreviation and acronym should be defined (the exceptions being those that are understood by everyone, such as *Mr.* and *scuba*). It is conventional to write out the term first, followed by the letters you will use to refer to it later:

> At our company, the Documentation Department Manager (DDM) is responsible for all documents that go outside the company. The DDM is also responsible for training technical writers.

If the next appearance of the term occurs much later in the text, don't assume that the reader will remember the meaning of the abbreviation or acronym. Restate the whole term, again putting the letters you will eventually use to refer to it in parentheses after the term. If you never use an abbreviation or acronym for the term, then don't put one in parentheses after the term.

As for technical terminology, there are no hard rules about what terms need to be defined in any given text. This is a judgment call, based on audience analysis. In general, you will want to define a term if both these conditions exist:

▌ the term is crucial for understanding the text

▌ there is a chance that some readers will not be familiar with the term and will not be able to figure out its meaning from the context.

The same is true for scientific symbols. Everyone knows the symbol for addition, but not all readers will recognize the symbol for infinity.

Some writers create a glossary, in table form, specifically for abbreviations, acronyms, terms, and symbols used in the text. This kind of glossary, if it isn't too long, will often be placed in an introductory section, before the running text begins.

You should provide a "stipulative definition" for any ordinary word or technical term that is being used in a special way in your text. Our earlier discussion of *activate* provides an example of an ordinary word used in a special, stipulated sense.

Several types of definition are available to the technical writer: the short parenthetical definition, the short formal definition, and the extended definition. Each is discussed below.

The Short Parenthetical Definition   In this approach, you provide a definition in parentheses or within parenthetical commas, using a synonym or a brief explanatory phrase. Sentence (1) below uses parentheses to set off a synonym definition for *diacritical* and an explanatory-phrase definition for *anglicized*:

(1) Telemax style avoids diacritical (accent) marks for foreign expressions that have been anglicized (fully adopted into the English language).

This sentence uses parenthetical commas to set off the definition of *bridge*:

(2) The bridge, a device that assembles calls, is required only for multipoint conferencing.

The Short Formal Definition   Use full sentences to formally define a term, either within the text or in a glossary. Some texts begin with a short glossary of key terms; however, if the glossary is long, it must be placed at the end of the chapter or the end of the book. Box 5.3 shows an excerpt from a glossary at the end of Houghton Mifflin's *A Guide for Authors.*

Formal definitions typically classify the term (put it in a category) and then show how it differs from other members of its category:

(3) A Spiffy drive is a small, removable-disk disk drive. It looks like an ordinary floppy drive, but it stores on its disks 1 gigabyte of information,

about 700 times as much as a high-density (1.44 megabyte) floppy drive will store.

The author of the above definition decided to distinguish between the Spiffy drive and a similar device on the basis of storage capacity. In other circumstances, the writer might have made a distinction on the basis of technology or price. The point is, you must carefully choose how to differentiate your term according to what will be most useful for your reader and most consistent with your purpose.

BOX 5.3 ▼ Excerpt from a Glossary

acknowledgments   A section in the preface of the book in which the author acknowledges the people who contributed to the book; for example, colleagues, reviewers, student assistants, typists, secretaries, and particular people on the publishing staff who made special contributions to the project.

alignment   The arrangement of elements so that lines drawn along their respective edges would coincide to form a single straight line; for example, captions are often aligned with one edge of the photo.

art proofs   Copies of final artwork sent to the author for review. If any corrections are needed, one set of proofs showing revisions will be returned to the artist.

art specifications (specs)   Original manuscript artwork prepared by the author for the artist to use as a model when drawing the final art. They should include any explicit instructions needed to render the art accurately.

author's alterations (AAs)   Changes made by the author, or on the author's behalf, after the manuscript has been set. Charges for these changes that exceed a certain percentage of the cost of composition will be deducted from the author's royalties.

backing page   The print on the back side of a page; for example, p. 2 backs up p. 1, and vice versa.

bad break   Division of a word on the wrong syllable at the end of a line or division of a paragraph so that only one line, or part of a line, carries over to the next page. (See **widow**)

baseline   The imaginary line that runs along a line of type touching the bottom of each letter.

bibliography   A list of reference works (books, periodical articles, etc.) that relate to the material covered in the text. It usually appears at the end of the book or chapter.

Instead of distinguishing between a term and other members of its category, formal definitions sometimes name conditions under which a term belongs to a category:

(4) A transmission glitch is an error when it sets off an alarm.

Here is one such definition from the *Police Officer Manual* for the city of Pittsburgh:

(5) A **motor vehicle pursuit** is an active attempt by a law enforcement officer, operating a motor vehicle and utilizing siren and emergency lights, to apprehend one or more occupants of another moving vehicle, **when** the driver of the fleeing vehicle is aware of the attempt and is resisting apprehension by maintaining or increasing speed in excess of the legal speed limit. [emphasis added]

The Extended Definition Some terms and abstract concepts require extended definitions running anywhere from a paragraph to several pages in length. Use techniques like the ones below according to what will best serve your purpose and your audience:

1. **Classification and differentiation:** NASDAQ is a stock market for new, growing companies.
2. **Etymology:** The word *telecommunication* is based on the Greek root *tele* meaning "far" and the Latin root *com* meaning "together."
3. **Negative definition:** An incident report is not a complaint.
4. **Contrast:** The Spiffy drive is much more expensive than a regular floppy drive.
5. **Comparison:** The external Spiffy drive looks like a regular floppy drive.
6. **Figurative comparison:** Owning a personal computer is like having a second brain, one that's less creative but faster and bigger.
7. **Examples:** A Trouble Clearance is a response to a serious problem, such as a customer complaint, an alarm, a trouble report, or an abnormal TTY printout.
8. **Purpose:** In magic, a false cut is a division of the deck designed to leave at least one portion, such as the top stock, in the same position.
9. **Physical description:** An icon looks like a child's drawing.
10. **Functional description:** A mailing-label program works by reprinting the same file over and over again, drawing data consecutively from a list of names and addresses.
11. **Components:** Your username consists of the first three letters of your last name and the last four digits in your SS number.

5   Technical Writing Style

The following extended definitions of *card trick* and *mainsail* use several of the techniques just mentioned.

A **card trick**, when done professionally, is not just a single, hidden maneuver, but a psychological entertainment based more on misdirection than sleight-of-hand. The magician typically performs the mechanical part of the trick early and quickly, often during preliminary activities, before the audience realizes that the trick has really begun. For example, if the trick involves the magical exchange of two known cards lying face down on a table, you can be sure that the cards have been switched before the audience knows that this event is supposed to happen. In such circumstances, the purpose of misdirection would be to make the audience believe that the trick is just about to begin—the card switching is about to occur—when, actually, it is all over. Thus the magician can be standing far away from the two cards when giving the command for the magical act to commence. In fact, the magician may make a big show of standing back, because he knows that "a certain skeptic in the audience won't believe this is really magic if I am within reach of those cards." That sort of patter is a part of the misdirection. Patter adds time between the sleight and the final effect. It creates a drama which is completely irrelevant to the actual trick, helping to embed in the audience's mind, by the time the trick is over, a false memory of what happened. For example, the joke at the skeptic's expense and the magician standing back will be remembered, but the exact way in which the faces of the cards were originally made known to the audience (the moment of sleight-of-hand) will be forgotten.

The **mainsail** is the large, usually triangular sail supported by the mast and the boom. Made of strong synthetic material, the mainsail for a 21-foot boat with a 35-foot mast might display 250 square yards of surface. The mainsail provides most of the locomotion for a small sailboat. It works the same way as an airplane wing does. An airplane wing is curved so that as the engines move the plane forward along the runway, air will rush more quickly over the top of the wing than the bottom, creating a relatively lower air pressure along the top, which causes the plane to be pulled upward—to fly, instead of just run along the ground. In the case of the mainsail, the air passing across the outside of the curved sail moves more quickly than the air moving across the inside. This differential in air pressure pulls the boat through the water. A sail is not just a surface to be pushed by the wind. If it were, sailboats could not sail towards the wind, which they can, up to 45 degrees. The mainsail's graceful curve and towering stature, of course, are not merely functional, but add beauty to the silent craft cruising by.

▲ *5. Eliminate Inappropriate Absolutes*

Qualify statements appropriately to make sure that your reader gets an accurate picture of what you are offering in proposals and advertisements. Many complex problems can never be solved, only ameliorated. Don't write that your proposed security policy will "eliminate employee theft"; write that it will "eliminate most employee theft."

Absolute statements can get you or your company in trouble. They can bind you to commitments that aren't going to be fulfilled. Don't write that your documentation will "prevent user error"; write that it will "reduce user error."

▲ *6. Cut the Deadwood*

You can shorten your sentences and make your text more readable by cutting deadwood. A. Lazarus, A. Mclean, and H. W. Smith (1972) define deadwood as "[w]hatever can be removed from a statement without altering its meaning or reducing the effectiveness of style" (p. 84). The authors note several kinds of deadwood, including expressions that implicitly or explicitly repeat information. Here are some examples with concise revisions:

> past experience → experience
> invited to attend → invited to
> circle around → circle
> short in length → short
> made a remark → remarked

Besides redundancy, deadwood takes the form of wordy conventional expressions for which there are brief alternatives:

> due to the fact that → because
> at the present time → now

Eliminate expressions that begin with *There is/are.* . . . Instead of writing

> There are three situations that require . . .

write

> Three situations require. . . .

Unnecessary detail results in extra verbiage:

> (1) When the opening screen appears, use your mouse to select the PowerDrive icon. This icon measures about three-quarters of an inch and looks like a hammer with a gray curved head, a yellowish stock, and the letters PD in red crossing the stock just below the head.

Users could find the PowerDrive icon if told, simply, to "look for a hammer with PD written across it."

Richard Lanham (1992, pp. 3–4) makes an amusing game of reducing the deadwood from your prose. He asks you to revise by cutting unnecessary words and then to figure out the "lard factor," the percentage of the original text that was "lard" (his term for deadwood). Lanham's formula looks like this:

$$\frac{\text{Number of words in the original} - \text{Number of words in the revision}}{\text{Number of words in the original}} \times 100 = \% \text{ lard}$$

Here's an example of revision and lard factor analysis:

Wordy statement
(2) You would do well to make a study of the above guidelines, and then you should follow them with care. (20 words)

Revision:
(3) Study the above guidelines and then follow them carefully. (9 words)

Analysis:
$$\frac{20 - 9}{20} \times 100 = 55\% \text{ lard}$$

ASSIGNMENTS FOR 5.2

1. *Nouns, Simple Vocabulary, Consistent Terms* Rewrite these sentences to create a clearer style by substituting nouns for pronouns, simple words for big words, and consistent use of terms for inconsistent use.

   a. The Telemax CommStation 18+ uses a tactile feedback membrane on the front panel. It allows the user to join with or drop out of any displayed conference; it also allows the operator to switch between monitor and talk-listen modes during conversations.

   b. The new policy abrogates the use of technical writing employees for ordinary business writing activities, which will now be carried out by management and marketing personnel.

   c. Software initial configuration is contingent upon the original hardware setup.

2. *Definitions* (a) Identify the methods of definition found in the *card trick* and *mainsail* examples at the end of section 5.2(15). (b) For an audience of tenth-graders, define one of the following terms using all three forms of definition discussed above (short parenthetical definition, short formal definition, extended definition): *floppy disk, modem, scanner, Web home*

page, Internet, English handbook, bibliography, front matter, back matter, clear style. (c) Write a short formal definition of a term of your own choosing; assume a context in which price is of paramount importance. (d) Write all three kinds of definition for an important term that first-semester students at your school must understand (e.g., *Incomplete* as a grade). Your purpose is to help these novices avoid harmful mistakes.

3. *Absolutes* Revise the following sentences by introducing qualifications or eliminating absolutes where necessary:

   a. People who don't use computers are afraid of technology.

   b. Our company offers the best deals anywhere.

   c. Never buy the latest technology; it is always unproven and buggy.

   d. Today, the field of technical writing is the right career for students who like to write.

4. *Deadwood* Revise these sentences to eliminate deadwood; then figure out the lard factor for each original sentence.

   a. Dear Sir: I am a person who is interested in test-driving your product, the Deluxe Power Tracktor, which I saw advertised in a magazine that I was reading.

   b. I hope that by next year we will be able to have the new version available for customers who have indicated an interest in having an update.

   c. By comparing the models in the table, you can see that there are noticeable differences between the computers. The Mark BH 400 offers a faster modem speed and equivalent memory for a lower price.

   d. Your suggestions that you have mentioned are good ideas and they should help us to solve our problems with the parking situation.

   e. There are some technical writers who spend all of their time at work reviewing pieces of writing and other texts that will be sent to readers outside of the company.

5.3 >—— Formatting Numbers and Formulas

Technical information is often numerical. Technical writers need to know how to present numbers and formulas clearly and conventionally.

▲ 1. Big and Small Numbers

Blake and Bly (1993, p. 21) state the problem this way:

> [D]oes that transmitter in your communications system weigh three-quarters of a ton, 3/4 ton, 0.75 ton, 75/100 ton, 1, 500 pounds, 1500 lb, or 1,500 lbs? Did it cost twelve and a half million dollars, 12.5 million

dollars, \$12 1/2 million, 12.5×10^6 dollars, or \$12,500,000? Can you write these numbers any way you please? Or is there a well-defined format for handling mathematics in writing?

The answer to Blake and Bly's final question is yes. Conventions exist for writing numbers in technical writing. Here is a review:

▌ Normally use numerals for all numbers above nine:

(1) At least two workers will be needed to complete 18 window frames in a week.

(2) A fourth of the students were working on their 12th lesson.

Some exceptions:

(3) Twenty-two citizens are registered to vote. (For the first word of a sentence)

(4) Many thousands of people were on hand. (For estimates: hundreds, thousands, millions)

(5) Subjects were 8 females and 4 males. (For comparison)

(6) The card player held 3 eights in his hand. (For contrast)

(7) He's 3 years old, and the school accepts only 4-year-olds. (For age)

(8) We remember the 1960s fondly. (For dates)

(9) The return on investment was 2:1. (For ratios)

▌ Use commas to separate thousands in large numbers: 34,955,310. Note the absence of a space after the comma. Exception: Don't put commas to the right of decimals.

▌ Use numerals and words if doing so will clarify very large amounts:

It was 13 billion light years away.

▌ Write out common fractions such as *one-half, two-thirds, one-fourth* when referring to only one or two fractions:

(10) Two-thirds of the males were beyond puberty, but only one-fourth of the females were that old.

A note of caution here: Writing out fractions sometimes implies inexactitude, a rough estimate.

He ate half a loaf of bread.

If it is important for your audience to understand that you are citing exact amounts, use decimals or numerical fractions. On the other hand, writing .33 when you mean one-third is also inexact; for exactitude, write *one-third*.

▮ Prefer decimals to numeric fractions:

The worm was 0.65 cm long [*not* 65/100 cm].

Note the zero before the decimal when the number is less than one. Note also that units of measurement are always singular:

2 lb, 6 oz [*not* 2 lbs, 6 ozs].

▮ Write percentages this way:

We gave no treatment to 5% of the participants [*not* 5 percent *or* five percent].

▮ Use the word *percentage* for inexact statements:

It was a larger percentage than we had expected.

▮ Use *percent* for exact statements:

The percent increase was 2.4.

▲ 2. Units of Measurement

Use a numeral followed by a singular abbreviation for the unit of measurement, with no period after the abbreviation:

1 oz of lead, 16 cm long, a 10-mg dose.

Note the hyphen to form the adjective.

For money, write $82, with no decimal point or zeros, if 82 dollars is the exact amount. If pennies are included, use a decimal point and go out two places: $6.50. For very large, rough-figure amounts, combine numerals with words:

Some of the congressmen wanted to cut $4.6 billion from the budget.

However, for an exact amount, use numerals only:

Congressman Smith offered a plan to cut $872,650,971 from the budget.

▲ 3. Formulas

Use these symbols when presenting formulas:

- * for multiplication
- / for division
- + for addition
- − for subtraction

Note: Often, the symbol for multiplication is omitted: 2x instead of 2 * x. Spreadsheets, which are commonly employed to create tables, use an asterisk (*) to mean multiply.

Understand the "order of operations":

1. Perform operations within parentheses before operations that apply to parenthetical elements.

2. Perform multiplication and division, in either order, before addition and subtraction.

> Therefore, if $x = 2$, then:
>
> $3 * x + 1 = 7$
>
> $3 * (x + 1) = 9$

ASSIGNMENTS FOR 5.3

1. *Answer Blake and Bly* Answer the specific questions posed by Blake and Bly at the beginning of section 5.3(1).

2. *Correct Errors* Correct the errors in the use of numbers in these sentences:

   a. Participants were eighteen female college students attending a ten-week seminar on the language abilities of four-year-olds.

   b. Through our five-day workshops, we helped hundreds of students in the nineteen nineties to raise their SAT scores by thirty points or more, a ten percent or better improvement rate.

   c. The fifth book on the shelf offers one thousand jokes, about five per page.

   d. Forty-two reports were summarized in the conference program, a third of them on the subject of writing three-part reports.

   e. Forty million dollars seems like a lot of money to someone who earns thirty-eight thousand dollars a year, but it is a mere drop in our country's one and a half trillion dollar budget.

   f. The catamaran was twenty-two feet long, eight foot in the beam, with a draft of one foot.

3. *Create Formula* Create a formula that will calculate the average price of three items (x, y, and z) minus a 10 percent discount.

5.4 ➤—— Communicating Internationally in IBE Style

Because English is often used for international business, many of your communications with foreign associates will be in English. If your communications are to be effective, you will need to take into account the difficulties that non-native speakers have with foreign languages, particularly English. By using International Business English (IBE) style, you can avoid misunderstandings and communicate more clearly with an international audience. IBE style includes the following principles.

▲ *1. Avoid Complicated Sentences*

Avoid sentences whose syntax may not be analyzable by someone whose knowledge is limited to basic sentence patterns. The following sentence might give your reader trouble:

> That project done, we can then focus on bringing in your contacts, the important link between the two enterprises.

For non-native speakers, full clauses are easier to understand than clauses reduced to phrases:

> When we have finished that project . . . [*instead of* That project done].
> These contacts are an important link . . . [*instead of* the important link].

▲ *2. Avoid Idioms*

Idioms are expressions that do not mean what the words literally say. For example,

> That enterprise bought the farm

might leave a foreign colleague wondering about a real-estate purchase. For the same reason, avoid sarcasm. Recognition of ironic effects requires a sensitivity to tone that your audience may not possess when reading English. If you say disparagingly that

> our first efforts were *wonderfully successful*, weren't they? [meaning *quite unsuccessful*],

your reader might take you literally and misunderstand.

In particular, edit out verb-particle idioms, expressions that combine verbs and prepositions in idiomatic ways:

> If you *run across* any additional problems with the contract that *bear on* your obligations, *run* them *by* me, and I'll *go over* them with you before you *sign off.*

Encounter is easier to understand than *run across; relate to* is easier than *bear on; show* is easier than *run by; review* is easier than *go over; agree to the contract by signing* is easier than *sign off*.

There is nothing wrong with putting prepositional phrases after verbs. *Run up a hill* is easy to understand. But *run up a lot of debts* consists of a difficult verb idiom (*run up*) followed by a noun phrase.

Avoid slang. It is too informal, and slang words may not appear in your reader's translation dictionary.

▲ 3. Proofread Carefully

Native speakers of a language are able to recognize and ignore spelling and grammatical errors, but non-native speakers, operating from reference books that describe only correct forms, may be lost when they encounter a mistake. Avoid or explain abbreviations and acronyms. Don't use nontraditional spellings (*thru, lite*).

Note: When communicating internationally, you should consider, in addition to IBE style, the principles of cross-cultural communication discussed in Chapter 4, section 4.8.

ASSIGNMENT FOR 5.4

1. *Revise to IBE Style* Revise these sentences to a style more fitting for an international audience.

   a. Unless forced to do so, don't back down on your negotiating positions on the issues we went over last week.

   b. Re the pow wow at Jack's office tomorrow AM, we're glad you're able to fill in for Gunther and we look forward to meeting you.

5.5 ⟩—— The Promise of Simplified English

In the 1920s, language philosopher Charles Ogden developed a simplified version of English for the purposes of helping non-native speakers learn English (Ogden, 1968). Ogden's "Basic English," as he called it, consisted of 850 words and a few grammar restrictions. Nowadays, these abbreviated languages are sometimes called "constructed languages" or "controlled languages." Many are based on Ogden's work; one, known as "Homer," offers a vocabulary that consists mainly of Ogden's 850 words plus the first 1,000 words of a frequency list.

Ogden's purpose was political: He wanted to foster an international language—namely, English—to improve communication and relations among peoples around the world. Ogden's effort was unsuccessful. However, text rewritten in Basic English could sometimes be more readable than the originals (see Box 5.4). Because of that, companies have created their own versions of simplified English to make their documentation easier to read by foreign clients. For example, Caterpillar Tractor Company created Caterpillar Technical English for its repair manuals. Caterpillar now considers their controlled language important proprietary information; as one spokesman put it, "It has given us a competitive advantage as we standardize our authoring process" (personal communication, January 22, 1999).

BOX 5.4 ▼ Two Examples of Revision to Simplified English

Revision of a Linguistics Passage to Ogden's Basic English

ORIGINAL TEXT:

It is precisely the indispensable elements of [the English] language that have undergone the strongest Scandinavian influence, and this is raised into certainty when we discover that a certain number of those grammatical words, the small coin of language . . . which are nowhere else transferred from one language to another, have been taken over from Danish into English. —From Otto Jespersen's *Growth and Structure of the English Language*

REVISION:

In fact, the most necessary parts of the [English] language are the very ones on which the effect of Scandinavian languages has been the greatest. We become certain of this when we see that a number of working or structure words, the small change of language, have been taken into English from the Danish. There is no other example of such words being taken over from one language to another. (Both versions appear in Richards, 1943, p. 46.)

Revision of a Technical Text to Ericsson's Controlled English

ORIGINAL TEXT:

When the two bi-metal springs have room temperature a gap should be provided, however, max. 0.1 mm, between the lower side of the link and contact spring 3. The distance is measured using a feeler gauge. Adjusting is executed by bending the adjusting tongues on the stiffened spring 4 using spring bender LSH 2602 or LSH 2603. After adjusting a check should be made of the simultaneousness of the twin contacts. No bending of the bi-metal springs must be made.

REVISION:

Let the temperature of the two-metal springs become the same as room temperature. The springs will then open. The maximum acceptable distance between the lower side of the link and the contact spring 3 is 0.1 mm. Measure the distance with a feeler gauge. If you need to adjust the springs, use spring bender LSH 2602 or LSH 2603. Bend the adjusting tongues on spring 4. Do not bend the springs. Then check that the two contacts operate together. (Both versions appear in Kirkman et al., 1978, p. 161.)

A team of experts in technical communications, J. Kirkman, C. Snow, and I. Watson (1978), created a successful simplified English for a Swedish company, L. M. Ericsson. Kirkman and his colleagues point out that translations of technical documents are expensive and time consuming. They speculate that a simplified version of English will be not only easier to read by non-native speakers but also easier to translate into foreign languages, especially if the foreign company creates a simplified version of its own native language to be the receiver of the translation.

Versions of simplified English include not only a limited dictionary but also a set of rules governing grammar and style. Box 5.5 provides an example of such rules (from Thomas, Jaffe, Kinkaid & Stees, 1992, p. 71). Notice that the rules reflect some of the ideas about clarity presented in this chapter.

ASSIGNMENT FOR 5.5

1. *Translate* Translate a short text, such as a paragraph from one of your own writings, into Ogden's Basic English and send your translation to your instructor in a memo. Ogden's Basic English can be found in books by him and by I. A. Richards; it can also be found on the Internet. You may use technical terms that don't appear in Ogden's 850-word corpus, but define each term in a glossary, using only words from Ogden's corpus for your definitions. Comment on whether you feel that the result is easier to read. Include a Fog Index analysis of the original and your translation.

5.6 >——Company Style Guides

A company style guide typically describes standards for style, terminology, and layout to be used in the organization's documents. In addition, many style guides cover a broad range of topics, such as the contributions of various departments to document production procedures for maintaining privacy for both classified documents and documents written for individual customers.

One major purpose of a style guide is to maintain an appropriate and respectable company image. The company projects an image of competence when all documents leaving the premises have the same professional appearance and style.

This competent image includes a consistent use of vocabulary. *The Microsoft Manual of Style for Technical Publications*, for example, consists of a 292-page dictionary of terms showing how Microsoft writers are to

BOX 5.5 ▼ **Rules for Simplified English**

The Grouping of Words
▌ Break up noun clusters that have more than three nouns.
▌ If possible, put an article or a demonstrative adjective before a noun.

Verbs
▌ Use the following verb forms:
  • The infinitive
  • The present tense
  • The past tense
  • The simple future tense
  • The past participle as an adjective
▌ Do not use the *-ing* form of the verb.
▌ Use the active voice.
▌ Do not use the past participle with a helping verb to make a complex verb.

Sentence Length
▌ The maximum length of a sentence is 20 words.
▌ To determine sentence length:
  • The colon and the dash count as a full stop.
  • Each word in a hyphenated group counts as a word.
  • Text within parentheses is a separate sentence.

General
▌ Write only one instruction per sentence, unless two actions must be done at the same time.
▌ Write the verb in the imperative (commanding) form for instructions and warnings.
▌ If you start an instruction with a dependent clause, you must separate that statement from the rest of the instruction with a comma.
▌ Do not leave out a verb to make a sentence shorter.

Source: Reprinted with permission from *Technical Communication*, the Journal of the Society for Technical Communication.

understand and use terminology. (This manual is now offered to the general public as a standard for technical writing.) Here are two typical entries from *The Microsoft Manual*:

hexadecimal (adj)
Do not abbreviate as *hex*. Use *h* when abbreviating a number, as in "Interrupt 21h." Do not insert a space between the number and *h*.

highlight

In general, avoid using *highlight,* unless you are specifically referring to the highlighter feature in some products that users can apply to emphasize selections. Use *select* instead.

Correct
Drag the pointer to select the text you want to format.

Incorrect
Drag the pointer to highlight the text you want to format.

Over the past two years, Louis Frapp has been developing a company style guide for Telemax. Frapp researched style guides and borrowed ideas from several sources, among them an article by Durthy A. Washington (1993). Washington says this about the value of the style guide:

> Its primary function is to streamline the document development process and thus significantly reduce the time required to create new information products. But an effective style guide can also serve as a training tool for new writers, editors, and documentation managers and enable companies to realize significant cost and time savings. (p. 505)

Andrea Sutcliffe (1996) offers another advantage to having a style guide within one's organization:

> A style guide saves time spent settling arguments, both within the publications department and with others in the organization—as long as users understand that many of a style guide's points are arbitrary and the goal is consistency, not editorial absolutes. (p. 179)

Wendy Smith will rely heavily on the *Telemax Style Guide* in the first months of her employment. The *Telemax Style Guide* includes the following specific content:

FRONT MATTER:
1. a cover with the company logo
2. a title page indicating authorship, copyright, and date of latest update
3. a table of contents and list of figures
4. a forward written by Howard Stone, president of Pittsburgh Telemax, endorsing the guide and requiring employees to follow its precepts
5. an introduction by DDM Marge Mendoza explaining the purpose of the guide, what it covers, and how to use it effectively.

THE BODY:

1. overview of the document development cycle showing the contributions and responsibilities of various departments and individuals

2. the usability testing process

3. rhetoric and style: how to write clear, effective prose

4. standards for controlled language: the technical terminology specific to Telemax's documents and image, preferred word choices and spellings

5. descriptions and models of standard company documents—product documentation, business proposals and reports, marketing texts, and so on—showing the layout, organization, conventional content, fonts, use of logo, and use of conventional phrasing; this section covers such issues as when to use vertical lists and how to format them (Box 5.6)

6. standards for visuals in printed documents, including how figures are displayed and labeled

7. standards for online, nonlinear hypertext documents, with examples

8. editing and proofreading processes

9. processes for documentation maintenance and security

10. the technical writer's code of ethics (see Box 2.2).

BACK MATTER:

1. appendices

2. a glossary of technical terms and abbreviations

3. a bibliography of cited and recommended sources

4. an index.

The *Telemax Style Guide* is itself a model of technical writing. Its style conforms to the precepts that appear in its own discussion of technical style. The formatting of titles and subtitles, figure captions, and other elements of page design are consistent. The ring binding and modular chapters make it easy to add and delete pages without affecting the rest of the package. It is comprehensive enough, with a well-designed table of contents and index, to be useful to all employees who write extensively on the job.

BOX 5.6 ▼   Excerpt on Lists from the Telemax Style Guide

Rule 1: Make all elements in a list as parallel in structure as possible.

Rule 2: Generally, format a list of four or more items vertically, using hanging paragraphs.

Rule 3: Format any list of two to three items vertically when it contains elements of some complexity or importance. The two elements in the bulleted list below (under Rule 4) are sufficiently complex to justify vertical formatting.

Rule 4: Set off each vertical element with a number in parentheses or a round bullet. Use numbers when:

- The elements in the list have an inherent order, such as steps in a procedure or a list of priorities, or

- You will need to refer to one or more elements in the list.

Otherwise use round bullets, as above.

Rule 5: Separate vertical lists from the running text with a blank line above and below.

Rule 6: After the bulleted or numbered first level, set off the first sublevel list with em dashes, the second sublevel with asterisks:

- XXXXXXXXXXXXXXXXXX
  — YYYYYYYYYY
  — YYYYYYYYYY
    * ZZZZZZZZZ
    * ZZZZZZZZZ

Exception: Use lowercase letters semi-enclosed with end-parentheses if an inherent order exists, as in this example:

(1) XXXXXXXXXXXXXXXXXX
  a) First, YYYYYYYYYY
  b) Next, YYYYYYYYYY
    * ZZZZZZZZZ
    * ZZZZZZZZZ

Rule 7: Punctuate elements in a list with a period if they are complete sentences. If phrases, put a period only after the last element. Don't capitalize the first word of phrasal elements, unless they are boldfaced.

Rule 8: Break up a vertical list of eight or more items into groups with headings.

ASSIGNMENTS FOR 5.6

1. *Examine Style Guides* Using resources in your school's library and the Web, examine company style guides. Two book-length style guides that may be available in your library are (a) Sun company's *Read Me First: A Style Guide for the Computer Industry* and (b) *Wired* magazine's *Wired Style: Principles of English Usage in the Digital Age.* In a memo to your instructor, report on ideas for style guides that don't appear in the section you just read.

2. *Plan a Style Guide* Create the table of contents for a style guide for your fictional company or for your technical writing class. Include any information that might be useful to a beginning employee who must do some writing on the job or to a student who will be writing texts for the course.

3. *Write Section* Write the section covering controlled language for one of the style guides mentioned in assignment 5.6(2). Do so by creating an alphabetically organized list of terms.

Tools of the Technical Writer

Not long ago, you could do technical writing for an organization if you understood the subject and could write well. While technical writers still need subject knowledge and writing skill, nowadays they also need to know how to use a broad set of electronic tools to carry out their numerous responsibilities.

This chapter provides an introduction to the hardware and software routinely used by technical writers to create, standardize, and maintain documents. Hardware tools include computers, printers, scanners, and digital cameras. Software tools include word processors, desktop publishers, graphics editors, screen capture utilities, and optical character recognition (OCR) utilities.

We understand that you may not have access to all of these tools. But our aim in this chapter is to give you a sense of the tools you will be using when you do sophisticated writing in the workplace, and to inspire you to take advantage of courses, workshops, and other means available to learn how to use these tools.

6.1 >——Hardware Tools

In this section we review the hardware tools of the technical writer.

▲ 1. Computers

The computer is the basic hardware tool of any professional writer. At Telemax, computers are connected through local area networks (LANs). In such an environment, the individual computer doesn't have to be particularly powerful, since it can draw on the power of the server and the rest of the network (see Figure 2.2 in Chapter 2).

The single technical writer who works alone in an office, or the freelance writer who works at home, will benefit from a more powerful system. A professional-level desktop computer will have large disk storage and computer memory, a high-speed CPU, a good keyboard, and an oversized monitor to permit a readable full-page display of text. The exact specifications for a high-end system change almost annually, as companies continue to produce ever more powerful microcomputers.

▲ *2. Printers*

The technical writers at Telemax use laser printers. Laser printers work by heating large numbers of very tiny dots on a piece of paper and applying ink to the paper. The ink sticks to the heated dots, creating an image. Modern laser printers can reproduce documents at resolutions as high as 1,200 dots per inch. Resolution this fine is typeset quality.

Different types of laser printers are distinguished by the nature of the language used to pass information from the computer to the printer. Most modern publishing systems use Postscript printers because the Postscript language is extremely efficient and accurate.

Companies like Pittsburgh Telemax set up very-high-quality printers on their LANs, with each printer shared by a small group of employees. This is a much better arrangement than having individual, less powerful printers attached to each terminal. High-quality printers print at high speeds, generally use the Postscript language, print on both sides of the page, and sort multiple copies.

▲ *3. Scanners*

Scanners are devices that reproduce printed text and images electronically. Technical writers use scanners to transfer printed texts to computer files that can then be edited, reprinted, or stored like any other word processing file. For example, requests for proposals (RFPs) that arrive at Telemax in a nondigital format are scanned into the Telemax network. This procedure saves a lot of typing time, since large portions of an RFP will be reprinted in Telemax's proposal. It also allows the DDM to easily pass on sections of the RFP to appropriate departments for their comments.

Although scanners are fairly accurate nowadays, imperfect original texts or texts with odd fonts may scan poorly, leaving numerous mistakes. However, a word processing program that underlines "misspelled" words throughout the text makes editing easy, since the underlining locates the mistakes that occurred during scanning.

A technical writer can also use the image-scanning capability of a scanner to scan a line drawing or a printed photograph to make it part of a word processing or desktop publishing text. (Such copying may require the permission of the creator; see section 2.6.)

Like most computer products, scanners are available in a broad range of quality and price. A low-resolution scanner is sufficient if you intend to display captured images only on a computer screen—for a company homepage, for example. A computer monitor displays images at only about 75 dots per inch, both vertically and horizontally. For images that will appear in commercial-grade publications, however, a high-quality scanner is essential.

Most scanners today are TWAIN compliant. TWAIN is an industry standard for scanner driver software. Any vendor can develop software to support any TWAIN-compliant scanner. Corel Photo-Paint, for example, supports TWAIN-compliant scanners. To capture an image using Photo-Paint and a TWAIN-compliant scanner, you simply select the Acquire command from the Photo-Paint File menu.

▲ 4. Cameras and Digital Cameras

High-quality photographs are common in marketing materials. Such photographs are taken by professional photographers. Technical writers frequently take photographs to illustrate steps in assembly. These are then scanned into computer files for record keeping and future use.

Digital cameras capture images electronically as "bitmap images" (discussed below in section 6.2). These captured images can be edited with software programs like Corel's Photo-Paint and Adobe's Photoshop. By using a digital camera you can spare yourself the trouble of developing a photograph and scanning it into a computer file. Digital cameras are now "standard equipment" in many professions, including technical writing.

At Telemax, DDM Marge Mendoza uses a digital camera to photograph the disassembled parts of a Telemax hardware system before the system is assembled and shipped to the customer. This procedure is necessary because products created for individual customers are often shipped before the documentation is completed. Without a photographic record, the technical writers might not be able to document all components and methods of assembly. Mendoza makes a computer folder for every photograph. The folder contains the image itself along with a text file describing the contents of the picture, the product line represented in the picture, the writing project for which the picture was taken, and the date on which the picture was taken.

High-quality digital cameras capture images at extremely high resolutions. When evaluating digital cameras, keep in mind how the captured images will be used. As we have said, since images intended to be displayed on a computer screen do not need to be captured at a high resolution, they can be taken with a less expensive digital camera, whereas images intended to be reproduced in commercial publications must be captured at very high resolutions.

▲ *5. Tape Recorders*

All technical writers at Telemax own a micro-cassette tape recorder that they use to keep a record of important meetings and, especially, of their interviews with engineers. Those interviews provide technical writers with much of the content of their writings. Accuracy is crucial, and accuracy is what the recorders provide. The recorders also allow writers to share with others in the documentation department the exact statements of managers and engineers, so that those statements can be discussed and carefully interpreted.

DDM Mendoza uses her recorder in training sessions as well. Occasionally, Pittsburgh Telemax contracts with an educational firm to do training in telecommunications theory and use of equipment. Telemax instructors record these sessions and later review them to improve their training methods. When Telemax engineers give in-house training to describe a new product to the Telemax staff, Mendoza records the session for later reference. Every important Telemax tape is eventually turned over to Mendoza, who breaks the overwrite tab, labels the cassette, and files it.

When handing Wendy her tape recorder, Mendoza informs her of the necessity to warn people that they are being recorded. This is true even in training sessions, where the person doing the recording is also doing most of the talking. A participant in any kind of meeting might ask that the recorder be temporarily turned off, in which case it should be.

Lately, Mendoza has been experimenting with videotaping in-house presentations. In some situations, videotaping seemed foolishly elaborate, and it distracted the engineers. But in other instances—when the presentation included a complex visual element—videotaping worked effectively.

ASSIGNMENTS FOR 6.1

1. *Learn Hardware* Find one of the pieces of hardware discussed in section 6.1 and learn a feature previously unfamiliar to you. Write a memo report to your instructor on your experience.

2. *Use a Tape Recorder* Interview two potential users of the piece of documentation you are writing for your Big Project, asking a few well-planned

questions designed to reveal their knowledge of the subject. Or interview two users of existing systems on your campus, such as the library's computerized indexes, to determine how well your respondents understand the system. For one of the interviews, use a tape recorder; for the other, do not. Take notes during both interviews. Put together a short report for your instructor. Comment on whether or not the tape recording was useful.

6.2 >——— Software Tools

In this section, we look at five classes of software tools used by the technical writer:

- word processing
- desktop publishing
- bitmap graphics
- vector graphics
- hypertext publishing.

These tools can be used in combination with one another. In fact, most commercial publishing packages combine two or more of these tools into a single suite. In addition, stand-alone word processing and desktop publishing programs can incorporate graphics and save a file in hypertext format.

Pittsburgh Telemax uses the Corel suite of graphics tools, which includes Corel Draw, Corel Photo-Paint, Corel OCR-Trace, and Corel Capture—all the graphics tools needed for a small documentation department.

▲ *1. Word Processing Systems*

Pittsburgh Telemax uses the Microsoft Word word processing program for all in-house communications, and it uses the Adobe FrameMaker desktop publishing program for all documentation. Note, however, that powerful word processing software like Word can be used by itself for most kinds of technical writing, including documentation.

Besides basic drafting, editing, saving, and printing capabilities, contemporary word processing programs include advanced features of importance to technical writers. Here are a few of them:

- **Change Views** Word processing software allows the author to view a composition in standard text format, WYSIWYG format, or outline format. Many word processing software systems can also display a document in online format, which may include hyperlinks or command buttons.

■ **Macro Languages** Advanced word processing software allows you to compose macros. A macro is simply a list of instructions. For example, you can compose a macro that tells the software to insert your name and address. You may even be able to create a dialog box to prompt for input, in which case the macro would insert the input at a specific point in the document.

■ **Autotext** In word processing terms, autotext is a saved range of text that you can quickly insert into a document. After assigning an autotext entry to a toolbar button, you can insert the autotext entry into the document merely by clicking on the button.

■ **Templates** Most word processing software systems allow you to save document files as templates that retain default text, formatting styles, and macros. You can then base new documents on existing templates.

■ **Paragraph Styles** Styles are a set of formatting parameters that describe what a paragraph looks like. Generally, styles include information about the font, the point size, the margins, the tab settings, and the line spacing. Word processing systems have default, built-in styles for running text, bulleted lists, and so forth. You can also create your own styles. If a built-in style does not exist for a paragraph type that you use often, you would create a new style and save it as part of a template.

■ **Bookmarks and Automatic Cross-Referencing** In word processing terms, a bookmark is a name associated with a particular spot in a document. A bookmark name can refer to a single point in a document, or it can refer to a range of pages within a document. Bookmarks are often used for building indexes. They are also useful for keeping track of references. For example, advanced word processing software can record information about captions, including the caption label (such as Figure or Table), the caption number, and its current page number. If the document is altered such that the page number of a caption changes, the word processing system automatically learns the new page number and updates all cross-references to it.

■ **Automatic Numbering** Full-featured word processors allow you to number headings and paragraphs. The advantage of automatic numbering is that when you insert a paragraph or heading within a numbered list, the word processing software automatically renumbers all other paragraphs or headings within the list. There are two types of numbering: single-level numbering and multilevel numbering.

Single-level numbering is typically used to number steps in a procedure or to number items in a logically ordered list, such as a list of priorities. Multilevel numbering is typically used for proposals, legal documents, and complex procedures. Multilevel numbering resembles outline numbering. It consists of a set of numbered lists, each one of which is associated with a level.

▌ **Tables** Technical writers create many kinds of tables, as illustrated throughout this book. Tables can be used to compare products on the basis of features, to display a budget, to organize a work schedule, or to create a troubleshooting guide. Note that a table consists of a number of blocks, called cells, aligned in a grid. Cells are logically grouped into rows and columns. However, each cell can have distinct content, and text within each cell can be individually formatted. This makes it possible to format heading cells uniquely, to make them stand out. Cells can contain formulas that show the results of mathematical operations performed on the content of other cells, such as the sum of those cells in a budget table.

▌ **Borders and Shading** Advanced word processing systems allow you to apply borders and shading to paragraphs. This feature is very useful in emphasizing special text. For example, a certain block of text may be intended as a warning. Applying shading or top and bottom borders to the paragraph distinguishes it from running text.

▲ *2. Desktop Publishing Systems*

Desktop publishing systems usually include most of the features of word processing systems. Adobe FrameMaker, for example, supports paragraph formatting, automatic numbering, automatic cross-referencing, and automatic captioning. It also supports advanced table functions. FrameMaker includes a number of basic document templates, and you can create your own templates.

However, desktop publishing systems do not support all word processing functions, and because desktop publishing systems are primarily page layout programs, they do not have the inherent flexibility that writers find so useful. Therefore, many writers prefer to develop documents using word processing systems and then import the document into a desktop publishing system.

Below are some advanced features of desktop publishing useful to technical writers:

▌ **Text Flows** Text flow is one of the properties of text frames. A frame is an area drawn on a page. The area inside a frame is reserved for a specific purpose: It can contain either text or graphics. Text frames can be linked with one another such that when one frame is filled, the text wraps to the linked frame. You can place that linked frame on the same page (for example, to create a dual-column text) or many pages later (as happens when text is continued from the front page of a newsletter to a page later in the publication).

❚ **Page Types** Most desktop publishing systems work by overlaying different page types. Adobe FrameMaker includes the following page types:

Body Pages Body pages comprise the majority of the actual document content. The content is contained within text frames or graphics frames positioned on the body page or the associated master page. The content displayed on a document's body pages is the same as the content of the printed document.

Master Pages Master pages are template pages that contain fixed formatting. The formatting may include graphics, such as top and bottom borders, or specialized text. You can define as many master pages as you want, although many documents require no more than three: one for the first page, one for all subsequent even pages, and one for all subsequent odd pages. You can attach any master page to any body page. When you attach a master page to a body page, the body page automatically takes on the properties of the master page. Any text, graphics, or frames positioned on the master page appear in the corresponding locations on the body page.

Reference Pages Reference pages are special-purpose pages that contain graphics, boilerplate text, and headings, among other elements, any of which can be called up and placed in body pages.

▲ *3. Bitmap Graphics Tools*

Bitmap graphics tools are used for working with pictures. Bitmap images (also called raster images) consist of a large number of very small dots called pixels, short for "picture elements." Pixels vary in color and intensity.

Bitmap images come in different formats identified by the filename extension. The two most commonly used on World Wide Web pages are GIF and JPG (or JPEG) files. GIF stands for Graphic Interchange Format; JPEG stands for Joint Photographic Experts Group. If you examine the source code for Web pages that contain these images, you will find references to file names with the GIF or JPG extension. Other industry-standard still-image formats include TIF (or TIFF), PCX, PIX, WMF, ICO, and BMP.

Some companies have developed proprietary formats. For example, the default format for Corel Photo-Paint is labeled CPT, and the default format for HiJaak is labeled IGF. It may not be possible to use one company's application to export a file to the proprietary format of a different company.

Technical writers regularly use four types of bitmap graphics tools: bitmap graphics editors, optical character recognition (OCR) software, screen capture utilities, and moving-image bitmap tools. Each is discussed below.

Bitmap Graphics Editors Bitmap graphics editors allow you to manipulate bitmap images. These are the basic tools that you find in painting programs. They are included in many software packages, such as Corel's Photo-Paint and MS Paint; the latter comes with Windows. Many other companies distribute limited-function bitmap editors along with their primary product. For example, a company that sells digital cameras must include software to transmit bitmap images from the camera to the customer's home computer. That company may also include a bitmap editor so the customer can manipulate the images to some degree.

Bitmap editors allow you to crop images (cut away unnecessary parts), rotate images, and make numerous adjustments to color and shade, such as changing color, blending colors with a brush or with mathematical formulas, smudging or clarifying borders, and adjusting the contrast between colors in an image.

Many bitmap editors allow you to apply special effects such as embossing. These effects can be useful in designing artistic graphics such as those that might adorn the cover of a document.

Optical Character Recognition Software Optical Character Recognition (OCR) software allows you to convert a scanned image to a text file. Figure 6.1 depicts the Corel OCR-Trace program in operation. Within the window, you can see a portion of a request for proposals (RFP) to which Telemax intends to respond by submitting a bid (a process discussed in Chapter 8). The image on the left is the scanned image; the image on the right is the converted text.

Nearly all OCR programs allow you to save the results in a standard ASCII text file. Many OCR programs also allow you to select from a variety of popular word processing formats, such as Rich Text Format (RTF), which is Microsoft's proprietary word processing file format.

Unlike the simple OCR programs that typically come with inexpensive scanners, Corel OCR-Trace offers many advanced features of value

FIGURE 6.1 ▼   Using OCR Software

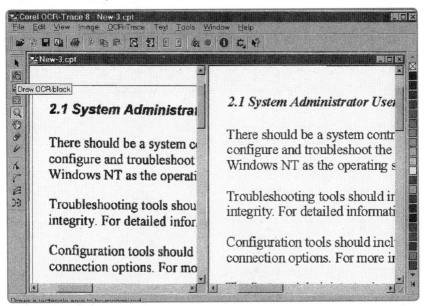

Source: Corel OCR-Trace is the registered trademark of Corel Corporation. Screen shots, copyright 1997 Corel Corporation and Corel Corporation Limited, are reprinted with permission.

to technical writers. It converts bitmap to vector images, and it offers numerous parameter settings to control conversion. For example, Corel-OCR Trace permits you to trace the outside edges of lines or the centers of lines, and allows you to create special-effects images, such as woodcut.

Screen Capture Utilities   Software documentation is an important specialty in the technical writing profession. Documents that describe software usually include supporting visuals that display the computer screen at crucial moments during the program operation. Some manuals have screen images on almost every page. Software tools that allow you to duplicate a screen image are called screen capture utilities. Figure 6.2 provides an example of screen captures (or "screen shots") used to clarify instruction.

The image you see on a computer monitor is a bitmap image displayed electronically. When you execute a screen capture, you save the electronic image in a file. In doing so, you can crop the area to be saved, specify the format for the saved image (such as GIF or JPG, if you will be displaying the image on the Web), and specify the disk-drive storage location for each captured image.

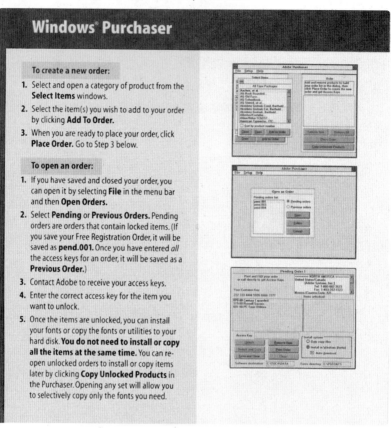

To create a new order:

1. Select and open a category of product from the **Select Items** windows.
2. Select the item(s) you wish to add to your order by clicking **Add To Order.**
3. When you are ready to place your order, click **Place Order.** Go to Step 3 below.

To open an order:

1. If you have saved and closed your order, you can open it by selecting **File** in the menu bar and then **Open Orders.**
2. Select **Pending** or **Previous Orders.** Pending orders are orders that contain locked items. (If you save your Free Registration Order, it will be saved as **pend.001.** Once you have entered *all* the access keys for an order, it will be saved as a **Previous Order.**)
3. Contact Adobe to receive your access keys.
4. Enter the correct access key for the item you want to unlock.
5. Once the items are unlocked, you can install your fonts or copy the fonts or utilities to your hard disk. **You do not need to install or copy all the items at the same time.** You can re-open unlocked orders to install or copy items later by clicking **Copy Unlocked Products** in the Purchaser. Opening any set will allow you to selectively copy only the fonts you need.

Source: From *Adobe Type On Call CD-ROM Quick Reference Card.* Used with expressed permission. All rights reserved. Adobe® and Type on Call® are trademarks of Adobe Systems Incorporated.

Moving-Image Bitmap Tools A moving bitmap image consists of a number of frames displayed in sequence, each for a specified period of time. The effect is a moving image, which may be incorporated into a slide-show presentation or added to a Web site. Moving-image editors allow you to modify the contents of each frame and to specify the display period for each frame.

The two most common file formats are MPG (or MPEG), which stands for Moving Picture Experts Group, and animated GIF, which stands for Graphic Interchange Format.

▲ 4. Vector Graphics

Vector graphics are quite different from bitmap graphics. While bitmap graphics produce images by positioning dots, vector graphics produce images by interpreting the mathematical characteristics of the image. For example, a bitmap image of a simple black rectangle on a white background would include definitions for every pixel. All the pixels would be white except those that lie within the lines making up the rectangle, which would be black. In this case, bitmapping is a brute-force method for depicting an image that can be more easily represented in mathematical terms using vector graphics.

A vector graphics file contains mathematical information that describes each component of an image. Normally, all colors are assigned numbers. In our simple image, the background color is white; therefore, the vector graphics file would contain a programming line that identifies the background color by its assigned number. The rectangle might be represented by two sets of coordinates (one for the upper-left corner and one for the lower-right corner) along with a number indicating its color and a number indicating the thickness of its line. The vector file would also indicate whether the square is filled.

Vector graphics editors are very important to technical writing because they are commonly used to create block diagrams and line drawings for assembly instructions and other kinds of illustrations. A wide variety of vector graphics editors are available, ranging from very simple to extremely sophisticated. Computer Assisted Design (CAD) tools such as AutoCAD are actually very sophisticated vector graphics editors. CAD tools are specifically designed for creating images that are exactly to scale. Designers use these drawings to indicate the exact specifications for a manufacturer. CAD programs, unfortunately, are difficult to learn and use.

Companies like Corel Graphics sell vector drawing products that are well suited for technical writers. Corel Draw includes all of the required drawing tools for creating vector graphics. Although Corel Draw is not intended for full-scale CAD drawings, you can use it to import and edit CAD drawings. You can then add callouts (labels), figure captions, or other objects. This is how technical writers generally create documents that require line figures drawn to scale.

Some typical features of vector graphics editors follow:

▌ **Draw Shapes** To draw a shape, you typically click on a button, then drag the mouse pointer across a page displayed on your monitor. For example, to draw a rectangle, you click on a button to change the mouse pointer to a rectangle tool, then you drag from the top-left corner to the lower-right corner. When you select an object in a vector drawing, a number of "handles" appear around its perimeter. For example, a selected rectangle typically has eight handles, one at each corner, and one at the middle of each side. To stretch or rotate a shape, you typically click on the shape to select it and then drag a handle.

▌ **Insert Text** Generally, you can use two types of text in vector drawing programs: artistic text and paragraph text. Artistic text is similar in its behavior to all other graphic objects. If you select it, handles appear around it. You can drag the handles around artistic text to stretch it or rotate it. Technical writers use artistic text to add callouts to line drawings and to label items in block diagrams, because artistic text can be dragged into place with the mouse easily and precisely. Paragraph text is more like the text in a word processor. To add paragraph text, you typically click on a paragraph text tool, then you draw a text box on the page. After you finish drawing the text box, you type inside the box. The text inside the text box can be formatted. For example, you can add bullets or adjust indents. Technical writers use paragraph text to add general comments to a drawing or to create legends.

▌ **Import Bitmap** You can use a bitmap image as part of a vector drawing. For example, if you take a screen capture, you can paste it into a vector drawing; then you can add callouts and other text. This technique is very useful for writing manuals describing software.

▌ **Layers** Some vector graphics editors allow you to draw objects on different drawing layers. For example, to develop a block diagram, you can draw the basic diagram in black on the first layer. You can then add callouts in a different color on the second layer and descriptive paragraph text on a third layer. You can also hide or display any combination of layers. This technique is similar to overlaying transparencies on an overhead projector.

▌ **Guidelines** Guidelines are straight lines positioned on the drawing page that allow you to line up objects with respect to one another. They are not necessarily a part of the drawing. However, guidelines have some of the characteristics of drawn objects. For example, you can move and rotate them. Normally, you can choose to display or hide guidelines as you wish. If you are working with many guidelines, you may want to hide them every so often to see how the drawing looks without them.

▌ **Grid** The grid is a matrix of points that can be used to align objects. Normally, you can choose to display or hide the grid, and you can specify the horizontal and vertical distances between grid points. You can also specify whether you want to snap to the grid. A grid is useful if you are drawing an array of regularly spaced objects, such as the pins on an electrical connector.

▌ **Snap** When you draw with snap turned on, the exterior lines of a square or rectangle attach to grids. This allows you to create objects that are identical or whose borders line up.

▪ **Align and Distribute** Most advanced vector graphics editors provide two methods for positioning objects with respect to one another. Aligning objects positions them in a row or column, and distributing objects equalizes the distance between them. Align and distribute tools are useful for drawing an object like an electrical connector, which has a number of pins that are evenly spaced.

▪ **Grouping** Vector graphics editors usually allow you to group a number of objects together so that they behave as a single object. To do this, you use the mouse to drag a rectangle around all the objects, then select a menu command or click on a button. Grouping can be useful for precisely placing a group of objects. For example, to draw an electrical connector, which consists of a number of pins and an enclosure, you would need to align the pins in the center of the enclosure. To do this, you would first group them, then move the group as a single object.

▪ **Templates** Many vector graphics editors allow you to create templates. Templates can contain drawn objects, guidelines, grid configurations, macros, and artistic and paragraph text styles. Once you have a library of templates, you can start most new drawings with one of the templates. This saves time and allows you to give long documents the uniformity of appearance so important in technical writing.

▲ *5. Hypertext Publishing Systems*

Hypertext is a method of electronically linking portions of an online document directly to other portions of the same document or to another document. Hypertext documents are designed to be displayed on a computer terminal. The document itself may reside on a microcomputer's hard drive, it may reside on the hard drive of a network file server, or it may reside on the hard drive of an Internet server. Therefore, a hypertext document may be available for use by only a single person, or a group of people, or every person in the world.

To display a hypertext document, a user enters a Web address in an Internet browser or selects a Help menu command. Once the document is displayed, the user can move from one portion of the document to another or from one document to another by clicking on links with the computer's mouse.

This is an extremely efficient way of organizing information because it yields control to the reader. However, it places demands on the technical writer, who must learn how to design hypertext documents.

Hypertext documents have generally been written in one of three mark-up "languages." The first, Standard Generalized Markup Language

(SGML), is powerful but difficult to use. Hypertext Markup Language (HTML) is a subset of SGML. It was developed as an easy, though not very powerful, alternative for creating Web pages. HTML remains very popular, and this is the one we will look at in detail. Lately, developers have been shifting to Extensible Markup Language (XML), a powerful, flexible refinement of SGML.

Many word processing programs, like Microsoft Word, will save an ordinary document in HTML, so that you don't have to do any programming to create fairly simple online pages. The newer versions of FrameMaker will also save to SGML and XML. Professional writers charged with working on Web pages, however, should learn markup languages like HTML in order to refine pages created with programs like Word. Writers also need to learn how to create help systems for online programs and documents. The sections below provide a short overview of HTML and online help systems.

HTML Hypertext Markup Language is a system for creating hypertext documents using standard ASCII text file format. Because it does not depend on a proprietary file format such as RTF, HTML is universal. Any computer that includes an Internet browser (Netscape, Internet Explorer) can display an HTML document.

HTML is actually a set of tags. Each tag is an instruction enclosed in angle brackets. For example, every HTML document begins with the <html> tag and ends with the </html> tag. These tags identify the document to an Internet browser as an HTML file. Within each HTML file is a head section, which is enclosed within <head> and </head> tags, and a body section, which is enclosed within <body> and </body> tags. Box 6.1 illustrates the HTML code used to create an early version of the Telemax homepage.

You can use markup tags to format text. For example, text that you want to emphasize is enclosed within <em> and </em> tags. Internet browsers can be configured to interpret these tags and display emphasized text in italics or boldface.

It is possible to use a standard text editor, such as Windows Notepad, to develop HTML documents. However, a number of HTML editors are also available. Netscape, for example, includes an HTML editor, Netscape Composer, with certain versions of its Internet browser, and Internet Explorer includes Front Page Express.

Online Help Technical writers create online help systems for software applications. A user can usually access online help documents by selecting a command from the application's Help menu.

BOX 6.1 ▼ **Creating a Web Page with HTML**

```
<html>

<head>
<meta http-equiv-"Content-Type"
content-"text/html; charset-iso-8859-1">
<meta name-"GENEARATOR" content-"Microsoft FrontPage Express 2.0">
<title>About Pittsburgh Telemax §</title>
</head>

<body bgcolor-'#F9F5DB">

<p align-"center"><a name-"top"></a><img arc-"Large%20Logo.gif"
width-"360" height-"129"></p>

<hr>

<p align-"center"><a href-"#about">About Pittsburgh Telemax</a>
§ <a href="#products">Products</a> § <a href-"#services">Services</a>
§ <a href-"#contact">Contact Us</a></p>

<hr>

<h1 align-"left"><a name-"about"</a><font size-"4" face-"Arial"> About
Pittsburgh Telemax<font></h1>

<p align-"left">Pittsburgh Telemax is a small business located in
Pittsburgh, Pennsylvania, that specializes in the development and
installation of state-of-the-art multimedia conferencing systems.
Applications for our systems include distance learning programs
```

Note: The near-center line beginning with "<p align..." contains the "img" command to import the Telemax logo.

WinHelp, a widely used online help system, displays help documents for applications running in the Windows environment. When a user selects a Help command, the Windows operating system starts the Win-Help application, which opens the requested help document. Normally, WinHelp displays an electronic table of contents or index for the document so the user can look up the appropriate subject. In context-sensitive applications, however, WinHelp can display the portion of the help document that pertains to the feature in use. Online help documents also sometimes include a set of definitions for difficult terms. When the reader clicks on the term in running text, its definition appears in a pop-up window.

JavaHelp is an online help system developed by Sun Microsystems for use with Java programs. It is similar to WinHelp except that the help files are saved in XML or HTML format rather than Microsoft's proprietary Rich Text Format (RTF). Like WinHelp, JavaHelp has an electronic table of contents, index, and search tool. JavaHelp can also be implemented in a context-sensitive manner. You can download everything you need to start developing JavaHelp systems from the Sun Microsystems web site at **http://java.sun.com/products/javahelp/**.

Portable Document Format   Adobe Systems has developed a set of programs that recreate documents in Portable Document Format (PDF). PDF documents, regardless of how complex in appearance, show up on the screen essentially as they will appear in print. The PDF format is particularly useful for detailed layouts, such as you would find in a scanned tax form. Adobe's Acrobat suite of products allows you to create, edit, and manage PDF files.

PDF files can have thumbnails, which are icons representing each page; by clicking on the thumbnail, you automatically jump to the corresponding page. You can also add bookmarks and hyperlinks to a PDF document. Adobe Acrobat allows you to distribute a document for review by others, who can add comments or electronic signatures to the document. (At Pittsburgh Telemax, when in-house documents are distributed in electronic form for review and sign-off, they are sent in PDF format.)

Adobe Acrobat also allows you to protect a PDF file by assigning a password to it. You can use protection to prevent others from printing or editing all, or a specified part of, the document.

The Acrobat Reader program is used for viewing PDF documents. You can download the Acrobat Reader for free from the Adobe web site **http://www.adobe.com/products/acrobat**.

ASSIGNMENTS FOR 6.2

1. *Learn Software* Find one of the pieces of software discussed in section 6.2 and learn a feature previously unfamiliar to you. Write a memo report to your instructor on your experience.

2. *Practice HTML* Using a word processing program that saves to HTML, such as Microsoft Word, create a simple homepage for your technical writing class. Follow these steps:
   a. Open your word processing program.
   b. Type your homepage, using different-sized fonts and different-styled fonts.
   c. Save the file onto the desktop as an HTML file, giving the filename an **.html** or **.htm** extension.
   d. Close your word processing program.
   e. Find your **.html** file on the desktop and open it by double-clicking on it.
   f. If Internet Explorer is your default browser, skip to step h. Otherwise do step g.
   g. Netscape Communicator should have opened automatically. First, in the drop-down File menu, select Edit Page. Then, in the Tools menu, select HTML tools/Edit HTML Source. You will now be viewing the "code" or tags for your homepage. (Skip to step i.)
   h. Internet Explorer should have opened automatically. In the drop-down View menu, select Source. Notepad will open automatically to show your document with tags.
   i. Figure out the meaning of one of the angle-bracketed tags in the middle of your file and report that to your instructor in a memo.

6.3 >——— Presentation Tools

Technical writers often play a role in marketing products. For example, technical writers may participate in the development of written proposals—that is, formal bids for jobs. (Written proposals are discussed in detail in Chapter 8.) Companies also make oral proposals, called "presentations," in their efforts to interest clients in their company's products and services. Telemax, for instance, frequently sends marketing people to universities to describe its distance learning systems. For these on-site presentations, the team prepares a slide show using PowerPoint, one of the programs in Microsoft Office.

Technical writers at Telemax usually participate in the preparation of the PowerPoint presentation, and a writer will sometimes accompany a salesperson to the site to help answer technical questions. The Telemax team brings a notebook computer, a projector, and a screen to the site. The PowerPoint presentation is saved on the computer's hard disk. A connecting cord attaches the computer to the projector, and the presenter calls up each slide in sequence by clicking the mouse button. The presenter elaborates on each slide.

Besides rudimentary word processing, PowerPoint provides a set of background patterns, still pictures, and sounds with which to create slides. Most users, however, tap into the Internet to find sounds and graphics to enhance their presentation. PowerPoint is an open gate to the multimedia world. Its strength lies in the unlimited possibilities of insertions: images, voices, music clips, video clips, and links to web sites. Although PowerPoint offers simple editing for sound, visuals, and video, experienced users employ other more sophisticated software for those jobs, then insert their final product into a PowerPoint slide.

Graphics and especially video take up a lot of space, so the disk system being used has to have a large storage capacity. Video, for example, uses 30 frames per second. Suppose each frame uses 400 kilobytes; then a 30-second clip will require 360 megabytes of storage.

PowerPoint presentations can be set up to run by themselves, each slide change occurring after a designated number of seconds. Or the timing can be based on completion of an audio or video clip. Sometimes marketers set up a computer, projector, and screen at a convention booth and then walk away to conduct other business while the slide show runs, in a continuous loop, hopefully attracting the attention of those passing by.

ASSIGNMENT FOR 6.3

1. *Do Tutorial* Do the tutorial in Box 6.2. The tutorial ends with a printout of two slides. Turn in your printout to your instructor.

BOX 6.2 ▼ **Microsoft Powerpoint Tutorial**

Get Started

Step 1: Open PowerPoint: START / Programs / Microsoft PowerPoint

Step 2: Select: Blank presentation / OK

Create Layout and Titles

Step 3: Select Autolayout: click on upper-left option / OK

Step 4: Create title: Click inside dotted box / Type: My Professor

Step 5: Create subtitle: Click inside dotted box / Type: By Yourname (type your name)

Manipulate Text

Step 6: Highlight the main title / select **B** for **bold**

Step 7: Adjust the size of the highlighted title to 54 point using the drop-down menu to the left of **B** / change the subtitle to 24 point

Step 8: Shift the position of the title to the upper-left corner: Hold down the mouse button while pointing at the border of the box and slide the box / Adjust the subtitle so that it starts under the first **s** in 'Professor'

Beautify Slide

Step 9: Select from the topmost drop-down menu: Format / Background

Step 10: Use down arrow in the active window to select: Fill effects

Step 11: Select from the top of the new window: Texture

Step 12: Click on a texture of your choice / OK / Apply

Add Slide #2 with a Graphic

Step 13: Select: Insert / New slide

Step 14: This time, choose the left-bottom autolayout to allow for a graphic

Step 15: Create your title and text by clicking in the dotted boxes

Step 16: Add graphic by double-clicking on 'Double click to add clip art' and double-clicking on an image

Step 17: Add a background following steps 9–12

Show and Print Slides

Step 18: Select: View / Slide sorter

Step 19: Under view, select: Slide show

Step 20: View your slide show by clicking on each slide

Step 21: Save your work using: File / Save

Step 22: Print by selecting: File / Print / (under Print <u>w</u>hat:) Handouts (2 slides per page) / OK

Visuals

Technical writing always has a visual element, if only in the layout of the text. To make their documents more readable, technical writers use a lot of white space. They write in short sections with headings, and they put extra space between sections to emphasize the organization of the text. Templates for layout (discussed in detail in Chapter 9) provide a consistent, attractive appearance to the pages of a manual. The predictable textual appearance contributes to a document's readability.

Most technical documents are printed in black and white. However, when color is available, as in the case of Web pages, writers use it to create attractive backgrounds, to set elements apart, and to emphasize important text. In both print and online documents, a two-color text would typically use black for most text and then one color, such as blue, for headings. The color would also be employed to attract attention to sidebars, warnings, and other important elements outside the running text.

In technical writing, the most powerful visual effect comes from the use of illustrations and visual images, or "visuals" as we are calling them here. Visuals include graphs, drawings, photographs, icons, and the like. They can present complex information with clarity and brevity. Research shows that effective visuals help the reader to learn more and remember more, while making the text more interesting and getting the message across more quickly (Rew, 1999, p. 293).

Organizations usually don't expect their technical writers to be accomplished artists or photographers. Telemax's Marketing Department, for instance, includes professional artists and photographers who do the final work. Instead, the technical writer must produce a clear sense of what the visual should look like so that the professional illustrators can produce the appropriate finished product.

We begin this chapter with generalizations about visuals. Then, in a series of sections, we provide examples of the standard visuals used for describing or illustrating objects, processes, and relationships. Those sections provide a gallery of options available to you as a technical and business writer. Next we examine the use of visuals, such as icons, to represent ideas. Finally, we discuss the craft of writing descriptive prose as part of the visual element in technical writing.

7.1 ⟩——— Generalizations About Visuals

Before discussing specific types of visuals, we can offer some general rules that apply to all visuals:

▲ *1. Use Visuals for Legitimate Purposes*

Visuals are costly to create and print. Take time to consider whether a visual is needed. Visuals should not be included in your text for mere decoration. Simple ideas easily communicated in prose do not need visual support. For example, it is rarely worth the trouble and expense to use a graph to compare two items on the basis of one criterion. It would be easier to simply display such information within the text, like this:

> Last year's profits: 2 million
>
> This year's profits: 8 million

Consider trimming your visual. For example, to illustrate a step using a screen shot, you can reproduce just one drop-down menu rather than the whole screen.

Understanding the legitimate functions of visuals can help you decide whether you need a visual at any particular moment in the development of your text. Effective visuals serve these legitimate purposes:

1. They convert running text into more comprehensible "visual text." When there are many decision points in the text, a decision table or flow chart can often be more effective than paragraphs of prose. Table 9.1 in Chapter 9 and Figure 7.7. later in this chapter provide examples of such information effectively presented in a table and a flow chart, respectively.

2. They present key information, supported by textual explanation. Important quantifiable results in experimental reports are presented in tables, which are then explained in the running text. Table 7.2 on page 181 provides an example of such a table. The running text would make a statement like this: "As the table shows, unemployed females were much more likely to feel satisfied with their lives than unemployed males." The explanation and the data presented in the visual complement each other. The same situation occurs in product comparison tables (Table 7.1). The important

data will show up in the table, and the text will state what conclusions can be drawn from those data.

3. They clarify text. When describing how a machine or system works, a visual may help the reader to correctly visualize what the text is describing. Figures 3.2, 6.2, and 7.6 provide examples of visuals used for this purpose.

4. They add to the text. Often the text will tell part of the story and the visual will tell another part. In Box 6.1 (page 157), the text describes how HTML works, and the visual presents a picture of the outcome so that the reader can see the effect of following the prose directions.

5. They summarize the text. Figure 2.1, the organizational chart for Pittsburgh Telemax, provides a visual summary of the departments and their relationships, while the text in that section of Chapter 2 provides a detailed description of the departments and their relationships. The visual summary helps the reader understand and synthesize the detailed information.

If a visual would effectively serve any of the five purposes listed above, consider adding the visual to your text. Do not use visuals that cannot be justified.

▲ 2. Choose the Appropriate Visual

Often the same information can be presented with more than one kind of visual. One of the purposes of visuals is to clarify text. If the visual is so complex that it doesn't clarify—as can easily happen with photographs, big tables, or graphs generated by computer graphics programs—then reconsider your approach. A simple line drawing might focus attention on the object better than a photograph. Two medium-sized tables might present the data better than one big one; or part of the data might be graphed and part placed in a table. This chapter provides a gallery of possible visuals for your technical writing. Review your options before deciding on what kind of visual will work best for you.

As you would expect, audience analysis is important in choosing the appropriate visual. If your audience won't understand a particularly complex visual (such as a schematic drawing), the visual will be useless.

▲ 3. Reference Visuals in the Text

Refer to visuals in your text, using the term *table* for grids and *figure* for all other visuals. Place the visual as soon as possible after the reference.

The reference may consist of a simple parenthetical note:

... profits for the last three years (Table 7).

Try to use a consistent style for parenthetical references. In normal running text, this textbook adds the word see when referring to visuals that appear in other chapters. For this chapter we would write

(Figure 7.1)

but

(see Figure 9.1).

Alternatively, you can place the reference in the running text, indicating what the visual displays:

Table 7 shows the profits for the last three years.

In fact, your text can include an extensive explanation of your visual if that would be helpful.

If more than one figure or more than one table appears in your text, number each one consecutively. Try not to refer ahead to Figure 4 before introducing Figure 3. If you are using only one figure or one table, you can refer to it with a phrase like *the table* or *the graph* or *the photograph,* without numbering it.

The words *Table* or *Figure* are capitalized when numbered: *Figure 3, Table 2.* They are printed in lowercase when not numbered:

The table compares. . . .

Include the term *Table* or *Figure* in the caption only if it is numbered:

Table 2 A Comparison of Office Carpets

Note: Some modern formats, such as the format used in the Information Mapping approach, incorporate visuals into the text with no "references" in the traditional sense. See section 9.6.

▲ 4. Use Informative Captions, Headings, and Labels

The titles of visuals are called captions. Captions should fully identify the subject matter of the visual and, if possible, the point that the visual is making. For example, the drawing in Figure 7.1 on page 169 has the caption "Components of the Standard Microcomputer System." A shorter caption, like "A Standard Microcomputer," would indicate the subject matter but fail to convey the purpose of the visual—namely, to show the components of a standard system.

Sometimes a caption will consist of both a title and a subtitle. Look ahead to the graph in Figure 7.10 on page 175. It has a subtitle that provides an important fact not provided by the graph itself: "Total Gross Sales: $20.63 Million." Figure 7.12 on page 177 also has two levels of captions: The main title identifies the subject of the graph, while the subtitle states the point being made by the graph.

Tables not only have captions (main titles), they also have "headings" for the individual columns. Look ahead to Table 7.1 on page 180. The caption identifies what data the table provides and the purpose of the table—namely, a "Comparison of Features of Multimedia Projectors." The caption is two-tiered, the second level providing an important fact about the data—that they were current as of a certain date. Information in a product comparison table can change suddenly, as prices drop and features become more powerful, so the date in this particular case is important.

Headings in tables identify columns in the table structure. Table 7.1 has a single set of headings: Model, Price, Lumens, and so forth. Some tables will have two or more subheadings under the main heading, creating internal columns within each main column. For example, Table 7.1 could be reconstructed so as to show last year's and this year's prices for each model of projector, in which case the column under Price would be split into two columns, one showing last year's price and one showing this year's, as illustrated below:

Model	Price	
	Last Year	This Year
JAAP: 8700MP	$6,345.00	$7,619.95

▲ 5. Indicate Outside Sources

If using a visual borrowed from an outside source, or based on information from an outside source, you must indicate that. You can use a "permissions" statement as part of the caption:

Figure 7.3 Exploded Drawing
Reprinted with permission of Compunetix, Inc., Monroeville, PA

When reproducing a visual, you must contact the copyright owner (often a book publisher or professional journal) to get permission. The copyright holder may not give permission, or may give permission with conditions, such as payment of a fee or use of a particular phrasing for a permissions statement to be included in your text.

For sources that don't require written permission to reproduce, such as government documents, you can put a "source" line under the visual:

Source: U.S. Government Health Service

If using a photograph that has identifiable people in it, get permission from those people to use the photograph.

▲ 6. Be Accurate and Consistent

The information presented in the visual should be up-to-date and should come from a reliable source. Any data that seem odd should be double-checked.

Check figures and mathematical operations for accuracy. Percentages, for example, should total 100. Make sure that information in the visual matches information in the text. Check the figure or table number to be certain it is correct, and check the reference in the text to make sure the numbers match.

Objects and maps, if not drawn to scale, should be roughly proportional (unless you are deliberately magnifying a section). Provide a distance scale with maps.

Choose one style for presenting visuals and stick to it throughout the text. If the first visual has a box around it, put a box around all the others. The same applies to captions and headings. For example, if you printed the first caption in 14-point Helvetica and placed it above the visual, do the same for all other captions.

▲ 7. Be Neat and Clear

Even if you are not an artist, you can design visuals that will come out neat and clear when the professionals are done with them. Avoid a crowded look. Leave out unnecessary detail. Carefully consider what needs to be labeled and what doesn't, and keep labels to a minimum. But bear in mind that the opposite is also true: Labels should be added where they will contribute to understanding. For example, if it would be useful for a reader to get a sense of not only the relative size of elements from the bars in a graph but also the exact amounts, then label those amounts—perhaps by putting them at the top of each bar, as in this example (640 and 612 are the exact amounts):

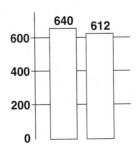

Generally avoid using computer programs that automatically generate graphs and tables: They tend to make visuals too fancy, while giving you too little control over the placement of labels. You will usually do better by using an art program and drawing your own visual.

Familiarity contributes to clarity. Follow conventions. Orient maps so that north is at the top. Use conventional shapes for stages in a flow chart. Put the biggest segment of a pie chart to the right from 12 o'clock. Use an exclamation-point icon to mean "Attention!" and a light-bulb icon for "Smart Idea."

ASSIGNMENTS FOR 7.1

1. *Critique a Visual* Find an interesting visual in a news or business maga-zine. Imagine that you are an editorial assistant for this publication. In a memo to your boss, critique the visual in terms of the seven points made in section 7.1. Conclude by recommending changes or no change, based on your critique.

2. *Revise a Visual* Find an interesting visual in a news or business magazine and represent the same information by creating a different kind of visual. For example, put tabled information in a graph. Or turn a photograph into a line drawing. Photocopy the original and submit a memo report to your instructor on why your version or the original version was the right choice for this visual.

7.2 >—— Visuals That Examine Objects

Technical writers use visuals to show the appearance and structure of objects, such as machines. The most common kinds of visuals for this purpose are box diagrams (see Figure 2.2) and line drawings (Figure 7.1). A box drawing consists of basic shapes, like boxes, connected perhaps by lines. Line drawings use basic shapes but also include some artistically drawn shapes using lines and shading. Box diagrams and line drawings should be as simple as possible, with sufficient but no unnecessary detail.

Figure 7.1 shows a line drawing with callouts. Callouts are words naming key parts of a visual. They are often connected to the appropri-ate part of the drawing with lines, called leaders, as in Figure 7.1. A call-out may also take the form of a legend, which is a list of numbered identifiers corresponding to numbers placed inside the drawing (Figure 7.2).

FIGURE 7.1 ▼ **Line Drawing with Callouts**

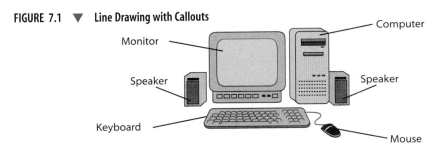

COMPONENTS OF THE STANDARD MICROCOMPUTER SYSTEM

FIGURE 7.2 ▼ **Line Drawing with Legend**

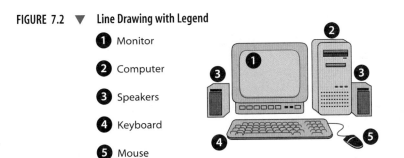

1. Monitor
2. Computer
3. Speakers
4. Keyboard
5. Mouse

COMPONENTS OF THE STANDARD MICROCOMPUTER SYSTEM

You should keep the number of callouts per drawing down to as few as possible, so as not to obscure the drawing itself with numbers or leader lines. Avoid crossing leader lines.

Be careful how you word your callouts. As noted by Caroline Rude (1994), a technical editing expert, "callouts on the illustration must match the terms used in the text" (p. 73). Rude writes that if a part is called a *casing* in the text, readers will search an illustration for the word *casing* but may never locate the part in the drawing if the writer used another term in the callout, such as *cover*.

Figure 7.3 shows an exploded drawing, in which an object is broken open or pulled apart to reveal its structure and possibly how it is assembled. The cut-away drawing in Figure 7.4 provides an interior view. And Figure 7.5 shows how a particular section of an object can be magnified to make detail visible. Notice that the enlarged image reproduces the orientation of the detail, even when it is upside down.

Occasionally only a photograph will do when precise detail is important. Technical writers working in marketing often use photographs to show off the attractiveness of their products. When using photographs

FIGURE 7.3 ▼ Exploded Drawing

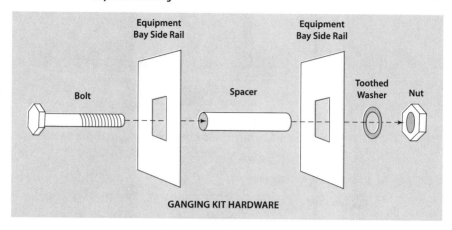

FIGURE 7.4 ▼ Cut-Away Drawing

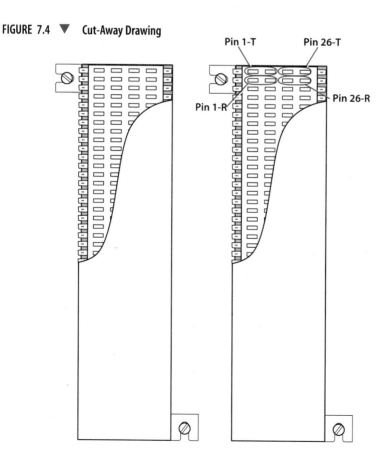

FIGURE 7.5 ▼ Magnified Drawing

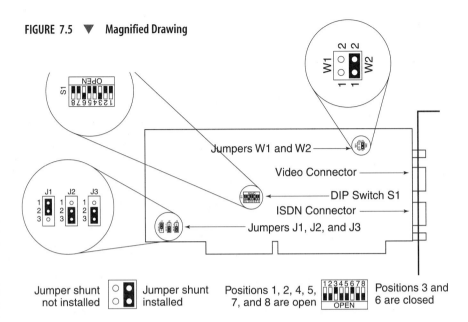

that have been reduced or enlarged, you may wish to place a ruler or some other familiar object (such as a human hand) next to it to show its scale.

ASSIGNMENTS FOR 7.2

1. *Create a Box Diagram or Line Drawing* Create a box diagram or line drawing using callouts and magnification. One possible subject: the area in the back of a microcomputer where most of the electrical cords are attached. Or draw a product, or part of a product, produced by your fictional company. Or, if you are engaged in a long project, make a drawing that you can use in the resulting document.

2. *Reveal Structure* Use cut-away or explosion techniques to reveal the interior, or assembly sequence, of a simple object such as a ballpoint pen or a flashlight.

7.3 >—— Visuals That Show Processes

Processes often involve physical motion, so a method is needed to indicate motion. A technical writer can use video for presentations or online texts, but in printed texts the technical writer usually uses arrows to indicate motion and the direction of that motion, as in Figure 7.6.

FIGURE 7.6 ▼   Drawing Showing Movement

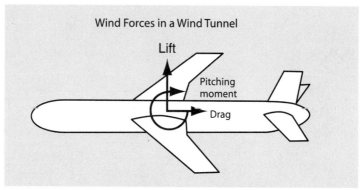

Source: NASA http://ccf.arc.nasa.gov/ao.page2html, Accessed March 14, 1999.

Gantt charts show the flow of work (see Figure 9.1). Flow charts are used to show decision-making paths (Figure 7.7) and to plan projects (see Figure 3.1). Schematic diagrams can indicate not only the structure of a system but also the flow of activity within it (Figure 7.8).

When creating instructions for computer software, writers sometimes print screen shots from the program. See Figure 6.2 for an example from a quick reference card.

ASSIGNMENT FOR 7.3

1. *Illustrate a Process* Create a visual or series of visuals that illustrates a process, such as registering for classes, appealing a grade, pledging a sorority, opening a program under Windows's menu system, or the heat flow in a building. Use an appropriate kind of visual.

7.4 ⟩——Visuals That Show Relationships

Graphs are perhaps the most familiar kind of visual showing relationships. Graphs are very common in business documents, where they might display information about company profits over time, relative product sales, and other financial trends. Technical writers need to understand how graphs work, and they need to be aware of the types of graphs available for presenting data and relationships.

▲ 1. Bar and Line Graphs

Bar and line graphs show changes and make comparisons using a vertical and horizontal axis. In a simple graph, the horizontal axis is marked

FIGURE 7.7 ▼ Flow Chart for Problem Solving

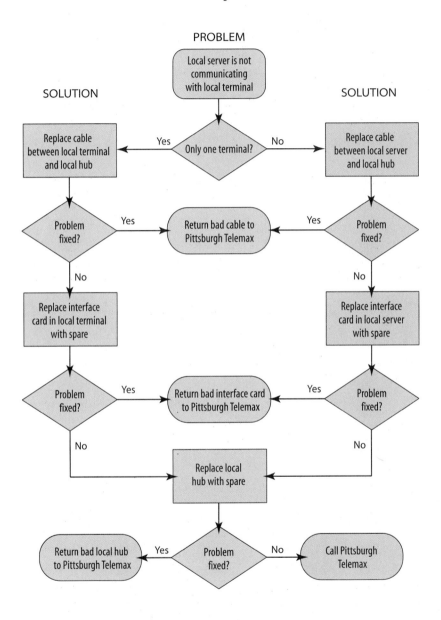

by textual (non-numerical) identifiers, such as company names or increments of time, while the vertical axis shows numerical changes. Figure 7.9 shows a bar graph and a line graph presenting the same information.

Writers sometimes rotate bar graphs (turn them on their side) so that the textual entries lie along the vertical axis and the numerical entries lie

FIGURE 7.8 ▶ Schematic Diagram

A CIRCUIT BOARD

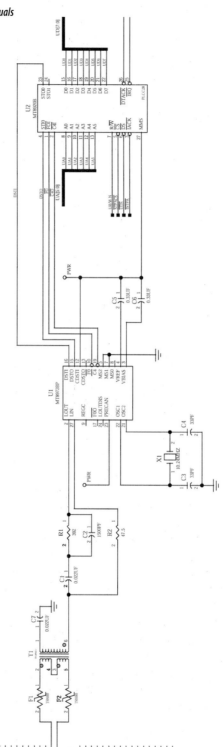

along the horizontal axis. Thus, a bar graph may have bars shooting out horizontally from the vertical axis instead of rising from the horizontal axis. This makes for natural, left-to-right reading of long labels, as in Figure 7.10. You should avoid printing long identifiers vertically, forcing the reader to rotate the page to read the text.

A graph might compare the performance of several entities over time, as in Figure 7.11.

In a correlational graph, the horizontal axis is called the *x*-axis and the vertical axis is called the *y*-axis. *Both* display numerical changes. Figure 7.12 shows that as you add months to the length of your auto financing loan, you pay a higher interest rate. As one figure goes up, the

FIGURE 7.9 ▼ **Two Basic Graphs**

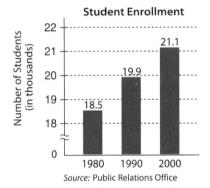

Student Enrollment

Source: Public Relations Office

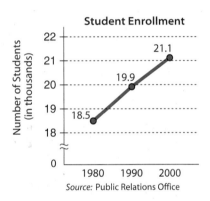

Student Enrollment

Source: Public Relations Office

FIGURE 7.10 ▼ **Horizontal Graph or "Pictogram"**

Breakdown of Telemax Gross Sales, 1999

Total Gross Sales: $20.63 million

U.S. government

U.S. educational institutions

U.S. commercial

Canadian commercial and educational sales

European sales

Asian sales

equal $500,000

FIGURE 7.11 ▼ **Multiple-Comparison Line Graph**

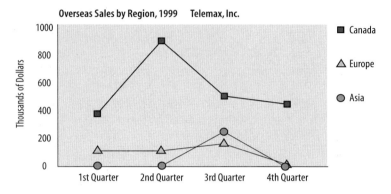

other goes up in a positive correlation. A note of caution here about correlation. Correlation does not always reflect a cause-effect relationship. The fact that the number of bars in a new town increases at the same rate as the number of churches does not mean that drinkers feel a greater need for religion or that religion drives people to drink. Instead, those increases are probably independent effects of another cause altogether, an increase in population. Adding months to your car payments, however, does directly affect the interest rate of your payments, as the graph in Figure 7.12 implies.

Sometimes the vertical axis begins with an initial jump larger than the other increments. For example, in a graph showing growth in the student population of a large university, most of the change might take place in the range from 18,000 to 22,000. If you used increments of 500 and started from 0, your line graph would be very tall (you'd have to have 36 increments before getting to 18,000). Therefore, you would want to skip to 18,000 as your first increment, as in Figure 7.9. In such cases, you should alert your reader to the jump by putting a break or jag in the vertical axis. (Note the base of the vertical axis in each of the graphs in Figure 7.9.)

When constructing bar and line graphs, indicate what quantities are being compared: dollars or millions of dollars, inches or miles. Clearly label both the vertical axis and the horizontal axis, and use an informative title above the graph. You can also put labels elsewhere on the graph for clarity.

In the same way, you can label points on line graphs. Sometimes writers draw dotted lines from the points down to the horizontal axis to specify exact values, and sometimes they go further and shade in segments

FIGURE 7.12 ▼ Correlational Graph

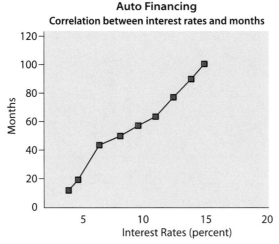

Source: D & D Auto Dealer, Inc.

formed by the dotted lines and the graphed line; but that kind of tinkering can make a visual look crowded or messy. Put values at the points, if that would be helpful (as in Figure 7.9), and leave out the dotted rules and shading.

Underneath the graph, indicate the source of the data being graphed if you have borrowed information from outside your organization (again, as in Figure 7.9).

Instead of bars and lines, you can use images to jazz up your graph, as in Figure 7.10; this sort of figure is sometimes called a "pictogram." Many of these enhancements are visually impressive, but they sometimes reduce clarity. As a technical writer, you should probably stick to the straightforward presentation of information in the simplest visual form possible. Leave the decorative embellishments to the art department.

▲ *2. Dishonest Graphs*

It is easy to distort information with a graph. Figure 7.13 depicts a correlational graph in which small increments (0, 5%, 10%, . . .) stretch the graph line upward. The crunching together of increments along the x-axis contributes to this effect, giving the impression of a large and continuing increase in revenues (when in fact the increase is flattening out). Figure 7.14 shows the same information graphed so as to provide a more honest representation of the data.

FIGURE 7.13 ▼ Dishonest Graph

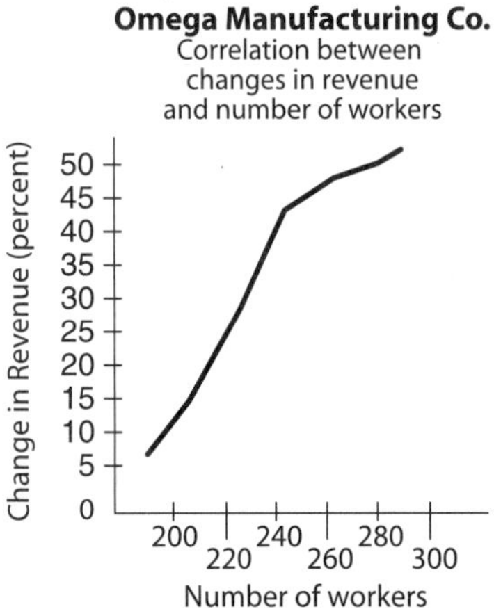

Omega Manufacturing Co.
Correlation between changes in revenue and number of workers
Change in Revenue (percent)
50
45
40
35
30
25
20
15
10
5
0
200
220
240
260
280
300
Number of workers

FIGURE 7.14 ▼ Honest Graph

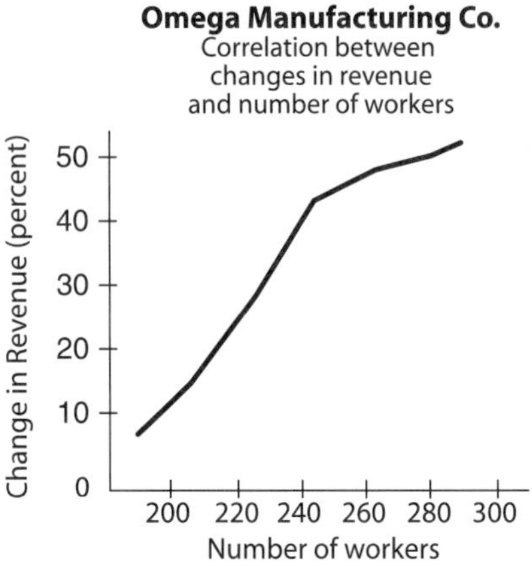

Omega Manufacturing Co.
Correlation between changes in revenue and number of workers
Change in Revenue (percent)
50
40
30
20
10
0
200
220
240
260
280
300
Number of workers

7 Visuals

As a writer, you need to judge what the data mean and then accurately represent that meaning with the shape of your visual.

▲ 3. *Charts*

Percentage charts show the breakdown of something into parts and the relative size of each part as a percentage of the whole. Pie charts do this with a circle (Figure 7.15), and bar charts do it with a bar (Figure 7.16). In the case of pie charts, begin with the largest portion, moving from 12 o'clock to the right. Continue in descending order to the smallest portion

FIGURE 7.15 ▼ Pie Chart

TELEMAX GROSS SALES, 1999
1%
2%
11%
20%
40%
26%
U.S. government sales
U.S. educational institutions
U.S. commercial sales
Canadian commercial and educational
European sales
Asian sales

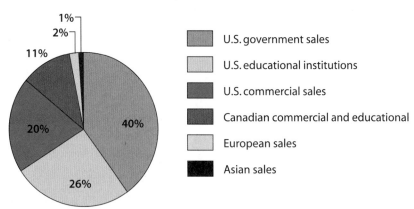

FIGURE 7.16 ▼ Bar Chart

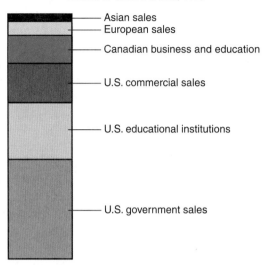

TELEMAX GROSS SALES, 1999

— Asian sales
— European sales

— Canadian business and education

— U.S. commercial sales

— U.S. educational institutions

— U.S. government sales

at the top left. However, leave the very last segment for unspecified contents, such as "miscellaneous" or "other," even if that segment is larger than preceding segments. To keep the segments proportional in size relative to their percentage of the whole, use 3.6 degrees of the arc for each percent. A 10 percent segment, then, would take up 36 degrees of arc.

Shading or color should be used to provide clear contrast between neighboring segments. You can progress from light shades to ever darker ones, or alternate dark and light shades. You can also identify the segments with callouts and leaders, or with a legend. Figure 7.15 uses both methods. Or you can write labels inside the larger segments, saving callouts for tiny segments, as in Figure 7.15.

Bar charts present the largest segment at the bottom, then the next largest above it, and so on to the smallest segment at the top (Figure 7.16). If the chart is turned sideways, the largest segment should be on the left, to take advantage of normal left-to-right reading in Western culture.

Organizational charts show the relationships among departments or personnel (see Figure 2.1). Note that such charts include both horizontal and hierarchical relationships.

▲ 4. Tables

Many comparisons that can be graphed can also be put into tables. A table typically presents a vertical list of comparable items along the leftmost column of the graphic, called the stub, with a set of criteria for comparison listed horizontally across the top. The data are placed in appropriate intersections in the resulting grid. You can create tables that display words only (called word tables), numbers only, or a combination (as in Table 7.1). Symbols and other visuals can also be placed in cells, if doing so would help summarize information.

Tables are particularly useful for precisely comparing many items on the basis of many criteria. However, giant tables with twenty or so stub entries and the same number of criteria for comparison can be unreadable. The reader would be overwhelmed by the amount of data—defeating the goal of clarification.

Very simple tables can clearly contrast a small set of numbers, such as the means in the outcome of an experiment. Table 7.2 shows one of the APA formats for presenting such data. The APA discourages the use of vertical rules, which is a way of discouraging overly complex tables. For easy reading, it advises writers to place a horizontal rule after every fourth or fifth row when their table contains long vertical columns of numbers or words.

You should put a horizontal rule between the heading and the data. Note in Table 7.2 that the main heading, "Work Categories," is separated from subheadings with a rule (not necessary but often helpful) and that the subheadings are separated from the data with a rule (necessary). Shading may replace rules, as in Table 7.1.

Tables, like figures, should be carefully labeled so that every part is comprehensible to the reader. When placing numbers in the cells, for example, be sure to indicate through your labeling whether you are

TABLE 7.1 ▼ Table Comparing Qualities

Comparison of Features of Multimedia Projectors
October 23, 1998

Model	Price	Lumens	Resolution	Min/Max diameter (inches)	Input S-Video	Weight (pounds)
JAAP: 8700MP	$7,619.95	1100	SVGA (800 x 600)	20/300	Yes	32.1
Emery: 5600C	$7,125.00	650	SXGA (1280 x 1024)	23/300	Yes	14.7
Maximus: DT9460	$4,955.00	700	SVGA (832 x 624)	20/640	Yes	14.1
Darwin: 245SP	$3,199.99	400	SVGA (800 x 600)	20/300	Yes	12.6
TND: 4200M	$2,721.99	300	SVGA (800 x 600)	40/200	Yes	17.5

TABLE 7.2 ▼ Table Showing Experimental Results

Life Satisfaction Ratings of Males and Females

	Work Categories		
	No Job	Job	Two Jobs
Males:			
M	4.1	7.9	4.8
SD	4.0	6.0	2.0
Females:			
M	7.1	7.3	3.1
SD	2.0	3.0	4.0

giving totals, averages, or percentages. You should also label the unit of measurement: dollars or Yen, meters or millimeters. You can identify such items in the title, in the headings, or in the cells:

Title identification:	Height in Feet and Cost in Dollars	
Head identification:	Feet	Cost $
	4	12.00
Cell identification:	Height	Cost
	4′	$12.00

In the case of numerical entries, take all numbers out to the same decimal place. Use zeros if necessary:

2.5   4.0

or

1.34   1.20   2.00

Align decimals, and use a single zero to the left of the decimal in the absence of a whole number:

incorrect	*correct*
.42	0.42
3.60	3.60

ASSIGNMENTS FOR 7.4

1. *Bar Graph* Put this information in a bar graph with an irregular initial increment on the vertical axis:

a. Student enrollment at Greenbower Junior College for 1999: 8,602

b. Student enrollment at Bryant Technical College for 1999: 8,870

c. Student enrollment at Loisburg College for 1999: 9,956

2. *Line Graph* Put this information in a line graph with an irregular initial increment on the vertical axis: Student enrollment at Maysville Junior College for 1960: 795; for 1970: 1,161; for 1980: 2,156; for 1990: 1,893, and for 2000: 1,789.

3. *Multiple-Bar Bar Graph* Put this information about students' grades in a technical writing class into two bar graphs. First, divide each of four bars into three segments, one segment for each type of score; then divide each of three bars into four segments, one segment for each type of student. Be prepared to discuss which graph is more effective.

   a. Male traditional students: Average Test Score: 75 / Average Quiz Score: 84 / Average Paper Grade: 80

   b. Male nontraditional students (26 or older): Average Test Score: 89 / Average Quiz Score: 91 / Average Paper Grade: 86

   c. Female traditional students: Average Test Score: 87 / Average Quiz Score: 90 / Average Paper Grade: 86

   d. Female nontraditional students (26 or older): Average Test Score: 94 / Average Quiz Score: 97 / Average Paper Grade: 95

4. *Co-Relational Line Graph* Put this information in a co-relational line graph: Percentage of nontraditional students (26 or older) at Pumpkinville College and the average GPA for all students: 4% / 2.6 GPA (1980); 8% / 2.8 GPA (1985); 15% / 3.1 GPA (1990); 18% / 3.3 GPA (1995).

5. *Pie Chart* Determine the percentages of your technical writing class that fall into these age groups, and then create a pie chart to represent those percentages: 18 or younger / 19–20 / 21–25 / 26 or older.

6. *Bar Graph* Your company makes ice cream sticks. Create a bar chart illustrating the breakdown of sales by flavor: cherry: 45%; blueberry: 31%; orange: 18%; lime: 6%. If you're in a creative mood, you can shape the chart to look like the product and use appropriate colors to represent the flavors.

7. *Table* Put this information in a table:

   a. Cartwright File Cabinets: weight—42 lb; height—4 ft; width—3 ft; depth 3 ft; colors—tan only; price—$295.50.

   b. Maxwell File Cabinets: weight—48 lb; height—4.5 ft.; width—4 ft.; depth 3 ft; colors—brown, gray, white; price—$350.00.

7.5 >—— Visuals That Symbolize

Symbols used in computer software and in printed documentation are called "icons." Icons stand apart from the text, either in the menu bar of a computer screen or in the margin of a page of writing. Smaller versions, called "glyphs," may appear within a line of text, as in

Keep your on the ball

The printer image used to represent the "print" command and the magnifying glass used to represent the "enlarge" command are familiar icons found in menu bars:

A triangle with an exclamation point in it, in the margin of a text, is easily recognizable as a signal that a warning note is appearing in the text:

The warning icon in the margin prevents readers from skipping the important notification of a dangerous situation.

At Telemax, not much thought has gone into the use of icons in documentation. Because technical writer Wendy Smith has drawing ability, Marge Mendoza has asked her to improve and extend the set of icons used in Telemax documents and computer screens. (This is the sort of activity a technical writer would take up during the downtime between major writing assignments.) In her spare time, Wendy researches the topic and looks for ideas in books like William Horton's (1994) *The Icon Book: Visual Symbols for Computer Systems and Documentation.* She also checks Internet sites displaying public domain icons, such as those accessible through Land of Links, whose address at the time of this writing is **http://www.wworld.com/users/jcamp/links.html.**

Wendy draws a number of lessons from her research, including the following:

1. Icons exist in a context. Take advantage of that context when designing an icon. Don't hold yourself to a standard of making the icon so recognizable that it can be understood alone, out of context.

2. Employ synecdoche, the poetic technique whereby a part represents the whole ("hired hands"). For example, a telephone receiver can represent a telephone.

3. Depict consequences. The image of an explosion warns of the dire consequences of a particular action or mistake.

4. Learn and use the standard symbols developed by the arts, the sciences, and other professions. Here are well-known symbols that caution about electrical hazard and warn against emitting static electricity:

5. Use familiar public symbols, such as the circle with a diagonal line for "prohibited" and the circle with a smile for "correct" or "OK."

6. Use images related to things and activities, such as a mailbox for "electronic mail," an open book for "read," and a clef or quarter note to represent "music."

7. Use letters and punctuation marks: **I** for "information," **Del** for "delete," **?** for "get help."

8. Indicate motion and direction with arrows ⇨, not pointing fingers ☞. Hand and finger images can have unsuspected bad connotations in other cultures.

9. Develop a consistent style. The level of detail should be about the same for all representations. Diagonal icons should all angle from low left to high right or high left to low right. Use borders to box in all icons, or leave them all unboxed. Choose the same kinds of arrows and the same fonts for lettering throughout the icon system.

ASSIGNMENTS FOR 7.5

1. *Create Tool Bar Icons* Create a set of icons that would be useful for a tool bar in a particular kind of software program, such as an accounting program, a monster-destroying game, or a music composing program.

2. *Create Documentation Icons* Create a set of icons for a manual. Include icons to alert readers to caution, important points, shortcuts, help notes, advanced notes, cross references, and so forth.

7.6 ⟩── Writing Physical Descriptions

Technical writers cannot rely entirely on visuals to get their points across. They must also know how to describe static entities (objects, places) and changing entities (mechanisms, processes) in the prose of their running text, conjuring up images in the reader's mind. This is the case even for prose that is supported by visuals.

You should never describe anything in its entirety. To do so would take you, absurdly, from the micro-level of subatomic particles to the macro-level of global positioning. The key principle underlying descriptive writing is, first, to establish a clear purpose and, then, to create a level of detail and approach appropriate to that purpose. Consideration of audience, as always, is an important factor here. A technician needs more information about the internal workings of a mechanism than a business manager needs.

▲ *1. Level of Detail*

You choose what details to mention according to what the reader needs to know—any other descriptive information is, at best, distracting. If your purpose is to help a reader find a particular part amidst all the others in a disassembled set of parts, you need only focus on the categorizing and distinguishing characteristics of that part. If all the parts are metallic gray, you don't need to mention the color. If all are about the same size, you can ignore size. If the part in question is grooved in a way that other parts are not, then that detail would be included in your description.

The language of descriptive writing should be precise and fairly concrete. Avoid vague words if more specific phrasing will help the reader identify or see what you are describing. Describe a display using eight shades as "grayscale," not "black and white." Of course, it is also possible to go too far toward the concrete end of the descriptive spectrum. To refer to one or another kind of wordiness as *prolixity* or *periphrasis* or *pleonasm* is to make distinctions that are rarely necessary. The trick, then, is to be specific enough to provide a useful picture without being so specific as to confuse. In most cases, what cognitive scientists call the "middle level" of specificity is the most effective in creating a clear picture for a nonexpert (a *penny* rather than a *coin* or an *Indian head*).

The passage in Box 7.1 describing a sailboat hull, written for novices, introduces some terminology but avoids many highly specific terms like *shrouds* for the wire lines supporting the mast or *sheets* for the rope lines used to manipulate the sails. A reader drowning in nautical terminology would have a hard time visualizing the boat. On the other hand, the writer uses the phrases *wire lines* and *rope lines,* instead of just *lines,* since that degree of specificity is necessary to understanding the different functions of the lines.

BOX 7.1 ▼ Descriptive Passage

The Hull of a Sailboat

From a distance, the hull of a small sailboat looks like the hull of a rowboat. A closer look reveals important differences. To begin with, the bow of the sailboat is covered, not open. This is crucial because the solid cover supports the mast, the tall vertical pole holding the sails.

The sailboat requires rope lines running along the edge of the hull to control the sails and wire lines attached to the hull to support the mast. The strong wire is necessary to hold up the mast and its sails, while the lighter, more flexible rope is appropriate for pulling in and letting out sails. This array of lines gives even a small sailboat a complex look, though a knowledgeable sailor sees the simple logic of it all.

The seating arrangements are different in a sailboat than in a rowboat. The rowboat has a seat that crosses the hull in about the middle. The sailboat has seats running along both sides of the hull, not across it. These dual seats allow sailors to shift their weight from one side of the boat to the other, to maintain enough weight upwind to prevent the boat from being blown over.

Close up, it is easy to see that a small sailboat has additional hull components not found on a rowboat. For steering, a tiller attaches to a rudder at the back of the sailboat. Inside the hull, just forward of the middle, a box called a centerboard trunk supports the centerboard, a removable flat piece of wood or fiberglass that extends through the bottom of the hull several feet into the water. The centerboard prevents the boat from sliding sideways when the boat is angling toward the wind or on a run across the wind.

▲ 2. Approaches to Description

In addition to decisions about detail, you must decide on an approach to the object or process being described. Here are three options:

1. The relational approach. You can focus on how the entity might be broken up into components and how the components relate to each other physically and functionally.

2. The spatial approach. You can describe from far to near, around the outside, top to bottom, or outside to inside.

3. The natural-order approach. You can follow a process from beginning to end, or show what happens in a process chronologically.

Many of the standard methods of definition are used in descriptive writing. For example, you can describe an object or mechanism in terms of how it appears to be similar to, or different from, a more familiar one.

Or you can describe it in terms of its function. A "thin blade" becomes a more comprehensible image if your reader is told how it carries out its function of shaving a chin, or removing paint from glass, or gutting fish, or scoring tile. As you begin to describe the functioning of the particular blade, the reader gets a clearer mental picture of the tool.

Similar to the far-to-near approach is the approach that begins with an overview and then moves on to specifics. A description of a distance learning room could proceed in that manner, starting with a discussion of what such rooms do and how, along with a box diagram of the whole setup. Next the writer might provide a physical description of such a room from a single perspective (perhaps the doorway), moving next to a close-up of one work station and, finally, to the inner workings of the electronic devices and the software programs.

▲ *3. Special Case: Describing for Marketing Purposes*

Companies like Pittsburgh Telemax produce a lot of marketing texts that include descriptions of their products. The purpose of such documents is to get people to buy the product, and details are selected with that in mind.

Figure 7.17 shows the front side of a marketing document used by Compunetix, Inc., a Pittsburgh-area telecommunications firm. Notice the limited focus on those physical features of the KPI Communication Station that reflect the device's ability to handle a large number of conferences. The selection of limited detail imposes this quality on the mind of the reader. Physical dimensions and appearance options (metal or oak enclosure) are presented in a list apart from the main text. Similarly, detailed specifications are listed on the back side of the document (Figure 7.18), apart from the front, which is designed to provoke interest.

ASSIGNMENTS FOR 7.6

1. *Analyze a Passage*   In a memo to your instructor, discuss the different methods of description at work in the passage in Box 7.1.

2. *Describe a Product for a Novice*   Choose a high-tech product with which you are familiar, such as your own personal computer, and assume that you work for the company that sells it. Write a description of the product for a novice who has little experience with this kind of product. Begin with an overview and progress to functions and features. Use one visual.

3. *Describe a Product for an Experienced Audience*   Do assignment 7.6(2), but write your description for an experienced, knowledgeable audience.

FIGURE 7.17 ▼ **Front Side of a Polybag**

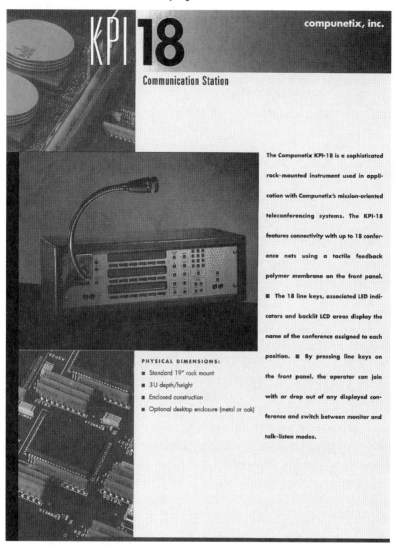

Source: Reprinted with permission from Compunetix Inc., Monroeville, PA.

FIGURE 7.18 ▼ Back Side of a Polybag

As a conferencing instrument, the KPI-18 allows the operator to participate in any number of assigned nets at the same time in either talk/listen mode or monitor mode. The KPI-18 operator can access public address keys for making announcements in designated zones, an intercom function for calling other users on the system or dial line keys for connecting with outside lines. In addition, the KPI-18 features Direct Voice Link (DVL) mode, which allows very quick connections between pre-determined parties, and a 10-button Function Key Keypad for easy and efficient operation.

All operational software for the instruments is maintained and downloaded by the host system, CONTEX® 500T, or 1000T. The instrument key assignments and access levels are downloaded from the host system. Instrument configuration changes made at the CONTEX® Maintenance Administration Terminal (MAT) are updated in real-time on the associated instrument. All instrument functions are software controlled to provide a very versatile configuration of hardware.

PHYSICAL FEATURES:
■ Function Key Keypad*
■ Panel Microphone
■ DTMF Keypad
■ Headset/Handset Jacks
■ Line Key Status and Activity LEDs
* The Function Key Keypad allows the operator to access special system functions with push-button ease.

■ Backlit LCDs
■ Foot Switch Selector Key
■ Independent Volume Control Keys
 – Panel Speaker
 – Headset/Handset
■ Public Address Key:
 Activates the KPI-18 in public address mode
■ Master Mute Key:
 Instantly mutes all line keys in monitor mode
■ Signal Key:
 Creates a hook flash
■ Radio Key:
 Activates an assigned radio port
■ Hold Key:
 Places a line on hold
■ Function Keys:
 Generates programmable alarms

ELECTRICAL CHARACTERISTICS:
■ Input Voltage:
 nominal 48 VDC, minimum 36 VDC, maximum 59 VDC
■ Amperage: nominal 0.50A, minimum 0.38A, maximum 1.0A
■ Signal: ISDN "U" Interface 2B+D with optional RS422 and fiber optic link
■ Optional 110VAC power supply module

Compunetix is a subsidiary of Compunetics, Inc. Compunetics maintains design and manufacturing facilities that include a premier Printed Circuit Board fabrication facility as well as board drafting. Compunetics employs over 200 people, including over 30 software and hardware engineers, and is registered as a small business concern.

Our partial client list includes:
■ NASA
■ FAA
■ U.S. Senate
■ Rockwell Space Operations
■ Boeing Computer Support Services
■ Social Security Administration
■ Allied-Signal Aerospace Company
■ Jet Propulsion Laboratory

compunetix, inc.
federal systems division
for mission control
2000 eldo road
monroeville, PA 15146
phone: (412) 373-8110

7 Visuals

Source: Reprinted with permission from Compunetix Inc., Monroeville, PA.

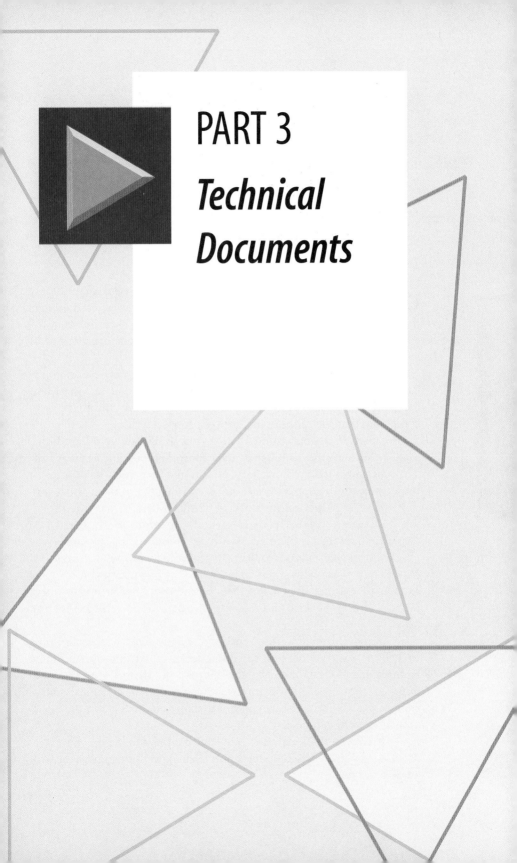

PART 3
Technical Documents

RFPs and Proposals

8

Organizations in need of an expensive product or service often publish "requests for proposals" (RFPs) in trade publications, or they mail their RFP to the companies specified on their list of likely suppliers. Government facilities, including state-supported universities, are required by law to put large contracts out for bid.

Companies like Telemax get most of their business by responding to RFPs with external proposals to provide products and service. Many companies outsource proposal writing to freelance technical writers or companies that specialize in the "art" of proposal writing.

Because it is a small company that tries to operate on a bare-bones budget, Telemax does as much of its own work as possible, reducing the need for outsourcing. The Documentation Department is ultimately responsible for developing proposals, even when the company hires outside experts to help with the proposal writing. Mendoza has taken training courses in proposal writing, and, in addition to her DDM responsibilities, this is the main type of technical writing she does.

When Telemax chooses to bring in professional proposal writers, that outside unit works with a "red team" within the organization. A red team consists of a group drawn together for a single, high-priority project. Mendoza heads the team and remains ultimately responsible for the proposal.

Although proposal writing has become a professional specialization, we believe that students in a beginning technical writing course should be introduced to the aims, the content, and the rhetorical strategies of technical proposals. An organization may expect its technical staff—engineers, technicians, or technical writers—to participate in the development of some proposals.

This chapter looks at how an RFP comes into being, how it is processed by provider companies like Telemax, and, then, how the proposal is written.

8.1 ⟩—— Writing an RFP

Let's assume that a small institution, Pumpkinville State College (PSC), has decided to create a distance learning program in order to expand course offerings at its satellite campus in a nearby city. The Campus Computer Committee has determined that PSC needs a point-to-point videoconferencing system with some customized features. The video-conferencing equipment will be used to include students at the remote campus in a class being taught at the main campus.

The classrooms at each campus will contain two large TVs, one displaying the main campus classroom and one displaying the remote campus classroom. Each student at the remote campus should have as much opportunity to ask questions and otherwise participate in the class as the students at the main campus. Professors using the main campus room must be able to control the TV cameras at both campuses—pointing them, as they wish, at the students, at themselves, or at the white board.

The committee has determined the approximate cost of developing such a facility by consulting with other schools that have similar setups. After further studies, the committee has found that implementing a distance learning program is feasible. The president of the college asks Henrietta Gartner, a technical writer assigned to the Purchasing Department, to develop a request for proposals.

The RFP that Gartner creates contains three sections: an introduction, a description of the project, and a list of technical specifications. The content of those sections appears below:

▲ 1. Introduction

The introduction states the required format for proposals and the deadline. It also outlines the procedure for submitting the proposal and includes the name, address, telephone number, and e-mail address for Gartner, the primary contact person at PSC. Gartner realizes that some of the requirements stated in the RFP may need to be clarified. Therefore, she includes in the introduction the telephone number for a technical contact person at the university and a procedure for submitting technical questions in writing or via e-mail.

▲ 2. Description of the Project

The second section of the RFP includes a general description of PSC and a discussion of how the college intends to use the videoconferencing system. It includes photographs and written descriptions of the class-rooms at both campuses that will be converted to distance learning rooms, and it locates and describes other relevant facilities, such as the main power source and telephone hook-ups.

▲ *3. Technical Specifications*

The final part of the RFP is the statement of requirements, or technical specifications. This section is co-authored by a number of people. A telecommunications expert writes the section on interfacing with the public telephone network, a computer systems analyst writes the section listing networking requirements, and a professor who teaches courses in multimedia technology writes the section on the user interface. Henrietta Gartner gathers all of these sections, edits them, and assembles them into a package.

After Gartner finishes the RFP, she advertises the project in several trade magazines for potential vendors. In the ad, Gartner includes a general description of the required system as well as her own name and telephone number. When a vendor contacts her, she mails a full copy of the RFP. Gartner records the company name and address for each vendor as well as the name and telephone number for the primary contact person. She uses this information to distribute the answers to technical questions as the various vendors develop their proposals.

ASSIGNMENTS FOR 8.1

1. *Examine an RFP* Obtain an RFP from your school's purchasing department. (Your instructor may have left a copy of one on reserve in your library.) In a memo to your instructor, indicate how your school's RFP is similar to and different from the RFP described in this section.

2. *Write an RFP* Select one of these scenarios and write an RFP:

   a. Write an RFP for a major project that your fictional company would be interested in responding to. (Examples: from your state's Highway Commission, an RFP to supply decorative trees and bushes for a 200-mile stretch of state highway; from a Canadian firm, an RFP to supply a home brew kit to be sold under the Canadian company's brand name in three provinces)

   b. Write an RFP from your company to be sent to local business equipment stores for 10 office phones with a set of specified features such as phone number memory, multiple lines, and speaker phone capability. Prepare for this project by searching through catalogues or by visiting local stores and learning about office telephones. Develop a list of features and learn the terminology for them.

c. Write an RFP for a piece of equipment that you would like to see purchased for your school. Prepare by thinking about where the equipment would be installed and who would use it for what purposes. Research the features of such equipment and learn the terminology for them.

8.2 >——— Processing an RFP

The members of the sales staff at Pittsburgh Telemax monitor the video-conferencing trade magazines. They look for new features offered by competitors, and they look for potential new markets for their own products. They also scan the advertisements for RFP opportunities. A salesperson at Pittsburgh Telemax notices the advertisement placed by Henrietta Gartner and brings it to the attention of his supervisor, Beverly Yoshida, who calls Gartner. Gartner records Yoshida's name and telephone number and sends a copy of the RFP to Pittsburgh Telemax.

When the full RFP arrives at Pittsburgh Telemax, Yoshida distributes copies to DDM Marge Mendoza, to the Sales and Marketing staff, and to the appropriate engineers and department managers. All of these individuals read through the proposal very carefully. As the engineers read the RFP, they think about the feasibility of providing a solution; as the salespeople read it, they consider what sort of pricing will be competitive.

At the proposal kick-off meeting, chaired by DDM Marge Mendoza, the committee members evaluate the requirements and compare notes. They determine that Pittsburgh Telemax can provide a solution to the RFP requirements at a reasonable cost with a reasonable effort. In short, they determine that Pittsburgh Telemax should respond to the proposal. They are able to make this decision fairly easily because they are experienced at creating systems like the one that Pumpkinville State College wants.

The committee asks Wendy Smith to develop a feasibility report, to be submitted to the company president, Howard Stone. This report will contain a summary of the RFP as well as a summary of the discussion at the kick-off meeting. It will clearly state the committee's final conclusions and recommendations.

ASSIGNMENT FOR 8.2

1. *Analyze RFP* Form an RFP evaluation committee consisting of several students. Assign roles (e.g., technical expert, DDM, marketing person).

Examine one of the RFPs created for assignment 8.1(2). Based on that discussion, write a feasibility report to your company president explaining why your company should respond with a proposal. (After discussing this matter with your committee members, write your own individual reports to turn in.) Begin with an executive summary that states the problem and gives your recommendation. In the middle section, provide details and lines of reasoning that back up your recommendation. In the final section, briefly restate your recommendation and the strongest reasons for it. Be persuasive.

8.3 >———— Writing a Proposal

Since Henrietta Gartner did not provide a copy of the RFP on computer disk, Marge Mendoza scans the original print copy and converts it to a computer file using OCR software. Mendoza assigns a proposal number and sets up the required word processing files.

The word processing files follow Telemax's standard proposal format modified by the directives in the RFP. The standard proposal includes the following parts:

Front Matter
Letter of Transmittal
Title Page
Table of Contents
List of Figures and Tables

Body
Executive Summary
Overview
Technical Specifications
Project Management
Budget
Conclusion

Back Matter
Appendices

▲ 1. Letter of Transmittal

All Pittsburgh Telemax proposals include an introductory letter from President Stone. In this letter, the president thanks the client for the opportunity to respond to the RFP. He also indicates why he believes

Telemax's proposed solution is worthy of serious consideration.

The president may list a number of product awards that Telemax has won. He will certainly include references to satisfied customers willing to speak on behalf of Telemax. This information will also appear elsewhere in the proposal. Proposals contain a lot of repetition, because it is impossible to know who will read which sections. The writers must assume that each section may be read out of context.

Mendoza writes the first draft of this letter, based on versions of the letter written for earlier RFPs, which she has stored in the object library. The president then reads it over, adding his own flourishes. Later, Mendoza will discreetly review the letter to make sure that President Stone hasn't added any grammatical errors or odd punctuation. She is not being disrespectful. Stone is aware of his ignorance of the details of correct writing, and he relies on Mendoza to save him and the company from embarrassment.

The letter of transmittal is just the first of many sales pitches that permeate the proposal. (Several of the methods of persuasion discussed in Chapter 4 are routinely used in proposal writing.)

▲ 2. Title Page

The title page displays the names of both the vendor and the client. It also displays the proposal number, the RFP number, and the projected delivery date. Since Mendoza already knows all of this information, she is able to complete the title page immediately.

▲ 3. Table of Contents

Each section following the table of contents is preceded by a tabbed separator. The table of contents lists all sections, using the same phrasing as in the tabs, and provides page numbers.

▲ 4. List of Figures and Tables

In this list, all figures and tables in the RFP are identified by number, title, and page number.

▲ 5. Executive Summary

The executive summary (Box 8.1) is aimed at the highest-level administrator concerned with the project—in this case, the president of the college. It provides a brief description of the solution—a distance learning facility—that Telemax will provide in response to the RFP. This is the most general description of the system that Telemax will provide; the most detailed description will appear later in the technical specifications section of the proposal. The executive summary is meant to be more persuasive than informative. It asserts that Telemax will meet the demands of the RFP, and it emphasizes the sophisticated technology that Telemax brings to the project, providing high-quality performance and maximum flexibility. Whoever reads the executive summary should come away from it thinking that Telemax can do the job—that it can fashion the system to work the way the college wants.

Marge Mendoza sets up a skeleton file containing only the format for the executive summary, not the content. Wendy Smith will write the content in consultation with the Product Development Department manager. Mendoza will edit.

▲ 6. Overview

The overview introduces Pittsburgh Telemax and includes a brief history of the company as well as a brief description of its products. Since this part of the overview is standard, Mendoza is able to copy it directly from the object library, making small modifications to fit the situation.

Needless to say, the overview strongly sells the company.

The overview also discusses the needs of the client company, demonstrating Telemax's understanding of those needs and how to address them. This analysis is based not only on information in the RFP but also on information obtained through phone calls to the client company and other types of research. The Telemax Sales and Marketing Department aggressively seeks out information on potential clients, using the Web, libraries, personal contacts, and every other ethical avenue of research.

The overview is aimed at professors and middle-level administrators directly concerned with the project. It covers the proposed system in more detail than the executive summary, but in less detail than the technical specifications section.

▲ 7. Technical Specifications

The technical specifications section is the longest part of the proposal and the most important. It is aimed at the computer experts on campus who have been assigned to this project. Although these experts don't have the final say, their evaluation will strongly affect the purchase decision.

In the technical specifications section, Pittsburgh Telemax will indicate exactly how it plans to meet the needs of the client. Box 8.2 shows

BOX 8.1 ▼ **Executive Summary for a Proposal**

> Pittsburgh Telemax has carefully reviewed Pumpkinville State College's RFP for a point-to-point multimedia teleconferencing system. The solution we propose meets all of the general requirements stated in the RFP. We also propose some alternatives in the details of the system to take advantage of new technology and lower cost.
>
> The **Communicator DL 1000** system, which we propose here, is a distance learning system designed to be flexible and adaptable. It is off-the-shelf, but, being off *our* shelf, it reflects the highest quality in manufacturing and is at the cutting edge in technology. The setup includes the specified number of personal computers and two digital cameras. The computers include a local server (which is also the professor's computer), a remote server, and the specified number of student terminals. All of these computers have interface modules installed in them to allow them to interface with one another over an Ethernet network. The local and remote servers also have special interface modules that allow them to interface with the ISDN network and with the local and remote cameras. The cameras are high-quality digital video recorders that can be independently controlled by the professor.
>
> The heart of the **Communicator DL 1000** system lies in the proprietary software that we have developed to drive the terminals and maintain records on the servers. Each computer has a polished graphical user interface that is intuitive and reliable. All functions can be accessed using the mouse. The system includes training manuals and user manuals that fully describe how to use these terminals. We also offer training courses, either at your location, here at our headquarters, or via teleconferencing.
>
> All records are stored in a relational database located at the professor's terminal. Access to this database is restricted by login. The database can be used for maintaining student attendance records, grades, and any other statistical information, as well as for course sites for sharing of student writings, submission of papers, and posting of handouts. Because the database is relational, we can customize it to maintain any specific type of information our customers require. We can also customize our user interface to access database fields in a logical and intuitive manner.
>
> The solution we propose here is optimal for the distance learning facility you describe in the RFP. However, Pittsburgh Telemax offers a wide range of solutions for applications such as yours, so we can also modify this proposal to meet any "second thought" changes you may want to make in your requirements and specifications.

the outline of this section for the Pumpkinville project. Box 8.3 provides an excerpt consisting of the text for the first part of subsection 2 within that outline.

For each requirement in the RFP, Telemax makes clear whether its proposal "complies" with the requirement, "will comply," "partially complies," or "cannot comply." (Companies like Telemax are sometimes hired to complete only part of a project, so it may not be necessary for the company to be able to do everything.)

BOX 8.2 ▼ Outline of the Technical Specifications Section of a Proposal

> **Section II Technical Specifications**
>
> 1. Network
> 2. User interface
> 3. Exam capabilities
> 4. Troubleshooting
> 5. System configuration
> 6. Training

Given the technical nature of this section, the initial draft will be assigned to the appropriate project managers and engineers. Mendoza intends to assign the editing to Louis Frapp.

▲ 8. Project Management

The management section provides a detailed analysis of how the project will be carried out. It includes sophisticated flow charts showing who will do what, and by what dates, to meet specified deadlines. It also includes a general description of the personnel involved and their qualifications. (Detailed vitas appear in the appendices.) Mendoza can pull laudatory paragraphs about personnel from the object library, but actual development of the project plan will be the responsibility of the red team.

This section is almost as important as the technical specifications section. Companies want to know that the organization they hire can do the project on time, with no glitches. That requires management competence, not just technical competence.

▲ 9. Budget

Although it doesn't come last in the proposal, the budget section is the last section to be completed. Mendoza creates a word processing file for it, but she cannot yet determine the final content. Since this section generally includes a standard pricing table (Table 8.1), Mendoza creates the table but leaves it blank. The left column of the pricing table is auto-numbered, as shown in the table. If Mendoza needs to add a new row, the item number will be inserted automatically. The second column is formatted to accept only numbers, the third and last columns are formatted to display dollar amounts, and the fourth column ("Discount") is for-

BOX 8.3 ▼ Excerpt from the User Interface Subsection

2. USER INTERFACE

2.1. General

RFP: All user interface computers should use the Windows 98 or Windows NT operating system, although other proposed solutions will be considered.

Comply: The system proposed by Pittsburgh Telemax runs on Windows 98 (professor terminal and student terminals) and Windows NT (system administrator terminal) computers.

2.2. System Administrator User Interface

RFP: There should be a system control computer (SCC) user interface to allow a technician to configure and troubleshoot the system.

Comply: The solution proposed by Pittsburgh Telemax includes a Windows NT System Control Computer. This computer includes comprehensive maintenance and diagnostic functions, and it provides control over a robust set of configuration options.

RFP: Troubleshooting tools should include functions for testing equipment and database integrity. For detailed information on troubleshooting requirements, see section 4.

Comply: The SCC provides comprehensive maintenance and diagnostic functions, as described in the responses to section 4 of this RFP.

RFP: Configuration tools should include functions for setting user interface options and connection options. For more information on configuration requirements, see section 5.

Comply: The SCC provides control over a robust set of configuration options, as described in the responses to section 5 of this RFP.

RFP: The System Administrator User Interface should include functions for creating exams designed by the professor or the department. These exams are to be electronically administered to students at the remote campus, as described in section 3.

Will Comply: Pittsburgh Telemax has installed systems similar to the one described in section 3. (See the appendices of this proposal for a list of references.) We will make the required software modifications to fully comply with section 3 of the RFP.

2.3. Professor User Interface

RFP: A mouse-driven user interface should be available to the professor as she/he conducts the class from the main campus location. It should be intuitive and easy to learn so that a class can be conducted without a system administrator. The professor's user interface should have the capabilities listed below, starting with section 2.4.

Comply: The professor's graphical user interface is mouse-driven and intuitive, so it is easy to learn and use. Pittsburgh Telemax's design process includes an ergonomic review that verifies that the user interface is user-friendly, efficient, and flexible. Our standard training course shows professors how to conduct a class without a system administrator. The system can be configured to include a call button to alert a system administrator if there is a problem. For an additional yearly fee, a call button to the Pittsburgh Telemax technical support department can be configured.

2.4. Audio Capabilities

RFP: The professor must be able to speak so that all students at both locations can hear.

Comply: The solution proposed by Pittsburgh Telemax includes a clip-on microphone for the professor and speakers and 1/8″ headphone jacks at each student terminal. Any student at the remote campus can plug in a headset, which automatically mutes the terminal's speaker but has no effect on the speakers at other terminals.

RFP: The professor should be able to mute any microphone and/or speaker, including those in use by students at the remote campus.

Partially Comply: The solution proposed by Pittsburgh Telemax allows the professor to mute any student terminal's microphone but does not allow the professor to mute a student terminal's speakers. The system provides two options for achieving the same result: the professor can mute any source microphone and can temporarily halt the transmission of audio to the remote campus.

TABLE 8.1 ▼   Standard Pricing Table

Item	Quantity	List Price	Discount	Net Price
1.				
2.				
3.				
4.				
			Total Net:	
			Shipping:	
			Insurance:	
			TOTAL:	

matted to display percentages. The cells in the right-most column contain formulas that calculate the net price based on the list price and the discount, and the bottom "Total" cells contain formulas that add up the appropriate cells. Pittsburgh Telemax's obligation for shipping and insurance costs, if any, will be stated in the RFP.

▲ 10. Conclusion

This section contains a persuasive argument for selecting Telemax. Every company has its strengths. Telemax stresses the high quality of its personnel and their work (another company might drum on about its low prices). In a Telemax proposal, this section may repeat the references a third time, referring the reader to former clients who have agreed to speak on behalf of Pittsburgh Telemax. The Sales and Marketing people have found that when Telemax is in close contention with another company, these references can make the difference.

▲ 11. Appendices

At the end of every proposal, Pittsburgh Telemax appends sample user documentation, promotional literature, and press releases, as well as the professional vitas of all personnel to be involved in the project.

* * *

Mendoza records information about the RFP and the proposal in the document database. This information includes

▌ the name of the client

▌ the name and telephone number of the contact person

▌ the client's RFP number

▌ the deadline for submitting the proposal

▌ the location of the word processing files.

Finally, Mendoza, as head of the red team, prepares a Gantt chart that distributes responsibilities, establishes subtasks, and sets deadlines for the proposal writing. She reviews the Gantt chart with the engineers and sales staff before finalizing it. See Figure 9.2 in Chapter 9 for an excerpt from that chart.

Since Wendy Smith is involved in writing this proposal, Mendoza gives her some general advice on proposal writing. She makes these points:

▌ Adopt the customer's language. Notice that the Pumpkinville RFP uses the terms *main campus* and *remote campus,* instead of something more generic like *local site* and *remote site.* We will use their terms.

▌ Always explain why you do not fully comply with a requirement. If possible, leave the readers with the impression that full compliance is not necessary.

▌ For "will comply" responses, convince the readers that you can comply by citing experience and track record.

▌ Sometimes, instead of responding "cannot comply," you can respond "partially comply" by putting forward an alternative approach that is just as good as the one the RFP indicated.

▌ Be honest. If the readers think you are hedging the truth, they won't be sure of anything in the proposal, and that'll end Telemax's chances.

▌ At every opportunity, sell the company, its personnel, and its products.

ASSIGNMENTS FOR 8.3

1. *Analyze a Proposal Format* Find a real proposal written in response to an RFP. If you don't have access to one, use a model in a book (your instructor may have left one or more examples on reserve in your school's library). In a memo to your teacher, point to instances in which the proposal conforms to, and doesn't conform to, the format and approach described in section 8.3.

2. *Write a Proposal* Write one or more sections of a proposal (as indicated by your instructor) based on one of the RFPs developed in assignment 8.1(2). Note: Big Project #19 calls for the writing of a full proposal.

Manuals

The manual is the quintessential technical document. Technical manuals teach customers about the product they purchased. Manuals explain

■ how the product works, theoretically and mechanically

■ how to adjust the product or its defaults

■ how to use the product for specific tasks

■ how to recognize breakdowns and fix them.

Manuals tend to be long, often running hundreds of pages. This chapter describes the specialized development processes that technical writers use to achieve high standards when working on manuals and sets of manuals that accompany large systems.

Some of the information here will be particularly useful to students working on Big Projects.

9.1 ⟩——Project Planning

At companies like Telemax, technical writing occurs within a larger framework of concurrent product-documentation production, as we saw in Chapter 3. This approach, in which technical writers belong to development teams, allows technical writers to begin writing documentation for systems as soon as possible, before the engineering and software development are completed. That involvement, in turn, puts technical writers in a position to influence design in favor of ease-of-use. In short, the technical writers act as representatives of the user in the design process.

This approach also results in completion of the documentation soon after the product is ready to go out the door. That promptness satisfies engineers and business managers, who sometimes see the development of documentation as an inconvenience leading to frustrating delay.

On the down side, this approach requires technical writers to put in extra hours revising the documentation again and again as inevitable design changes occur during the development of the product (Lanyi, 1994). Fewer hours will be spent writing if technical writers wait until the product is finished before beginning writing. Some companies, therefore, involve technical writers only at the end of the product development process. Such companies often outsource technical writing rather than maintaining a large writing staff.

Regardless of approach, planning large documents, or sets of documents, is a top-down process. That is, the writing team begins with the largest considerations and works down to the smallest written sections. At Telemax, during the earliest meetings, technical writers and engineers discuss what components of the product need to be documented. The DDM then creates a schedule for getting the work done that coordinates with the project manager's "master plan" for the project.

For project plans and schedules, managers, including the DDM, often use a particular kind of outline called a Gantt chart. Figure 9.1 shows a very simple Gantt chart; Figure 9.2 shows an excerpt from a realistic Gantt chart for planning a writing project (in this case, the writing of a proposal). Looking at Figure 9.1, we can see that a Gantt chart shows *concurrency:* where in the process two or more activities are occurring at the same time. The bars representing tasks 1 and 2 (Invite Guests, Plan Food & Wine) overlap, indicating that Marsha and Sue will be working on two tasks simultaneously on Wednesday afternoon. The overlapping of bars representing tasks 3 and 4 (Buy Food, Buy Wine) also show concurrency, but with a division of labor: While Marsha is finishing up the food shopping, Sue is doing the wine shopping. A Gantt chart also shows *dependency:* where in the process one activity cannot begin until another is completed. Notice that task 3, food shopping, cannot begin until task 2, which includes food planning, is completed.

FIGURE 9.1 ▼ Simple Gantt Chart: Marsha and Sue Plan a Party

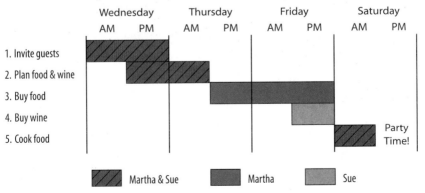

FIGURE 9.2 ▼ Excerpt from a Gantt Chart Made with Microsoft Project 98

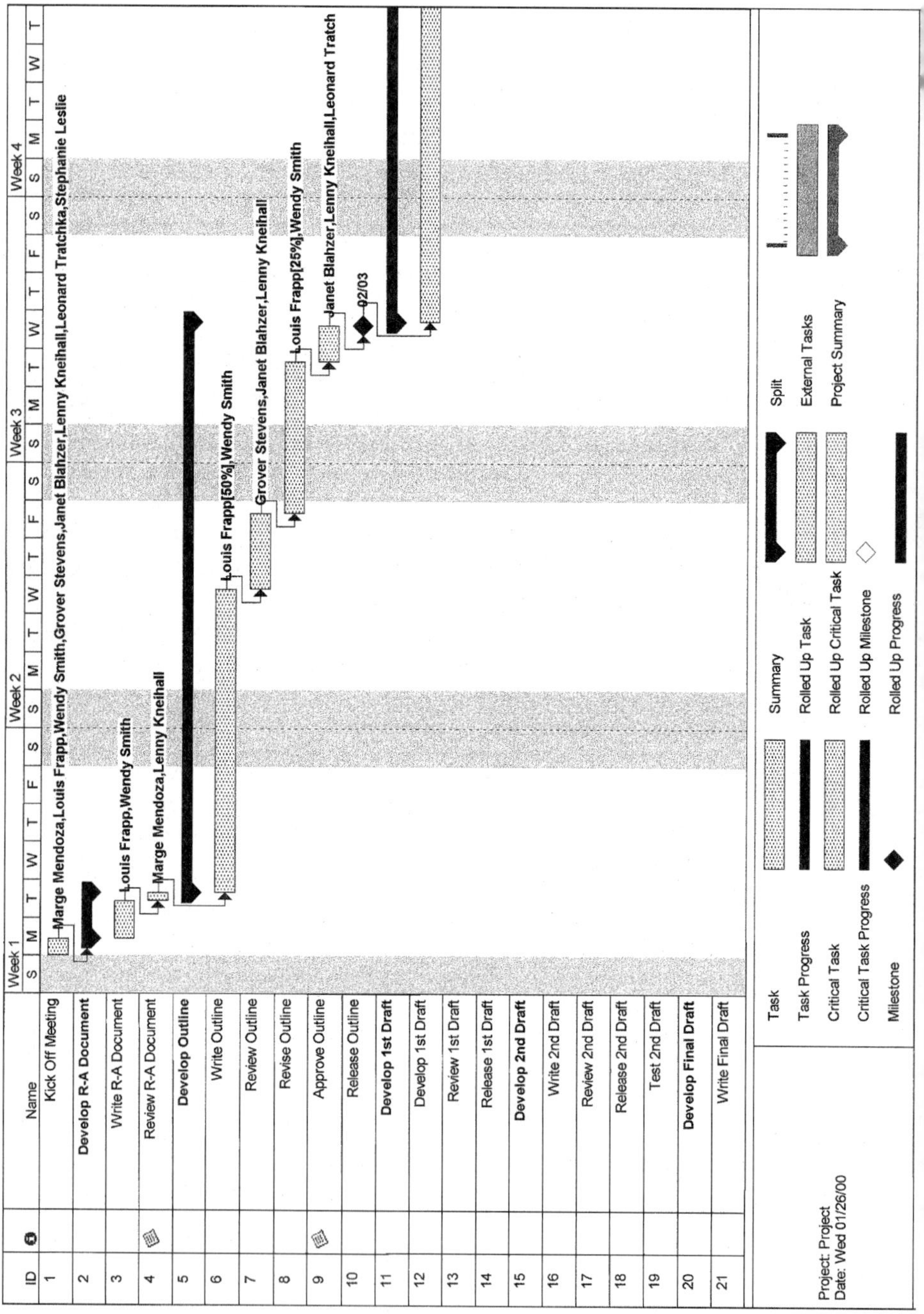

Gantt charts can display estimates of time for each task, and they can indicate who is responsible for what percentage of the differing tasks, as in Figure 9.2. Also note in this figure that diamonds demarcate milestones and that solid bars with downward tips embrace each group of activities that leads to a milestone.

ASSIGNMENTS FOR 9.1

1. *Recommend an Approach* Write a memo to the president of your fictional company recommending either a team approach to documentation development or a delayed-documentation approach. Justify your decision in terms of the unique character of your company and its business practices.

2. *Gantt Chart* (a) Create a Gantt chart for one of the writing projects you have undertaken so far in this course, showing what you (and possibly others) did to complete the project, sequentially and concurrently, over the period of time you spent on the project. (b) Create a Gantt chart for a new project that you are about to undertake. (c) Imagine that you and several friends have volunteered to develop a Web site for a local senior center. The site will include photos, text describing the center and its activities and services, and short biographies on each member of the staff. Create a Gantt chart for planning this project.

9.2 >——— Developing a Full Set of Manuals

At Telemax, a typical conferencing system created for a client will require at least five manuals, and each manual will have a standard content that changes only in the details, according to the particular system's features. The manuals, which may be bound together into one book or bound separately, are as follows:

Installation Manual
Maintenance Manual
Administration Manual
Module Manuals
User Guides

The fact that a similar set of manuals will be created for each large project gives full play to the object-oriented approach to assembling and writing manuals discussed in Chapter 3.

Other companies making different products will have their own standard set of documents, but in many cases that set will not differ greatly from those Telemax creates. The five Telemax manuals answer universal needs for customers of high-tech products.

Here follows a brief description of each manual's content.

▲ *1. Installation Manual*

The *Installation Manual* typically contains three important sections:

1. *A list of system components* This section describes the different components of the system. The Communicator DL 1000 system proposed for Pumpkinville State University consists of several components: local and remote servers, local and remote cameras, student terminals, and cabling. The local server also acts as the professor's terminal and the System Administration Terminal. The *Communicator DL 1000 Installation Manual* includes an illustation of each component. These illustrations include labels that point to specific features. Following an illustration, each feature is described in detail, including tables or more detailed illustrations, as required.

2. *The initial order configuration (IOC)* This section describes the defaults of the system—that is, how Telemax set up the system during installation. It includes all the default settings for the modules installed in each computer, and it indicates which version of each software program is installed in each computer. The *Communicator DL 1000 Installation Manual* describes the default switch and jumper settings for the network interface modules in the servers and the student terminals, as well as the default switch and jumper settings for the ISDN interface modules in the servers. If a client later removes a component (perhaps for repair), the client can use this section of the *Installation Manual* to reinstate the IOC.

3. *The installation procedure* This section describes the complete installation procedure, from unpacking the shipped components to assembly, system startup, and final testing. Pittsburg Telemax technicians typically install larger systems such as the Communicator DL 1000. Therefore, the *Communicator DL 1000 Installation Manual* does not include an installation procedure. However, Pittsburg Telemax has developed a separate internal document that describes this procedure to Telemax technicians. This document includes a check list so that technicians can mark each step as it is completed.

▲ *2. Maintenance Manual*

The *Maintenance Manual* always contains four important sections:

1. *Theory of operation* This section describes in general how the whole system works. It shows control signal distribution, timing signal distribution, and data signal distribution. Block diagrams illustrate each distribution process.

2. *Procedures for routine maintenance* This section explains how preventive maintenance should be carried out (e.g., how to check cable connections and how often they should be checked).

3. *Procedures for corrective maintenance* This section explains how to fix damaged parts (e.g., how to replace a camera if it fails).

4. *Troubleshooting* This section describes the alarm system. Telemax systems are fully alarmed. Whenever something unusual happens anywhere in the system, the affected component sends a message to the system administration terminal, which records the event. Since many harmless blips and glitches routinely occur when data are transmitted, some problems do not initiate alarms until a threshold of errors has been recorded. At Telemax, alarms fall into five categories. (a) Informational messages indicate that someone has changed defaults. (b) Minor warnings concern situations that are meant to be monitored, with no immediate action taken. Action is required for the more serious messages: (c) major, (d) critical, and (e) fatal (system shutdown). A technical writer working on the *System Maintenance Manual* will create a "decision table" for alarms, which lists problems and their solutions. This particular kind of decision table is called an alarm table (Table 9.1).

▲ *3. Administration Manual*

The *Administration Manual* tells the system administrator and other technicians how the system administration terminal works. It describes both the hardware and software features of the system administration terminal, and it describes the maintenance, diagnostic, and configuration functions associated with the system administration terminal. This manual includes illustrations that depict the terminal, and it describes the physical, mechanical, and operational features of the terminal. It also includes screen captures that show the user interface when the system administration software is running.

The *Administration Manual* also describes the local server, which doubles as the system administration terminal, and it describes the system administration software, which is one of the programs installed on the local server.

9 Manuals

TABLE 9.1 ▼ **Excerpt from an Alarm Table**

Number	Severity	Message	Cause	Corrections
000	Info	User [string] logged on at local terminal [dec]	A user has logged on at local terminal [dec]	No action required
001	Info	Bad login at local terminal [dec]	A user has attempted unsucessfully to log on at local terminal [dec]	No action required
100	minor	Local server lost communications with local terminal [dec]	Driver not responding	Reset local terminal [dec]
				Reset local hub
			Bad connection	Check cable connection at local terminal [dec]
				Check cable connection at local hub
			Bad cable	Replace cable between local terminal [dec] and local hub
			Bad network interface card	Replace network interface card in local terminal [dec]
101	major	Local server lost communications with all local terminals	Driver not responding	Reset local server
			Bad connection	Check cable connection at local server
				Check cable connection at local hub
			Bad cable	Replace cable between local server and local hub
102	critical	Local server lost communications with remote server	Telephone lines disconnected (call dropped)	Redial
			Bad connection	Check ISDN connection at local server
				Check ISDN connection at remote server
			Bad cable	Check all ISDN cables at local server
				Check all ISDN cables at remote server
			Bad ISDN modem	Replace ISDN modem at local server
				Replace ISDN modem at remote server

▲ *4. Module Manuals*

As mentioned earlier, large electronic systems nowadays are developed in removable modules. For each module type, the *Module Manual* describes

▮ its physical characteristics

▮ its theory of operation

▮ its read-only memory (ROM) program, including self-tests and light-emitting diode (LED) indicators

▮ its application software.

Some larger Telemax systems include an equipment rack that is populated with electronic modules. Telemax has developed a manual for every module that plugs into the equipment rack. When a physical or mechanical change is made to a module, only the section on physical characteristics in the module manual needs to be updated. When a change is made to the embedded software, only the section in the module manual that pertains to that software needs to be updated.

The Communicator DL 1000 uses only two modules: an ISDN interface module, which is installed in the local and remote servers, and a network interface module, which is installed in both servers and each student terminal. The network interface module is purchased from a different vendor, who supplies the documentation. Telemax simply passes this documentation along to the customer. Telemax designs and manufactures the ISDN interface module, however, so Telemax has developed a module manual to describe it, the *ISDN Interface Module Manual.*

▲ *5. User Guides*

A user guide describes the user interface for those who are not familiar with the technical aspects of the system. The *Instructor's Terminal Manual* for the Communicator DL 1000 describes how to use the software at the professor's terminal to control cameras, distribute and collect exams, take roll, and activate the online help system. Even though the manual is available online, Telemax provides printed copies of the *Instructor Terminal Manual* so professors can study the system by reading in the office or at home.

The student terminals are very simple to use—the students are not expected to read a manual before they enroll in a distance learning class. However, Telemax provides a printed quick reference guide for each student terminal. This guide describes how to perform the basis functions for the student terminal, including how to indicate attendance, how to respond to the professor's questions, how to fill out online exams, and how to activate the online help system.

A technical writer at Telemax may be assigned to any of the above manuals, or may be involved in producing parts of several of them.

ASSIGNMENT FOR 9.2

1. *Analyze Manuals* Write a memo to your instructor describing the set of manuals that came with one of the larger "systems" (computer or otherwise) on your campus. Possible systems include those for library indexes, a distance learning network, physical fitness equipment, or science lab equipment. How does this document set compare with Telemax's standard document set?

9.3 ⟩—— Determining Sections, Page Layout, and Packaging

Any long document typically has three broad sections that must be designed: the front matter, the body, and the back matter.

Front matter at Telemax may include, in this order:

1. cover with the company logo
2. title page indicating authorship, copyright, and date of latest update
3. table of contents
4. list of figures and tables
5. introduction explaining the purpose of the text, what it covers, and how to use it effectively. The introduction may also include an explanation of stylistic conventions for warnings and other notes, as well as a short glossary of terms and abbreviations.

Telemax produces lengthy in-house documents only on rare occasions. Most recently, the company created and distributed a 12-page sexual harassment policy statement. For such documents, the front matter may also include a *Forward* written by Howard Stone, the president of Pittsburgh Telemax, or Marge Mendoza, the DDM, or some other prominent person in the company, endorsing the content of the text.

Back matter may include, in this order:

1. appendices
2. extensive glossary of technical terms
3. bibliography
4. index.

The body consists of two elements: text and visuals. Technical writers plan the visual components at the same time as they plan the text. Table

3.1 in Chapter 3 shows the three-column "storyboard" that writers at Pittsburgh Telemax use for incorporating visuals into the planning process.

As an early step in the development of any long text, the Documentation Department, working with the Sales and Marketing Department, will decide on the physical shape of the whole document: the size of its pages, templates for page layouts, and the kind of binding and cover. Often these matters have been worked out a long time ago, and standards and templates exist for each type of document. For example, at Pittsburgh Telemax, templates exist for

▮ front and back matter

▮ ordinary running text

▮ first pages of chapters

▮ specialized text, such as steps in a set of directions.

The writers select the appropriate template from an existing set of standard designs so that the new document conforms to past practices. Telemax, like any other company, wants its documents to be consistent in structure and appearance in order to make them familiar and comfortable to work with, as well as maximally comprehensible.

Figure 9.3 shows the master template used by Pittsburgh Telemax for ordinary running text in large manuals. Notice that the design leaves

FIGURE 9.3 ▼ **Template for Manuals**

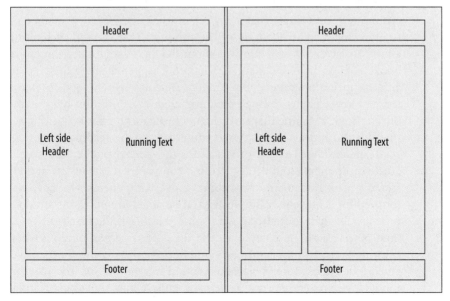

FIGURE 9.4 ▼   **Template for Illustration of Steps**

Installation Guide		Installation Guide	
Step 8 Text text text text text text text text text text text text text text text text text text text text text text text	Illustration for Step 8	Illustration for Step 12	**Step 12** Text text text text text text text text text text text text text text text text text text text text text text text
Step 9 Text text text text text text text text text text text text text text text text text	Illustration for Step 9		
Step 10 Text text text text text text text text text text text text text text text text text	Illustration for Step 10	Illustration for Step 13	**Step 13** Text text text text text text text text text text text text text text text text text
Step 11 Text text text text text text text text text text text text text text text text text text text text text	Illustration for Step 11	Illustration for Step 14	**Step 14** Text text text text text text text text text text text text text. Text text text text text text text text text text text text text text
Page 6		Page 7	

space in the left side-headers for headings, summaries of the text, comments on the text, definitions, tips, icons, and warnings. Figure 9.4 shows a layout for a set of instructions requiring illustrations for each step.

Besides determining page design, the writers, in consultation with the marketing department, must decide on packaging. For large manuals customized for a single customer, Telemax uses ring-binder notebooks, to allow for regular updating of the product. This method of binding allows replacement of sections without having to reproduce the entire book. For example, if Chapter 7 has to be altered and expanded to account for an upgrade in the product, Telemax merely sends the customer a new Chapter 7. Pages are numbered noncontinuously throughout the book, meaning that each chapter begins with page 1. The chapter number also appears on each page, somewhere in the heading or footing.

Telemax doesn't create products for the general public, but it does create components sold widely to other companies for inclusion in their systems. The documents describing those components are not customized for a single user but, instead, are printed in bulk. For such documents, Telemax uses strong wire spiral binding if the text runs more than 50 pages. Some companies use the scored perfect binding when printing a large number of copies. Perfect binding is the inexpensive, glued binding used for most books found in a bookstore. The scoring, visible in the covers as a crease near the spine, allows the book to lie flat when opened. Even soft-covered books can be scored. However, Telemax never uses perfect binding, because it is not as strong as wire binding and it doesn't allow the text to lie as flat as the wire binding does. The wire binding does have disadvantages, however: It is expensive, and it has no flat spine for a title (an inconvenience for shelving).

For short pieces of documentation, such as quick start guides, Telemax uses the staple-and-fold binding method.

The ultimate package is no package at all. Telemax, like many companies, is shifting away from paper documentation to sophisticated online documentation, at least for documents containing nonproprietary information. At this time, Telemax is wary of posting on the Internet, even with password protection, any information that it wants to keep secret.

ASSIGNMENT FOR 9.3

1. *Design a Manual* Design a 50-page manual for one of the products your fictional company makes. Indicate binding, list front and back matter, and create a template for as many of these types of pages as your instructor requests: (a) first page of chapters; (b) running text, left side and right side; (c) index. To find examples of layout, examine a number of real manuals, preferably those describing products similar to your product.

9.4 >——Developing Manuals and Guides for the General Public

We have been discussing the development of manuals that accompany systems designed for specific customers or for a market niche of high-tech companies. Those manuals use a conservative page design and a formal, neutral tone and writing style. By contrast, commercial manuals sold to the general public require a less intimidating format:

▪ a lot of white space

▪ large headings

▪ sidebars for tips, extended definitions, humorous examples, warnings, anecdotes

▪ numerous visuals, including screen captures.

In addition, manuals and guides written for the general public often use a friendly tone and informal style. Figure 9.5 illustrates a page design and writing style suitable for the general public from a book on Web page design. Note the considerable white space in this figure, as well as the informal style in the first paragraph ("You know what they say about assumptions, right?"), the humorous tone in the second paragraph ("Hey, it's not our fault—it's a UNIX thing"), and the colloquial grammar in the first bulleted paragraph ("If you're using an outside vendor as your Web site, they . . .").

FIGURE 9.5 ▼ **Example of Page Design and Writing Style for a General-Public Audience**

66   *The Web Page Design Cookbook*

It's also a good idea at this point to have other people look at the pages; run a simple usability test to make sure that your ideas on perfectly logical structure and sequence make sense to potential users. (You know what they say about assumptions, right?) If appropriate, you can use your browser's e-mail feature to distribute copies of the test pages within your internal network.

Overview, step 7: Install files on the server.

Once you've tested (and fixed) everything, you can transfer your HTML and other files to the Web server where they will reside. In technical terms, this is known as "mounting" the files. (Hey, it's not our fault—it's a UNIX thing.)

The mounting process varies from server to server:

- If you're using an outside vendor as your Web site, they should have fairly explicit instructions on how to mount files for public access. Check with the folks in technical support to see how they want you to proceed.

- If you're mounting your files on an internal Web server, or a proxy server outside your company firewall, check with your system administrator.

> **Some unsolicited advice**
>
> Regardless of your pride of authorship, your looming deadlines, or your urgency to get your Web pages out there, always approach the technical gods with empathy for their struggles. Put yourself in their position, and phrase your request for help accordingly. You'll be amazed at what friendly sympathy will do for your place in the mounting queue (but don't hesitate to buy them lunch again, if you think it will help).

When the files have been mounted, check to make sure that:

- Your files are placed in the correct directory, and that all the files are there.

- All the files have the correct permissions set.

- All your internal links reference the right locations and subdirectories.

Source: From *The Web Page Design Cookbook* by William Horton, Lee Taylor, Arthur Ignacio, and Nancy L. Hoft. Reprinted by permission of John Wiley & Sons, Inc. Copyright 1996 John Wiley & Sons.

For projects like documenting a word processing program, the manual would be written for a nontechnical user. In planning each manual, the technical writer has to take into account how the reader is going to use it: as a learning guide or as a reference. In other words, either the reader will use the manual to learn how to perform the functions of the product, or the reader will use the manual to look up parameters and other details that users of this product normally don't commit to memory.

Reference manuals and user's guides have traditionally employed different approaches to information. Note the following two statements about printing with Microsoft Word. The first is oriented to the structure of the program; the second, to a task.

REFERENCE MANUAL APPROACH:
Selecting <u>P</u>rint under the **File** menu opens the **Print** window. Clicking on **OK** prints according to the defaults in the window. The **Name:** window reveals the default printer, which can be changed by. . . .

USER'S MANUAL APPROACH:
To immediately print your document, select <u>P</u>rint from the **File** menu. When the **Print** window opens, click on **OK**.

In the first passage above, the style is impersonal. The assumed interest is in how the software works. This passage will continue until all options have been explained. The second passage uses the less formal second-person point of view, which brings the reader into the picture. It tells the reader how to do something, how to perform a specific task. It does not include all information about printing, only the information necessary to do the task.

Of course, many readers need both a learning guide and a reference. It is now common for companies that make high-tech products to package several types of documentation with products that go directly to end-users. Here are some typical types of documentation:

▲ 1. Setup or Installation Guides

Some devices must be set up and some software programs must be installed before they can be used. Setup guides for hardware typically include photographs or appropriately detailed drawings to accompany each step. An installation guide usually comprises a short set of numbered steps.

In creating these guides, technical writers follow principles like those discussed in Chapter 3 for writing short instructions.

▲ 2. "What's New" Sheets

This kind of documentation, written for users who are updating their version of the product, often consists of no more than a single sheet of paper that describes changes that show up in the latest version.

▲ 3. Reference Manuals

The purpose of a reference manual is to provide complete information about a product. Though usually not a learning guide, it may include some instructions for operations.

Despite the strong concern for audience in technical writing, a reference manual is typically organized according to the structure of the product rather than a reader's immediate needs. For example, in the case of an art software program, you might document each tool methodically, moving across the top of the monitor display from left to right, and then down the left-side tool bar from top to bottom. Here, your focus is on the product, not the reader. To give another example, suppose you were documenting an integrated office software package. At the highest level of organization, you would divide the text into the major component parts—let's say: word processing, art, database, and spreadsheet. In other words, your first consideration is the structure of the software. However, your next decision—which component to document first—might be made on the basis of user interest or ease of learning, which brings in the audience as a consideration. Or it might be made on the basis of which component needs to be learned before other components can be used. For example, the database may require word processing functions, in which case structure would continue to be the guiding principle for organization.

The reader, of course, is still served by such texts inasmuch as they provide a comprehensive set of answers to any question that may arise in the reader's mind. A reference manual of the kind described above will have a table of contents and an extensive index, so that readers can easily find what they're looking for. Indexing is usually outsourced to professionals, though sometimes technical writers on staff are expected to learn this craft. Telemax paid $650 to have Louis Frapp attend a workshop on indexing, after which Frapp became responsible for this important job.

The other major organizational pattern for reference manuals is the dictionary model, in which topics for discussion are presented as words or phrases listed alphabetically—for example, from *Alignment command* to *Zip drive*. This organization obviates the need for a table of contents or an index.

▲ *4. Quick Start Guides*

Quick start guides are task-oriented tutorials. They can be very brief, containing just a few pages; or they can be quite extensive, like the first edition of the *Getting Started* manual for Aldus PageMaker on the Macintosh (1988), which ran 95 pages.

In creating a quick start guide, the writer focuses on the reader's need to begin using the product productively from day one. No company wants office work to come to a standstill while employees spend a week learning everything there is to know about a new piece of equipment or a new piece of software. The focus of the quick start guide, then, is not on the product (as it is with the reference manual) but on the reader and what the reader needs to do immediately.

Quick start task-oriented manuals are designed to teach the most common operations. To plan a quick start guide, you must first decide which functions of the product are most commonly used. Then, once that crucial decision is made, sometimes on the basis of a field study, you need to decide on the order in which to present those operations as tasks for the learner to perform. Often simple necessity determines that order. For example, in the case of a word processing program, the user has to open a file before writing one, and write and edit one before printing it.

▲ *5. FAQs*

Another method of conveying orienting and startup information is the FAQ approach, whereby the writer poses "Frequently Asked Questions" and then answers them. The questions follow the order in which the problems arise for the user, beginning with questions about product registration, the nature of the product, and its installation; then, questions about carrying out functions; and, finally, questions about accessing online or phone help.

▲ *6. Reference Cards and Posters*

Once the product is being used and the basic functions have been learned, users can find important information by referring to flat (one panel each side) and fanfold (multiple panel) reference cards. Telemax sometimes distributes a packet of reference cards with each reference manual, so that many users can have their own cards. By printing on both sides with small print and by using a telegraphic writing style, technical writers can fit on fanfold cards almost all, if not all, of the information necessary for using the product. Often these cards have characteristics of both a reference manual and a user's guide. Though usually organized around the structure of the software, and stuffed with information such as a list of commands, reference cards may also include, here and there, a box with steps for performing an important function.

Some companies use posters as simplified reference cards—for example, to display function-key commands or the options that appear under drop-down menus.

ASSIGNMENTS FOR 9.4

1. *Analyze Reference Manuals* Find one reference manual organized by structure and another one organized by the dictionary method (your instructor may have left sample copies on reserve in your library). After browsing around in both, trying to find out how to perform some of the functions documented, write a memo report to your instructor discussing your experience—your success or lack of success. Which approach do you prefer, and why?

2. *Multiple Plans* Find a small device that you can take apart and whose structure you will understand. (Examples: a pencil sharpener, an electric toothbrush, a stapler.) Plan two pieces of documentation for this device: (a) a product-oriented document that focuses on the components and structure of the product and how it works, and (b) a task-oriented document that tells readers how to use the product. For each plan, create a storyboard to show where visuals will play a role.

3. *Revise to Task Oriented* Below is a description of a drop-down menu option quoted from a Ready, Set, Go!™ reference manual. Revise the passage to make it task-oriented. First indicate the purpose or usefulness of the process; that would be your definition of the task. Then include only the information necessary to do the task.

> **Put Text . . .**
> Saves text from a text block or chain of blocks in a Ready, Set, Go! document as a text-only (ASCII) file. This command saves all the text in the block or chain with an insertion point or text selected. The command is dimmed if no insertion point or text is selected.
>
> For a complete description of the dialog box you use to save text, see the Save As command in this section.
>
> After it's saved, you can open the file with any application that can open text-only files.

4. *Quick Start Guide* Create a quick start guide for using e-mail or for finding a book in the library at your school. Stick to the basics.

5. *FAQ* Write and answer a set of "Frequently Asked Questions" pertaining to one of these: (a) a product produced by your fictional company or (b) a service offered by your school (e.g., financial aid, library, computer lab, e-mail).

6. *Reference Card* Create a reference card for using e-mail or for finding a book in the library. List all, or almost all, functions available.

7. *Poster* Do 9.4(6), but create a poster. Remember, posters have to be read from a distance.

9.5 ⟩—— Designing Online Documentation

Most organizations now have their own sites on the World Wide Web. These sites describe the organizations and advertise products and services. They may also provide access to online documentation.

Figure 9.6 shows a common structure for a homepage. The banner displays the organization's name in dramatic fashion. The large center-right section talks generally about the organization and perhaps indicates what the Web site provides. The menu lists the major sections of the Web site; each block is a "link" that, when clicked on, takes the reader to one of the major sections.

FIGURE 9.6 ▼ **A Basic Design for Homepages**

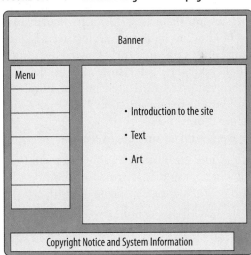

Banner

Menu

- Introduction to the site
- Text
- Art

Copyright Notice and System Information

9 Manuals

Within running text, words or phrases can be programmed as links. These words or phrases would appear underlined or in a color different from that of the running text. For example, in the text below, from a Web site offering a resume writing service, the underlined words would constitute a single link:

> Your first step will be to develop your own version of your resume, using standard headings. We will show you how to do that. Once we have read your version, we will send you a set of interview questions, which will help us develop a refined, professional version of your resume.

Clicking anywhere on standard headings will take readers to a discussion of standard resume headings. These internal links give readers flexibility in how they move through your text. A reader already familiar with the standard headings in resumes will not bother with the link, but someone who doesn't know that information might choose to follow up the link before continuing reading. In the case of online manuals for products, readers who already understand conceptual information, for instance, could skip a link to that information, while those who need that background could access it through the link.

When designing an ordinary printed text, a technical writer chooses for the reader a preferred order for consuming information. This is called "linear order." The reader reads section 1, then section 2, then section 3, and so on, in a linear fashion. Of course, readers may ignore that linear order and skip some sections and read others out of order; but in printed texts, readers feel pressure to read from the beginning to the end, following the arrangement created by the writer. By contrast, online hypertexts allow readers to jump around to different parts of the site or to different sites, putting less pressure on them to follow a particular linear order. Such texts are said to be "nonlinear." A technical writer designing a Web site or an online manual must think in terms of giving the reader choices, instead of making choices for the reader. Instead of asking "What parts of this information should I present first, second, and third?" the writer should ask "How can I bundle the information so that the reader will be presented with a useful set of choices?"

Nonlinear texts have several advantages over linear texts:

1. They serve multiple audiences better by allowing them to choose what to read and what not to read, or to decide how deeply to go into a subject.

2. They economically provide access to huge amounts of related information by providing links to in-house databases or to other Web sites.

3. They include multimedia (music, voice, motion pictures) not found in printed texts.

4. They are interactive, providing opportunities for readers to communicate with the author (or organization) in order to make comments, ask questions, answer questions, or place orders.

5. They are more economical in that they involve no printing or distribution costs, and no large cost for use of color and photographs.

On the down side, nonlinear texts put a burden on readers to create their own sense of organization, sometimes leading to confusion, frustration, and ineffective accessing of information. However, you can address that problem by presenting readers with a menu (functioning as a table of contents) that specifies a preferred order of reading. You can also provide "hot buttons" (links) that take readers back to the previous page or to earlier menus, thereby helping them to recover from wrong avenues. In short, as a technical writer designing a Web site or online manual, you have to worry about readers getting lost in your hypertext—something that doesn't happen in printed texts.

There's also the problem of attribution when Web pages are printed out. P. J. Lynch and S. Horton (1999), in their book on Web page design, make this recommendation:

> Each page should include a title, an author, an institutional affiliation, a revision date, copyright information, and a link to the homepage of your site. (p. 77)

As much as possible, Telemax follows these general rules for ease-of-use in online documentation:

▌ Keep scrolling to a minimum by limiting online page size so that, for most users, each page will fill only one screen. Assume that your user is viewing your work with a 14-inch monitor at 800 × 600 pixel density. Consider using a landscape page because most monitors are wider than they are tall. Box 9.1, based on a resume writing service site, shows how links can be used to compact information and avoid scrolling. In this box, after adjustment to a smaller screen size, all the terms under REQUIRED and OPTIONAL would be links to sets of information.

▌ Number online manual pages so they can be referenced.

▌ Use white space generously; present material in blocks, with space between the blocks.

▌ Place Forward, Backward, and Return to Menu buttons at the bottom of each online page.

▌ Select a proportional font, one that varies the distance between letters. Best choices are a fairly thick sans-serif font, like Helvetica, or a very readable serif font, like Times Roman. San-serif fonts use straight lines with no curls on the ends; they remind you of stick figures (see the word *Helvetica* above). Serif fonts have curls or small ledges at the tips (see the phrase *Times Roman* above).

▌ Use 12-point font size or higher for running text and 14-point font size or higher for headings. Even larger sizes may be appropriate for older audiences or audiences known to have sight impairments.

▌ Use visuals judiciously, or make them optional, since they slow downloading time.

▌ Provide a Drop-Down Help Manual or a search facility for Help.

▌ Provide context-sensitive Help, including definitions of technical terms.

Chapter 12 in this book continues this discussion of Web site design, focusing on marketing pages. (See also Shriver, 1997, pp. 506–517, for additional research-supported details on effective online design.)

Online documentation that is meant to be printed should appear in Portable Document Format (PDF). If space allows, you can create two copies of the document: one meant for on-screen reading that follows the bulleted guidelines above, and one formatted like a word processed document in PDF form for downloading and printing. Both have their appealing features. The on-screen version offers the advantage of non-linear design, allowing the reader to easily find information or explore ideas, whereas the printed text is easier on the eyes and allows the reader to make marginal notes while reading.

ASSIGNMENTS FOR 9.5

1. *Design a Homepage* Using the design in Figure 9.6, or your own creative version of it, create a homepage for your fictional company or for some other organization. Do a mock version on paper or an online version, whichever your instructor prefers.

2. *Design a Simple Web Site* Design the pages for a Web site for your fictional company or some other organization. From the homepage, offer three additional pages, and on one of those, create a link to a definition of a term or to another Web site. Use the principles in the bulleted list in section 9.5.

BOX 9.1 ▼ Adjusting Page Size to Screen Size

BEFORE ADJUSTMENT:

Standard Resume Sections

The Heading
   The heading should contain your name in a prominent position, your permanent address, your phone number, your fax number, and your e-mail address.

Objective (Optional)
   This line tells the resume reader what kind of job you are looking for. Don't be vague; tailor the line to the job you are applying for. Place it just below the heading.

Summary of Qualifications (Optional)
   This summary consists of a short paragraph naming your strongest assets. Place it just below the heading or objective line.

Education
   State your major or degree earned, followed by the name of the school. Begin with the school you are now attending or last attended. Mention college-related activities and achievements.

Experience
   Starting with your most recent employment, list employer and location, job title and duties, and any unique achievements, including promotion.

Awards, Honors, Memberships, Special Skills, Certifications (Optional)
   Use any of these generic headings, or invent a specific one for yourself (Charity Work, Military Service)

Personal Interests, Hobbies, Activities (Optional)
   Employers like active, social people to join their "family." Show that you are not a couch potato or a loner. Your interests may luckily coincide with those of the interviewer.

AFTER ADJUSTMENT:

Standard Resume Sections

REQUIRED:
   Heading
   Education
   Experience

OPTIONAL:
   Objective
   Summary of Qualifications
   Awards, Honors, Memberships, Special Skills, Certifications
   Personal Interests, Hobbies, Activities

9.6 >——— The Minimalist Approach to Manual Design

The minimalist approach to technical writing has been developing for several decades, ever since documentation writers began to wonder why nontechnical people had such trouble learning to use microcomputers (Carroll, 1998). Borrowing from cognitive science research as well as from their own applied research, technical writers have tried to create a type of documentation that matches how people learn and how they behave while struggling with new tasks.

For example, early research showed that novice and expert users consistently followed slightly different patterns in solving problems while working with computers, as described here by P. A. H. Anson (1998):

> [Novices] begin by looking on-screen, scanning the user interface for familiar or perceived relevant information. [Experts] go to Help depending on the type of task (conceptual, procedural, or problem solving) and their own knowledge and skill. . . . Novices are more likely to turn to paper documentation, and experts seek online help. This behavior pattern occurs if there is no acknowledged expert close by to answer quick questions. The local expert may be asked to help first if time constraints are pressing the user. This research strongly indicates that users take what they perceive to be the easiest, fastest, and most convenient path to find information first. (pp. 100–101)

As Anson points out, principles of minimalist documentation are consistent with that behavior. Here are the basic principles (see also Box 9.2):

1. Make documentation task oriented, use real tasks, and don't waste time with preliminaries (get right to the task instruction). In other words, teach procedures by having learners undertake the real-life tasks for which they will use the product. Skip all introductory and background discussions that aren't necessary for following your instructions for those tasks.

2. Take advantage of the fact that users will use their knowledge, intuition, inferencing skill, and perceptions to solve problems. Don't explain what the reader can quickly figure out or even learn through easy trial and error. This is called "involving the user in the discovery of information." (The traditional method tends toward overexplaining.)

3. Since users will be making some decisions with minimal information (see #2 above), support error recognition and recovery. For example, when writing instructions, use tables that indicate what the right outcome of a step looks like and what to do if things go wrong.

BOX 9.2 ▼ **Concepts for Information Mapping**

Chunking:
  Present information in small blocks, or chunks. For an example of chunking, examine Box 5.4 in this book: Excerpt on Lists from the *Telemax Style Guide*. The guidelines appearing in Box 5.4 require writers to break up long numbered lists into chunks.

Relevance:
  Put only one kind of information related to one topic in a chunk. For example, don't mix conceptual information with instructional information.

Labeling:
  Provide a label for each chunk. These labels are set in the left margin and serve as tabs for readers seeking information. They preview information and replace introductory and transitional sentences and paragraphs.

Consistency:
  Use the same terminology and formatting throughout. This principle lies behind the concept of "controlled language" (discussed in Chapter 5) and is in keeping with the efforts of companies like Telemax to standardize the formats for lists and the layouts of documents.

Integrated Graphics:
  Do not detach graphics as figures or tables; instead, integrate them into the flow of the text. Graphics, especially tables, frequently replace text in the Information Mapping approach. Mapped text sometimes looks like a series of decision tables.

Source: Summarized with permission of Robert E. Horn, Visiting Scholar (Program on People, Computers and Design), Stanford University. For further information, see R. E. Horn, *Visual Language: Global Communication for the 21st Century*, MacroVU Press, PMBox 366, 321 High School Road, Bainbridge Island, WA 98110 (www.macrovu.com), and R. E. Horn, *Mapping Hypertext: Analysis, Linkage, and Display of Knowledge for the Next Generation of Online Text and Graphics*, The Lexington Institute, Lexington MA, available from Information Mapping, Inc., 411 Waverly Oaks Road, Waltham, MA 02154 (www.infomap.com)

4. Use a modular approach that presents information only once, in short chunks with headings. (This approach can be fine-tuned during your planning stage, when you decide where each piece of information or each concept will be taught and then create a module for teaching it.) Avoid continuous text in which the same information gets introduced or the same concept gets explained many times. By using numerous top and side headings within the modules, you can help readers not only to find information but also to skip information they don't need at the moment. (Figure 9.7 shows a page from a minimalist document, illustrating top and side headings.)

FIGURE 9.7 ▼   Minimalist Documentation Presenting Information

About the Remote Procedure Calls

Introduction	E-Transport has developed the TAE Quotation Module RPCs using the Entera™ product by Open Environment Corporation (OEC). Entera provides the communications layer (that is, the transport medium) between your client application and the TAE.
Using RPCs	To use the TAE Quotation Module RPCs in your client application, you must first install the software that E-Transport has provided to you. The software includes runtime dynamic link libraries (DLLs) from OEC and RPC stub files from E-Transport. **Special note about the stub files** The stubs that E-Transport provides have different suffixes according to the development environment at your site. (Visual C++® developers receive stubs that end with "_c.c"; Visual Basic® developers receive stubs files with a ".vb" suffix, PowerBuilder® developers receive stubs with an ".srf" suffix, and so on.)
IMPORTANT: All RPC parameters required	When issuing a TAE Quotation Module RPC from within your client-application code, you must specify *all* of the RPC's associated (input *and* output) parameters *in the order shown*. The rule applies even for optional-input parameters, where those of type "char" can contain empty strings and those of type "long" can contain zeros. Most input parameters *require* non-empty-string pr non-zero values; others can contain empty strings or zeroes. For each description of an RPC, this reference clearly indicates which input parameters require non-empty-string or non-zero values.
For more information	The remainder of this document describes the RPCs used to save, retrieve and fax quotation information via the TAE. To learn more about developing client software using the Entera product and RPCs, see the *Entera 3.0 Client Developer's Guide* included in your TAE package.

Source: From *TAE™ Quotation Module™: Remote Procedure Call (RPC) Reference.* Reprinted with permission of E-Transport, Inc., Pittsburgh, PA.

A large body of research supports the claim that minimalist documentation is easier to use than traditional documentation designed around the structure of the product (Van de Meij & Carroll, 1998, p. 19). Telling users how to perform a real task that they are interested in performing is more effective than telling them how to use a particular feature of a computer program. Minimalist documentation is also cost-effective because it is brief. Anson (1998) reports that a set of Hewlett Packard documents for a printer that originally ran 650 pages came in at only 270 pages when revised to a minimalist version (p. 103). A brief text is not only cheaper to print, it is also more likely to be used. Several features of minimalism contribute to brevity:

1. It takes advantage of what users know or can infer. For example, why waste space telling users what is on the computer screen when they can see for themselves?

2. It doesn't repeat information.

3. It leaves out explanations in order to focus on action.

4. It leaves out preliminaries, going directly to the task.

5. Its modular approach doesn't require transitions. Each "chunk" of text is self-contained.

One feature of minimalist documentation that creates more text rather than less is the support for error recognition and recovery. With traditional documentation, learners "spend between 25 and 50 percent of their time correcting errors" (Van de Meij & Carroll, 1998, p. 32). Minimalist documentation decreases that wasted time. Statements like the one below appear regularly in instructional, minimalist text:

> If the message "Cannot find file" appears on the screen, you have typed the wrong drive letter. Hit F1 and then type in A: or C:, depending on where your file resides.

Information Mapping, Inc., trains technical writers in its version of minimalist documentation writing. The Information Mapping approach was developed by Robert E. Horn and his colleagues over several decades. Some of the basic concepts behind Horn's approach are summarized in Box 9.2.

Text that has been "mapped" looks quite different from ordinary paragraphs of running text. Figures 9.7 and 9.8 show pages from documentation written by writers after training in Information Mapping. In Figure 9.7, information is presented in paragraph form; in Figure 9.8, instructions are presented in table form. Note in these figures that every chunk is separated by a horizontal rule, and that each chunk has its own label to enhance accessibility.

Richard Fincham, a technical writer who consulted with the authors on this book, works for E-Transport, which produced the documents in Figures 9.7 and 9.8. Fincham began Information Mapping training as a skeptic and is now a believer. He says that he is seeing more and more "mapped" texts from sources outside his company as well.

9 Manuals

FIGURE 9.8   ▼   Minimalist Documentation Presenting Instructions

Quotation-fax RPCs	The following table briefly describes the RPCs for faxing quotation information to one or more recipients and shows where to look for more information about each RPC:

To initiate this action . . .	Issue this RPC . . .	Page
Fax a quotation to one or more recipients	QM1_QuoteSendFax01	46
Determine the status of a fax	QM1_QuoteGetFaxStatus01	48
Update the general status of a faxing request	QM1_QuoteUpdateFaxStatusA1101	51
Update the status of a fax sent to a specific quotation recipient	QM1_QuoteUpdateFaxStatus01	53

Source: From *TAE™ Quotation Module™: Remote Procedure Call (RPC) Reference.* Reprinted with permission of E-Transport, Inc., Pittsburgh, PA.

Minimalist documentation is not a miracle solution to all problems of teaching high-tech activities. But it is an important innovation that is gaining ground in the technical writing profession.

ASSIGNMENT FOR 9.6

1. *Revise Documentation*   Using the principles of minimalist documentation briefly presented in this section, revise a piece of documentation you have written, or a short section from a professionally written manual, or a piece of documentation developed at your school for use on campus. Make the text task oriented; present information in chunks and instructions in tables; use side headings.

Testing and Revising

10

Once the first draft of a manual has been written, technical writers turn to the extended process of revision. As we have seen, technical writers revise on the basis of document cycling, a process by which various groups (typically engineers, business managers, and marketing experts) review and critique developing documents, particularly for accuracy and completeness. In a technical writing course, this activity is comparable to reviews of your drafts by fellow students and the instructor.

Technical writers also conduct usability tests and field tests to assess how well end-users can understand the text and use the instructions. Because most students are already familiar with peer and teacher review, this chapter focuses on the testing approach to revision.

10.1 >——— The Nature of Revision in Technical Writing

In composition or essay-writing courses, students are often told that revision means "re-visioning" a text, seeing it from a totally new perspective. Such revision often leads to major changes, the writer sometimes altering the text to such an extent that the final draft looks nothing like the first.

Technical writers rarely make such momentous changes in their texts. The final draft of a piece of technical writing usually looks quite familiar to someone who has seen the first draft. This is mainly due to the elaborate planning that technical writers do. Revision as re-seeing is a technique used more often by writers who don't do much planning but, instead, quickly plunge into a first draft and then slowly develop their thinking and their text through multiple revisions.

That revision-heavy writing process is too slow for technical writing. The essayist likes to put the text aside and then come back to it later as a "stranger," to see how it sounds, before doing another major revision. Technical writers don't have time for that. Technical writers working for organizations must coordinate their documentation production with the work of engineers or managers. This requires working to a schedule.

Although technical writers read over their texts and make changes, they don't rely heavily on their own instincts as to how a text should be improved. Instead, they revise, first of all, on the basis of critiques by engineers and other experts, who focus on accuracy. Then they revise for usability on the basis of "usability testing," a procedure in which typical users of the product try out the documentation and, through their behavior and their comments, demonstrate the document's effectiveness and reveal its flaws. Finally, technical writers may also revise after "field testing," which involves visiting a site where the documentation is being used in order to observe and interview users.

For the essayist, then, revision often means "re-seeing the document after having set it aside," but for the technical writer, revision usually means "making necessary changes after a review or a test."

Nevertheless, we must recognize that technical writers are sometimes assigned projects to do on their own, with no review and no testing. In such cases, they may find themselves, like essayists, looking down at the text and realizing that their favorite passage is counterproductive or, worse, seeing that the whole approach is wrong. In those circumstances, the technical writer has to cut that favorite passage or even trash the draft and start over. That kind of revision requires honesty—and courage. But good writers have that tough-mindedness about their own prose.

ASSIGNMENT FOR 10.1

1. *Reflect on the Writing Process* The contemporary philologist Dennis Baron (1989) says that "[m]ost of the writers I have talked to—let us call them speculative writers for want of a better term—discover their subject as they write. Of course they have some idea of general topic . . . and they may even have sketched an outline of their work. But their plans invariably change with the writing, and . . . [as with] a good mystery they do not know what the outcome will be until the task is done. . . . Other writers, perhaps fifteen to twenty percent of those I know, do things just the opposite: they plan everything in their heads before pen ever touches paper" (p. 61). Which kind of writer, generally, are you—a speculative writer or a planner? In a memo to your instructor, describe the writing process you use for most writing tasks. Include personal details such as where and when you write, peculiar habits, and the use of others to critique your drafts. Indicate how you would have to change your writing habits to become a good technical writer.

10.2 >———— Usability Testing

At various stages in the documentation development process, especially near completion, technical writers may test the effectiveness of their text by having individuals inside or outside the organization try out the documentation. This process is called usability testing. On the basis of the usability test results, technical writers will revise and improve their documents.

Even after careful audience analysis and the extensive review process, usability testing is often necessary. We have already seen that audience analysis is, to some extent, a guessing game. And internal reviews, while useful in verifying accuracy, tell us little about how nonexperts, or even experts outside the organization, will read the documentation.

Some users avoid using written documentation, if at all possible. When they come to an impasse in using a product, their first instinct is to fiddle with the product, attempting by trial and error to solve the problem. If they feel obliged to get help, they are more likely to turn to a co-worker or call the manufacturer's telephone support than to try to solve the problem by turning to the written documentation. This is especially true if they have tried out the documentation and found it inconvenient.

It is crucial, then, for the documentation to work for the customer. Ineffective documentation means more calls to a company's technical support unit, which is costly. Usability testing, by taking the bugs out of documentation, helps to keep customers satisfied and self-sufficient— and that not only saves money but makes the company look good.

In the rest of this section, we present the series of steps used by Pittsburgh Telemax to plan, execute, and evaluate a usability test for a piece of documentation. We are assuming here that the product has been tested by the quality control engineers and that it works. The usability testing discussed below is applied to the documentation, not the product.

▲ 1. Establish Roles

Telemax usually uses a four-person testing team. Because of a shortage of personnel in the Documentation Department, members of the Marketing Department join the team. This collaboration has the side benefit of providing marketing people with a deep knowledge of the product and the documentation. Here are the four roles for this team:

▌ **Test administrator.** This person manages the whole process and reports to the DDM. The test administrator also functions as a secondary observer, taking notes on the test takers' behavior. (Hereafter, test takers will be called "participants.") At Telemax, Louis Frapp would assume the role of test administrator.

▌ **Technician.** This person operates the camcorder, videotaping the participants' performance. The technician sits near each participant and answers technical questions about the software and hardware, providing assistance when the participant cannot complete a task. At Telemax, a member of the Documentation Department would assume this role.

▌ **Proctor.** This person greets the participants who are testing the documentation, orients them to the process, and gives out and collects test materials and the post-test written questionnaire. The proctor functions as a close-up observer who keeps track of participants' successes and failures on a score sheet and takes notes on their behavior (confusion, hesitation, wrong choices). The proctor interviews the participants after the testing. At Telemax, a member of the marketing department would assume this role.

▌ **Data coordinator.** This person collects the videotape, evaluation sheets, interview notes, surveys, and any other data and puts them all together into a report and distributes the report to the members of the team. The data coordinator also functions as a secondary observer. At Telemax, a member of the marketing department would assume this role.

Figure 10.1 shows a diagram of a typical testing room.

FIGURE 10.1 ▼   Typical Room Design for Usability Testing

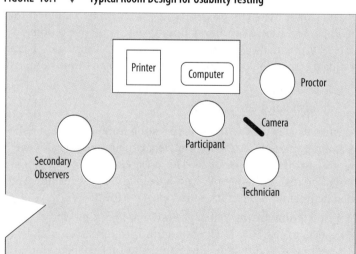

▲ *2. Establish Objectives*

At Pittsburgh Telemax, usability testing objectives are written out. They address the following:

1. what tasks will be tested
2. measurable ways of determining whether the customer can do those tasks
3. measurable ways of determining whether the documentation makes the product easy to use.

Tasks to Be Taught The objectives begin with an overview of what the product does for the customer. In the case of a word processing program, for example, the main functions of the program would be listed as "components to be tested," such as file creation, file editing, file saving, and file printing. A selection of more complex operations, such as creation of templates, would also be included in the testing. The usability testing will determine whether users can easily

1. find the appropriate sections in the manual in order to solve problems
2. learn how to perform various functions by using the manual.

In the case of long manuals, not all functions will be tested. Instead, since the instructional approach is (or should be) consistent throughout the document, the testers will be able to make inferences about the effectiveness of sections not specifically tested on the basis of test results for selected functions.

In the case of complex products, participants may test both a quick start guide (which gets them using the software quickly) and a reference manual. The quick start guide will be tested to determine whether it allows the customer to begin using the product immediately to carry out common tasks. The larger reference manual will be tested to determine whether users can find what they want in the manual and can understand the text once they have gotten to the right page.

Evaluation Methods Next, the objectives state how the testing will determine whether the customer can do various tasks, using the product and the documentation. For example, a test for a word processing program might include a task in which the user is asked to open an old file. Following the documentation, the participant either will or will not be able to do that, so a simple yes-no checklist may be used for such tasks. However, as we will see below, testers often want to know how long it takes a participant to complete a task, in which case the operation will be timed as well.

Another objective is to determine the degree to which the documentation makes the product easy to use. For this purpose, Pittsburgh Telemax uses both quantifiable measures, such as the timing of tasks, and subjective measures, such as open questions in interviews. The company has adopted criteria for the objective evaluation from the work of professional communicator Larry Queipo (1991). Marge Mendoza has adopted his list of objectives for the Documentation Department at Telemax:

Criteria for Objective Evaluation of Documentation

▍ Times to do such things as
    locating information
    learning relevant information
    performing individual tasks
    performing groups of tasks
    performing entire scenarios

▍ Number and types of errors

▍ Number of correct responses

▍ Frequency and types of assistance required by the evaluator [the participant]

▍ Percentage of users [participants] that must complete the task successfully

▍ Users' attitudes about the usability of doing the task (use a scale of 1 to 5 where 1 = very satisfactory). (Queipo, 1991, p. 187)

The testers are interested in user time-on-task because it constitutes a measure of ease-of-use. If it takes a participant 20 minutes to do a task that the testers thought would take 3 minutes, the testers know they have a problem. Keeping track of time-on-task also allows the testers to make an objective comparison between versions of the documentation. If their new version of the documentation reduces that 20-minute time-on-task to a few minutes, they know they have solved the problem.

Here are some sample test entries for the timed tasks mentioned under the first bullet in Queipo's list. Again, we'll assume that the documentation being tested is for a word processing program:

▍ **Locating information:** Find out how to change line spacing by point increment. Read the information aloud.

▍ **Learning relevant information:** Repeat an earlier task without referring to the manual.

▍ **Performing individual tasks:** Modify the paragraph on the monitor so that it is double-spaced.

▍ **Performing groups of tasks:** Open a new file, type your name, save, and print the file.

▎**Performing entire scenarios:** Your boss is dissatisfied with the flyer you created (filename: flyer2). She believes that the flyer needs bigger headings and more white space, including wider margins on both sides. Revise flyer2 accordingly, as quickly as you can, and print two copies.

The last bullet in Queipo's list refers to objective measurement of attitudes. Box 3.4 in Chapter 3 shows various types of questions used in attitude testing, including "closed questions," which request quantifiable information. For example, in reporting survey results, one can make a statement like this:

> Six out of eight participants rated the documentation for the first task "Excellent" or "Good," while the other two rated it "Adequate." This suggests that the documentation for the task needs no revision.

Besides measuring attitudes "objectively" with closed questions, testers can ask open-ended, subjective questions in the questionnaire or interview. Here are some sample "open questions":

▎ What terminology don't you understand in this section?

▎ Which places in the documentation momentarily confused you?

▎ What are the good and bad qualities of this part of the documentation?

It is possible to quantify open questions by reporting the most common responses: "Five of the eight participants stated that the best quality of the documentation is its clear style."

▲ *3. Develop Customer Profiles*

The documentation may have to serve multiple audiences. If possible, representatives of all such audiences should be recruited as participants for usability testing, including individuals from the "least proficient" category—that is, those who will have the most trouble using the documentation to learn the product.

When testing documentation designed for a particular organization, the testers would naturally prefer to use employees at that organization, if this is possible. When testing documentation meant for a large set of customers, Telemax turns to employment agencies to hire participants.

▲ *4. Write the Test Materials*

The test materials typically include

▎ a participant profile sheet to be filled out by each participant (Box 10.1)

BOX 10.1 ▼ **Participant Profile Sheet**

Participant number_____ Product _____

Document title _____

Your latest job title _____

Your company/organization _____

Attitude toward using high-tech products

_____ Confident   _____ Nervous

Familiarity with using documentation to learn about high-tech products

_____ Very familiar   _____ Some experience   _____ Inexperienced

Attitude toward using documentation to learn about high-tech products

_____ Confident   _____ Nervous

If you have used this or a similar product before:

Years experience working with this or a similar product_____

_____

Job(s) you perform with the product_____

_____

Major product functions used_____

_____

Product functions occasionally used_____

_____

❚ a task sheet listing the operations the participants will attempt

❚ an evaluation sheet (called a "test log") for evaluating and timing each
participant's performance

❚ a list of post-test interview questions

❚ a post-test written questionnaire.

For the post-test questioning, testers might choose to use an interview
only, or a written questionnaire only, instead of both.

▲ 5. Plan the Testing Process

Test planning usually consists of these steps:

1. Determine how to recruit appropriate participants.
2. Write a script for the proctor, so that all participants are introduced to the testing process and led through it in the same way.
3. Set up the test room with furniture and equipment.

▲ 6. Conduct the Usability Test

Once the testing begins, testers closely monitor the behavior of participants as they use the documentation to carry out specified tasks. The testers look for ways in which the participants misunderstand the documentation. They also watch for instances in which the participants accidentally overlook or inappropriately ignore crucial instructions.

The usability testers are quite active during the test session, as they carry out specific actions such as these:

▮ closely watch the participant use the documentation

▮ take notes, using a system for logging the time that it takes a participant to perform each action

▮ videotape the session with a camcorder

▮ ask the participant to think aloud, so that the participant's interpretation of the text can be noted

▮ help out when the participant is stuck so that the participant can continue with the testing.

The use of videotaping may seem intrusive, and indeed a camcorder does make some participants nervous. However, that nervousness usually disappears quickly. At Telemax, before beginning the real usability test, testers run each participant through some "warm up drills," unimportant actions that allow the participant to get used to working in the artificial environment of a testing room.

Janice Redish and David Schell (1989) explain the importance of audio- and videotaping, which they have used at their testing facility, the American Institutes for Research:

> [W]e use both videotape and audiotape to record what occurs during the test. Sometimes, actions happen so fast that no one is sure what the test subject [participant] or the computer actually did. We can review the videotape in slow motion to pinpoint the source of a problem. On audiotape, we capture both the subjects' statements and the researchers' observations. (p. 71)

Nowadays, both audio and video can be effectively captured with a camcorder.

Following the monitoring phase, the testers may interview participants or administer a questionnaire. One purpose of these post-test activities is to record the participants' general impressions of the documentation: Is it easy/difficult to find answers to questions? Is the language clear/unclear? Could you learn about the product on your own using this documentation?

▲ 7. Evaluate the Results and Plan Revisions

Once all the data are collected and printed in a single document by the data coordinator, the testers study them and then meet to discuss their meaning and to determine how the documentation should be revised.

ASSIGNMENT FOR 10.2

1. *Test Quick Start Beginners Guide* Write part of a quick start beginner's guide for a word processing program or some other piece of software used in your school's computer labs. Include one simple task and one complex one. Plan and carry out a usability test for your instructions. Write a memo report to your instructor on the results of the usability test, including your conclusions as to how your instructions will need to be revised. Attach to the memo your planning documents, testing materials, and survey and interview questions, as well as the raw data. To find novice participants for word processing software, you may have to write a guide for a Macintosh program and then select participants familiar only with the Windows platform, or vice versa.

10.3 ▷── Field Testing

Technical writers also use field testing as a basis for revision. In a field test, the testers go into the workplace where the product is being used and observe customers using the product in their work environment. The testers then interview customers and sometimes have them fill out a written questionnaire. Field testing is particularly useful for online documentation, which can be updated immediately after the test results have been analyzed.

Technical writers at Telemax usually include written questionnaires with their products upon delivery, along with a letter asking users to fill out and return the questionnaires following their initial experience with the product (see Box 3.6 in Chapter 3). Telemax cannot afford to send employees around the world, or even around the country, to visit customers' sites. Occasionally, however, opportunities arise to field-test the documentation in the Pittsburgh area. Telemax takes advantage of those opportunities to do thorough field testing of documentation, following this process:

1. Obtain permission from the appropriate manager to visit the workplace.

2. Arrange to observe and question several employees using the product and the documentation; select employees representing different audiences, if that situation exists.

3. Create an observation sheet to evaluate user proficiency with the product.

4. Create interview questions designed to determine customer satisfaction with the documentation, and/or create a written questionnaire for all employees using the product and the documentation.

5. Conduct the field test.

6. Evaluate the results.

7. Revise the documentation.

Even with all the planning illustrated by the list above, field testing has to be a flexible activity. You never know what you'll find when you enter another's workplace. You may discover that some of the employees assigned to be your test participants are still using their old product and thus aren't using your product, much less the documentation. Or that employees are using only the most basic features of your product. Or that employees have completely mastered the product and no longer even refer to the documentation.

ASSIGNMENT FOR 10.3

1. *Field-Test New Users* Find an individual on your campus who is using the documentation for a software program or a machine. (Your school may be running courses in basic computer use, in which case the textbook or teacher handouts could serve as the documentation for this assignment.) Plan and execute a field test to determine user satisfaction with the documentation. Write a brief memo report to your instructor on the test results. Make recommendations for revision of the documentation.

Editing, Proofreading, and Indexing

Some technical writers make their living doing nothing but editing or proofreading or indexing documents. In that role, they may work for the organization producing the documents, or they may operate as free-lancers.

Many technical writers responsible for document creation do not have access to experts in "production work," the final phases of document publishing. They are responsible for working on documents from beginning to end. Even engineers and business managers may be responsible for the final versions of some or all of their writings. Therefore, it is worthwhile for anyone who will be working on technical or business documents to know something about how professional editors, proofreaders, and indexers do their jobs.

In companies that distinguish between editing and proofreading, editors review a text for "high-level" problems of structure and style. An editor is responsible for seeing to it that the document is consistent with company standards, grammatically correct, and stylistically effective.

A proofreader looks mainly for sentence-level errors, such as misspelled or missing words, uneven indentations, too many hyphenated lines in a row, or inconsistent cross-references.

Despite that distinction, both editors and proofreaders may correct or query any serious flaws of any kind that they notice. There is some overlap in their work. Both scrutinize the text for violations of company standards for layout, for example. This overlap is useful in ensuring that few mistakes in the text will go unnoticed and uncorrected—though, in long texts, mistakes sometimes slip by all the guardians.

Indexing is a unique task, and a very important one. A good index substantially improves a manual's usefulness. Since reference manuals are not read from cover to cover, the index constitutes the most important user interface for these volumes.

To provide an overview of these activities, we discuss the topics of editing, proofreading, and indexing in general terms below. The serious technical writer would be wise to read books on each of these subjects and to attend courses or workshops on each of them.

11.1 >—— Editing

The responsibilities of a professional technical editor in an organization may be quite broad. Judith Tarutz, a former senior technical editor at Hewlett Packard, points out that one person may perform "the jobs of proofreader, copy editor, senior editor, production editor, and possibly managing editor" (1992, p. 10). In fulfilling those responsibilities, technical editors may engage in

> training new writers and editors; reviewing documentation plans; serving as consultant to writers on writing, editorial, and production matters; and representing their department and company on various committees, such as those formed to create style guides or implement government regulations. (p. 11)

A technical editor's editing duties may include editing not only printed documents but also "online help, online tutorials, user interfaces, videotapes, slide shows, speeches, and technical marketing brochures" (p. 11).

The professional technical editor might work on texts produced by professional technical writers, which are usually quite polished, or on texts produced by engineers, technicians, or management personnel, which can be quite rough. Because professional editors attempt to improve style, they sometimes come in conflict with writers, who may see stylistic changes as an insult to their writing skills or a distortion of their meaning. Effective editors manage to avoid most conflict. In exchanges with writers, such editors are able and willing to justify corrections, revisions, and suggestions, and they listen to what the writers say in response. Many changes can be negotiated. Good editors appreciate the monetary cost of changes and the psychological value of a light hand on someone else's text. Tarutz puts it this way: "Editing is not about making changes; it's about making necessary improvements and corrections" (1992, p. 28).

Despite the need to work well with writers, the technical editor's final responsibility is to the reader. Most organizations give technical editors the authority to make changes over the protests of writers, in order to carry out "necessary improvements and corrections."

In the course of reviewing documents, the technical editor looks for

▎ places where the format varies from the company standard or from the rest of the document (e.g., a 14-point level-two heading showing up in a document in which all other level-two headings are 13-point)

▎ places where the word usage varies from the company standard or from Standard English (e.g., use of an abbreviation of the company name when the full name should be used, or use of gender-exclusionary pronouns)

∎ places where syntax varies from Standard English or would cause problems for an international audience (for example, a breakdown of parallel structure or the use of reduced clauses instead of full clauses)

∎ places where phrasing is unclear

∎ places where phrasing is ugly

∎ places where phrasing may have the wrong effect on readers (e.g., scaring readers when the text should be calming and reassuring them)

∎ places where the text or the phrasing is illogical, or contradicts earlier statements, or is inaccurate

∎ places where more explanation or more examples or some other kind of clarifying element is necessary.

As you can see from the list above, some technical editing is rule governed. The technical editor follows standards appearing in the company style guide for decisions on layout, word choices, and various issues of correctness and style. But the technical editor also focuses on higher-order concerns, such as making the text logical, making it appropriate in its effect on the audience, making it clear, and making it attractive.

Professional editors use proofreading marks (Figure 11.1) to indicate needed changes. Each change is placemarked in the text and then explained in the nearest margin using a standard set of codes. For example, in Figure 11.1, eleven entries down from the top, *tr* in the margin means "transpose letters" and the curved line in the middle of *inidcated* shows where to do the transposing. The unique placemark and the unique marginal code constitute a double system of indicating a single change, which helps avoid mistakes.

Figure 11.2 shows a text with proofreading marks. It also shows how editors make large inserts. The caret at the end of the middle paragraph indicates an insert, the marginal explanation says "Insert A Attached," and Insert A appears below in a box.

ASSIGNMENT FOR 11.1

1. *Edit a Document* Photocopy and then edit the document appearing in Box 11.1 (page 247), applying each of the eight bulleted responsibilities listed near the end of section 11.1. As much as possible, use the conventional marks illustrated in Figure 11.1. In addition, raise questions or suggest changes in marginal comments. Turn in your marked-up, edited text to your instructor.

FIGURE 11.1 ▼ Standard Proofreading Marks

ꝺ	Correct a typ⌀.	Correct a typo.
⌐/m⌐/⌐ꝺ	Corⱡect ⱡore than one typ⌀.	Correct more than one typo.
t	Insert a leter.	Insert a letter.
or words	Insert a word.	Insert a word or words.
ℯ	Make a⌀ deletion.	Make a deletion.
ℰ	Delefte and close up space.	Delete and close up space.
⌣	Close up ex̣tra space.	Close up extra space.
#	Insertproper spacing.	Insert proper spacing.
#/⌐	Closeúp and insert space.	Close up and insert space.
eq #	Regularize proper spacing.	Regularize proper spacing.
tr	Transpose letters inⱡicated.	Transpose letters indicated.
tr	Transpose as words indicated.	Transpose words as indicated.
tr	Reorder shown as words several.	Reorder several words as shown.
⊔	Move le⌐ter(s) down.	Move letter(s) down.
⊓	Move le⌐ter(s) up.	Move letter(s) up.
⊏ ⊏	Move text to left.	Move text to left.
⊐ ⊐	Move text to right.	Move text to right.
¶	⌐Indent for paragraph.	Indent for paragraph.
no ¶	⊏ No paragraph indent.	No paragraph indent.
═	St^rai gh⌐en type horizontally.	Straighten type horizontally.
‖	‖ Align type vertically.	Align type vertically.
run in	Run back turnover⊃ ⊂lines.	Run back turnover lines.
⌐	Break line when it runs far⌐too long.	Break line when it runs far too long.
⊙	Insert period here∧	Insert period here.
⌄	Commas‸commas everywhere.	Commas, commas everywhere.
⌄	Its in need of an apostrophe.	It's in need of an apostrophe.
⌄/ ⌄	∧Add quotation marks,‸he begged.	"Add quotation marks," he begged.
;	Add a semicolon‸don't hesitate.	Add a semicolon; don't hesitate.
:	She advised‸"You need a colon."	She advised: "You need a colon."
?	How about a question mark∧	How about a question mark?
⌐=⌐	Add a slap‸dash hyphen.	Add a slap-dash hyphen.
$\frac{1}{N}$	1971‗2001 takes an en dash.	1971–2001 takes an en dash.
$\frac{1}{M}$	Add an em dash‸if you like.	Add an em dash—if you like.
(/)	Add parentheses‸as they say‸	Add parentheses (as they say).
lc	Sometimes you want Lower case.	Sometimes you want lower case.
caps	Sometimes you want upper CASE.	Sometimes you want UPPER CASE.
sc	Even small caps are used.	Even SMALL CAPS are used.
ital	Add italics instantly.	Add italics instantly.
rom	But use roman in the main.	But use roman in the main.
bf	Add boldface if necessary.	Add boldface if necessary.
wf	Fix a wrong font letter.	Fix a wrong font letter.
sp	Spell out all ③ terms.	Spell out all three terms.
∧	Change x to a subscript.	Change x to a subscript.
∨	Change y to a superscript.	Change y to a superscript.
(Au?)	Confirm or supply data.	Please do so.
stet	Let stand as is.	Let stand as is. (To retract a change already marked.)

FIGURE 11.2 ▼ Using Proofreading Marks

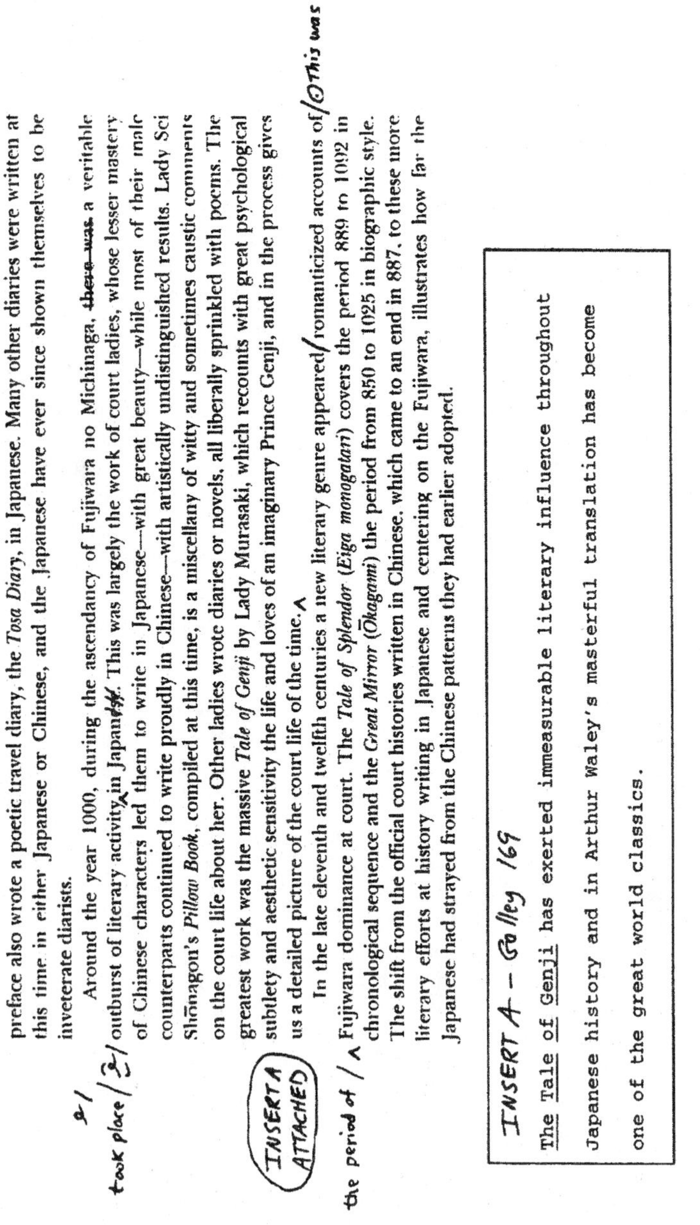

preface also wrote a poetic travel diary, the *Tosa Diary*, in Japanese. Many other diaries were written at this time in either Japanese or Chinese, and the Japanese have ever since shown themselves to be inveterate diarists.
Around the year 1000, during the ascendancy of Fujiwara no Michinaga, ~~there was~~ a veritable outburst of literary activity in Japanese. This was largely the work of court ladies, whose lesser mastery of Chinese characters led them to write in Japanese—with great beauty—while most of their male counterparts continued to write proudly in Chinese—with artistically undistinguished results. Lady Sei Shōnagon's *Pillow Book*, compiled at this time, is a miscellany of witty and sometimes caustic comments on the court life about her. Other ladies wrote diaries or novels, all liberally sprinkled with poems. The greatest work was the massive *Tale of Genji* by Lady Murasaki, which recounts with great psychological subtlety and aesthetic sensitivity the life and loves of an imaginary Prince Genji, and in the process gives us a detailed picture of the court life of the time.
In the late eleventh and twelfth centuries a new literary genre appeared romanticized accounts of Fujiwara dominance at court. The *Tale of Splendor* (*Eiga monogatari*) covers the period 889 to 1092 in chronological sequence and the *Great Mirror* (*Ōkagami*) the period from 850 to 1025 in biographic style. The shift from the official court histories written in Chinese, which came to an end in 887, to these more literary efforts at history writing in Japanese and centering on the Fujiwara, illustrates how far the Japanese had strayed from the Chinese patterns they had earlier adopted.
took place
the period of
INSERT A ATTACHED
This was
INSERT A – Galley 169
The Tale of Genji has exerted immeasurable literary influence throughout Japanese history and in Arthur Waley's masterful translation has become one of the great world classics.

Source: Houghton Mifflin College Division, *A Guide for Authors.* Copyright © 1998 by Houghton Mifflin Company. Reprinted with permission.

BOX 11.1 ▼ Text Requiring Editing

TO: Lois Fisher, District Manager
FROM: Greg Martin, manager of the Coaltown Bingo store
DATE: June 5, 1996
SUBJECT:A proposal to increase sales through a Frequent
             Shopper Program

New Solution: A Frequent Shopper Program

I wish to propose a Frequent Shopper Program to increase sales; twice a year, frequent shoppers who purchase a minimum dollar amount would be rewarded with voucherss for free groceries in our stores. The size of each certificate would vary according too how much the shopper exceeded the minimum needed to qualify.

This program should encourage infrequent shoppers to come to our store to try and meet the minimum, and it should work to retain loyalty of our regular shoppers, possibly even encouraging then to buy more stuff.

Background Sales in Decline

At this time, for the past year, sales have been increasing in our regoin. This negative trend has affected every store, including mine in Coaltown. Our effor to counter this decline, although well-conceived, has not been successful. Our coupon mailing have not brought in new customer's, nor, apparently, have they increased shopping from our old customers'.

It is time for us to try something new and daring for once. None of us wants the profits in this region to fall any further, if necessary. Higher management's conservatism may bring us all down.

Other Benefits

I would suggest giving free T-shirts to those who qualify for free groceries under our pro-gram with the slogan "I'm a Freakquent Shopper." This would provide our stores with free advertising.

The cards we would issue to keep track of customers purchase totals could also keep track of who buys which products, creating mailing lists which we could use to selectively advertise sales and which we could then sell to vendors.

Pilot Study

To reduce the risk of this adventure, I would be willing to conduct a pilot study at my Coaltown store. That way, if the project fails, regional profits would be effected only slightly.

11.2 >——— Proofreading

Proofreading is the last step in polishing a document, and it is especially important for all documents that will go outside the organization. The proofreader looks for errors that have somehow escaped the scrutiny of all those who have worked on the document so far. Some organizations outsource this work to professional proofreaders; others simply pass it on to the technical writers. The technical writers may therefore find themselves proofreading the works of others, as well as their own writings.

The following points provide an overview of how professionals do proofreading.

▲ 1. Comparison Proofreading

Not long ago, a proofreader would compare the typeset text, known as the "live copy," with the original, edited manuscript, the "dead copy," to make sure that no errors were introduced during typesetting. This process is called "comparison proofreading." Sometimes proofreaders worked in pairs, one reader reading the dead copy aloud while the other listened and read the live copy silently, looking for discrepancies.

Nowadays text production is fully computerized in organizations like Pittsburgh Telemax, so no typesetting takes place. The computer will locate places where changes have been made during the last editing session. The proofreader may first focus on those places to make sure that no mistakes were added in the course of implementing editing changes. Then the proofreader would examine the rest of the text for errors.

▲ 2. Solo Methods

Most proofreading nowadays is done solo, because it's cheaper and because there is less comparing going on. The proofreader typically uses a straightedge instrument, such as a ruler, to focus on one line at a time. Some proofreaders use a piece of cardboard with a rectangular hole cut out of the center for focused viewing.

Many proofreaders divide up a page into separate tasks, checking all headings, for instance, before reading the running text. It is important for proofreaders to read a text for meaning, in order to catch homophone errors (*affect* when *effect* is meant) and other errors in which a wrong word appears (such as *the* for *that*) or an inflection is missing (*walk* when *walks* is required). Computer spellcheckers won't pick up such errors.

The human mind has a strong inclination to read for meaning, and it is not necessary to see the whole text to capture meaning. For example, you can erase the bottom halves of words in a sentence and yet, in most cases, read the sentence fairly easily. The developing meaning of the text affects what we see. As we read, we see not only what is there but what we expect to be there, given what we have read so far. Proofreaders are acutely aware of this "problem." Therefore, after reading for meaning and making corrections, proofreaders often recheck their work, going over the page a second time, using some method to defeat the inclination to read for meaning. They may read slowly aloud, for example, or read the page bottom up.

As a student writer, one method you may find effective is to read sections out loud and tape-record them. Then play back the recording to hear how the text sounds. If you hear yourself tripping over the text while sounding out a passage, you can examine that passage for points of awkwardness and ungrammaticality.

▲ *3. What to Look For and Where*

Professional proofreaders succeed for two main reasons:

▌ They know what to look for.

▌ They know where to look.

Professional proofreader Peggy Smith (1997) provides a summary of what proofreaders look for (Box 11.2). Knowing the errors that writers make helps you to spot them.

Professionals are particularly alert for errors in certain places. They know that, to an almost uncanny degree, errors show up in headings and in the first lines of lists. In fact, any place where a text changes (e.g., a shift to indented text or a change in font style) is a likely location for error.

▲ *4. Dealing with Unauthorized Changes*

Besides finding errors, proofreaders provide a check on editors. Proofreaders look for unauthorized changes during editing, such as changes in terminology that have not been approved by the engineers. An editor trying to improve the style of a document might want to reduce the jargon, but the conversion of a technical term to an ordinary language term may not be appropriate. If engineers are developing a set of technical terms for a product, they don't want that effort undermined. Engineers concerned with accuracy and editors concerned with readability have different interests that may need to be negotiated.

BOX 11.2 ▼ **Errors That Proofreaders Look For**

The following list summarizes many of the problems proofreaders look for. If you can catch everything on the list and decide correctly whether to mark, query, or ignore a problem, you'll be well on the way to doing work of professional quality.

Mark the following for correction:

• Unauthorized deviations from the dead copy

• Unauthorized deviations from specifications

• Typos, including omissions of letters, transpositions of letters and words, doublets, repeaters, and outs

Decide whether to *mark, query* or *ignore* the following:

• Mechanical faults: misaligned characters, broken or dirty characters, rivers or lakes, smudges, dots, uneven ink color, and so on

• Spacing errors

• Positioning faults

• Word division errors

• Widows and orphans at page or column top and bottom

• Widows at paragraph bottom

• Other bad breaks (heads, text lines, short pages, and so on)

• Type style errors (typeface, type size, caps, Clc, italics or underscores)

• Poor graphics

• Nonstandard grammar or usage

• Punctuation errors and inconsistencies

• Editorial style discrepancies (inconsistencies in analogous items, capitalization, number style, cross references, abbreviations, symbols, units of measure, treatment of proper names, use of italics or underscores, and so on)

• Poor exposition

• Errors in alphabetical or numerical sequence

• Faulty reference

• Missing material

• Faulty headings

• Incorrect arithmetic

• Errors in equations and formulas

• Problems in tables, charts, graphs, exhibits

• Errors in front matter listings

• Blanks in text

Source: From *Mark My Words: Instruction and Practice in Proofreading*, 3rd edition, by Peggy Smith, EEI Press, 1997. Reprinted with permission of EEI Press, Alexandria, VA.

▲ *5. Responding to Errors*

As Smith (1997) points out, the proofreader has three choices when encountering an error:

▌ ignore

▌ tactfully query

▌ mark.

Proofreaders need to obtain authorization for marking and querying various types of errors. Smith suggests five levels of proofreading responsibility. At the lowest level of responsibility, the proofreader would query nothing and would mark only deviations from specification and typographical standards, such as awkward page breaks, deviations from the dead copy, misspellings, and improper word divisions at the ends of lines. At the highest level of responsibility, the proofreader would mark any error that might be noticed by a careful, knowledgeable reader or that "might confuse an inattentive reader" (p. 16).

ASSIGNMENTS FOR 11.2

1. *Proofread Text* Photocopy Box 11.3 and proofread it. Use standard marks. Mark all errors. Turn in your corrected, photocopied version to your instructor.

2. *Proofread Your Own Work* Using the methods provided in section 11.2, proofread one of your own papers, preferably one written for this course. In a memo to your instructor, describe the errors you found.

11.3 ⟩——— Indexing

This section provides a brief overview of the theory and practice of indexing. It concludes with a process for indexing documents created in a technical writing course. The information provided here should allow you to index a technical document with minimum competence—though, again, we recommend reading more thoroughly on indexing or taking a course in it.

Indexing is so important that high-tech companies often outsource indexing to professional freelancers. However, Telemax is always looking for ways to stay lean and save money. Since a manual typically costs the company $800 to $1,000 to index, Mendoza has had Louis Frapp trained in professional indexing. This investment of a few thousand dollars in employee training pays for itself quickly.

BOX 11.3 ▼ **Text Requiring Proofreading**

To: Pumpkinville School Board
From: Arnold Pringle, Superintendent, Pumpkinville Area Schools
Date: June 30, 2,000
RE: Conference Session on Zero Tolerence

On July 20th I traveled to Frostburg, ML, to attend a day-long conference on student misbehavior in schools.A full record of my expenses are attacked. In summary, the trip cost $345.80.

I. Purpose of the Trip

My main purpose was to attend the 3-hour mourning session on zero tolerance policies. We have discussed expanding our zero tolerance policies to drugs and sexual harassment. If found the session quite relevant to our concerns.

II. Suppor for Zero Tolerance

The federal Gun-Free Schools acts of 1994, requires us to have zero tolerance policy on guns in school. Violators must be expelled. This has worked well at Pumpkiville. It has also worked at other schools nation wide, according to the session leaders. The problem is toy guns Several students around the country have been suspended for bringing plastic toys to school, most notably a case in Seattle which a 10-year-old boy was suspended for bringing to school a one-inch plastic acessory to a G.I. joe doll. The press ridiculed school officials for for this action. The session leaders offerred these justifications for zero tolerance for toys: 1) guns are getting smaller, and (2) police have shot children who were waiving gun-like objects.

II. Keys for Implementing Zero Tolerance:

The session leaders advised that following for implementation of zero tolerance for guns, drugs, and sexual harassment:

1) Involve the community in deciding what will be banned absolutely.

2) Allow yourself some flexibility in punishment

3) Have an appeal process for students.

5) Train your staff.

III. Recomendations

The session convinced me the zero tolerance is an effective policy if done right. As a first step , I recommend that the board schedule a public hearing to inform locale citizens of our interest in expanding zero tolerance to other areas and to get their feedback

▲ *1. The Indexer as an Organizer*

In the simplest terms, an indexer does three things:

1. identifies and lists important topics
2. identifies and lists subtopics
3. identifies and cross-references related topics and synonyms.

The first step in indexing is to determine what the major topics are. For each major topic, the indexer must decide if the topic should be presented with subtopics. The information represented by subtopic may be scattered throughout the text. By bringing that information together under one topic, the indexer provides an organization for the text that is quite different from the one provided by the writer's arrangement. Each multilevel entry in an index, then, shows how and where a topic is treated throughout the book, as in this example:

> word processing
> > definition, 12
> > future of, 84
> > general features, 14–16
> > using Microsoft Word, 16

These subtopics show us that the body of the text does the following: defines and describes word processing in general, describes a particular word processing program (Microsoft Word), and talks about the future of word processing. This collation of the information on word processing will not appear in the table of contents or anywhere else in the book.

▲ *2. Organizational Levels*

Most indexes exhibit up to three levels for each entry. An entry may consist of a topic only:

> editing, 75, 156–58

Or a topic and a cross-reference to another, related topic:

> resumes, 42. *See also* job search.

The "word processing" example in section 11.3(1) shows two levels, topic and subtopics. Here is an entry with three levels:

> desktop publishing
> > definition of, 45
> > future of, 89
> > programs
> > > Corel Ventura, 47–51
> > > Framemaker, 45–47

Notice that page numbers do not appear at heading levels (*desktop publishing* or *programs*) if there are subheadings below them.

Indexers have to distinguish between subtopics and synonyms. Synonyms are the alternative terms a reader might choose to look up while searching for a particular topic. Synonyms should be cross-referenced to the word that the indexer chose for the topic. In the example below, the indexer chose *typing* for the topic, but the indexer suspects that some readers will look for the topic under *keyboarding.* Hence this entry:

> keyboarding. *See* typing

There is no page number after *keyboarding* because the indexer wants the reader to go to the place in the index where the topic is more comprehensively listed. There the reader would see all the relevant pages and subtopics for the topic. Remember, one of the goals of indexing is to show the reader how a topic is treated throughout the text. Simply putting page numbers after a list of words would not accomplish that purpose.

In some cases, the word or phrase an indexer uses to name a topic may not even appear anywhere in the text itself. For example, an indexer might want to list locations of discussions of Microsoft products under the entry *Microsoft products,* even though the author never uses the phrase *Microsoft products.* Obviously an indexer couldn't do that if indexing were nothing more than a list of words and the pages on which they appear.

▲ 3. Formatting Styles

Topics and subtopics are alphabetically listed. Some styles of indexing capitalize all topic and subtopic entries; some cap only topic entries; some (as in the examples above) don't cap any entries, except words normally capitalized in English, such as a person's name.

Indexes use the same font as the running text in the body, but one point size smaller. Subtopics and carry-over lines are typically indented one "em" (the width of the uppercase letter M).

▲ 4. Methods and Tools

Indexers read through a text, marking words for topic entries. Since they are usually working to a tight production schedule, with perhaps only two weeks to complete a book, they must perform under high pressure. Professional indexer Nancy Mulvaney (1994) describes the work as follows:

> The indexer becomes immersed in the flow of the writing. It is inevitable that the indexer will internalize the voice and tone of the author. At the

same time, though, the indexer must consider the reader's perspective, adding cross-references where needed and picking up on nuances that are not clearly stated. The indexing process is very intense. Chances are that no other reader will read the book in such a focused manner in such a short amount of time as does the indexer. . . .

For the length of time an indexer works on a book, the indexer lives and breathes the language of the book. . . . While indexers must be detail oriented, they must also be able to synthesize information and communicate that synthesis to the readers.

Contemporary indexers use computer software programs to aid in their work. Embedded functions in Microsoft Word, Adobe Framemaker, and similar software allow the indexer to either mark words in the text or actually write index notes in the text. Later, on command, the software will cull out those marked words or notes and use them to compile a tentative index. Using embedded indexing programs avoids the necessity of re-indexing the text for each future edition.

Dedicated indexing software programs allow indexers to type indexes as separate files. These programs have great flexibility and allow the indexer to choose any standard indexing style. Instead of working "in the dark" in regard to the whole index, "The structure of the index is constantly emerging" (Mulvaney, p. 272). Mulvaney believes that dedicated software is the most cost effective for professional work.

▲ 5. A Method for Indexing Short Documents

You can index a short document of the kind written for a technical writing course by following these steps:

Mark Key Words in the Text

1. Read the document through once, making a mental note of the major ideas.

2. Read the document through again, underlining or highlighting key words in headings and in the running text. For this pass, mark words related to ideas that are developed in the text *in more than one sentence.*

3. Do a final read, this time marking these entries as key words: 3.
   the names of authors that you have referenced
   other people's names
   place names
   brand names
   types of products and devices that you have identified.

Organize the Key Words

4. Write down the key words and their page numbers on 3 × 5 note cards; use a separate card for each word. Write the word in the middle of the card, leaving the top lines blank.

5. Alphabetize the cards.

6. Go through your stack of cards and look for words that could become subcategories of other more general words. If you find *at least two* subcategory words for a general word, write the general word at the top of all the related cards and keep the general word card and related-word cards together in a stack.

7. Go through your list of key words looking for instances in which a reader might seek the topic using a synonym. Create a set of synonym cards, placing the synonym and the cross-reference on the top line of the card:

> keyboarding. *See* typing.

Then insert the synonym cards into the alphabetized set. (Alphabetize by the synonym, not the cross-reference.)

Create and Test the Index

8. Choose a consistent format (you might want to use the one in this book), and create a model showing how main topics and subtopics and cross-references will be formatted.

9. Keeping one eye on the model, type up your index.

10. Check each entry to determine that the page reference is correct by finding each term in the text.

11. Ask someone to read your text and then to try to find topics by using your index. Note any topics or synonyms the person looks for that you haven't indexed.

12. Revise your index on the basis of the usability test in the previous step.

ASSIGNMENTS FOR 11.3

1. *Index Your Own Paper* Index a short paper you have written for course work. Use subtopics and cross-references for synonyms and related terms. Turn in a copy of the paper along with the index.

2. *Index a Long Document* Do assignment 11.3(1), but index a chapter in a book, such as this one.

PART 4

Business Documents

12 Marketing Publications

Large organizations have marketing departments employing professional writers and artists. These professionals know how to sell products through text and visuals, including effective layout. The kind of writing done in a marketing department is sometimes defined as "technical writing," and technical writers normally assigned to write documentation may be drafted to work with marketing personnel on specific projects.

If you are a technical writer in a small organization, you may be expected to do much of the design and creation of marketing documents. This chapter begins with principles of design and layout and then looks at how those principles can be applied to familiar types of marketing publications: flyers, posters, polybags, and brochures.

12.1 ▷—— Principles of Design and Layout

In a textbook like this, we cannot teach the knowledge and artistry that go into professional-level text design and layout for marketing, but we can cover some of the main ideas. Even the very general knowledge presented here will allow you to produce more attractive and effective marketing documents. For more information, you can consult some of the many excellent books available on this subject (e.g., Koren & Meckler, 1989; Meyer, 1997; Siebert & Ballard, 1992; Williams, 1994; Williams & Tollett, 1998).

Page design is usually understood in terms of four major principles: balance, emphasis, rhythm, and unity. We must add a fifth principle stating your license to deliberately break any of the first four principles to create a dramatic effect. Each of the initial four principles can be developed and controlled through the use of "line, shape, texture, space, size, value [degree of dark or light] and/or color" (Siebert & Ballard, 1992, p. 29).

▲ *1. Balance*

Balance means creating an equal presence on each side of the page, or between the top and bottom, or from corner to corner. If you have a lot of text on the left side of the page, you can balance that with a striking illustration or a heavy vertical border line at the right side of the page. Figure 12.1 contrasts an unbalanced page with two balanced ones.

▲ *2. Emphasis*

Emphasis means foregrounding a part of the page, making it stand out in contrast to the rest of the page. Designers do this to draw attention to important textual content or images. The reader's eye movements generally follow a Z-pattern across and down the page, so you can emphasize a visual or a piece of text simply by placing it in the high-left position, where the reader's eye goes first. You can also emphasize by using any of these techniques:

▌ oversizing

▌ reversing (such as white text on a black background)

▌ dramatic use of color or value

▌ isolating or surrounding with white space

▌ boxing or framing

▌ changing medium (a photo within a sea of text).

FIGURE 12.1 ▼ Balance

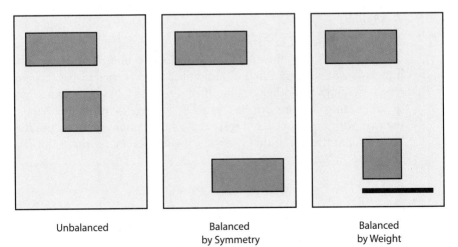

Unbalanced	Balanced by Symmetry	Balanced by Weight

FIGURE 12.2 ▼ Emphasis

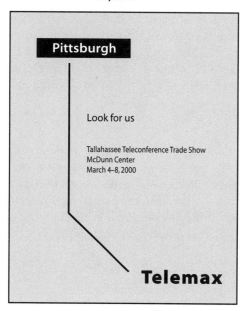

Notice how the name Pittsburgh Telemax is emphasized in the poster in Figure 12.2 by reversing and oversizing.

▲ *3. Rhythm*

Rhythm is a sense of movement created by repeating an element. Blocks of texts, if they are similar and follow close to one another, give the impression of rhythm. Rhythm also appears from page to page as you repeat headings and other graphic effects, such as tabs and borders.

Interesting rhythms can be created by varying elements in a regular manner within a sequence. Figure 12.3, for example, shows a gradual increasing of the size of the "telephone poles" as they approach the *T* in Telemax.

▲ *4. Unity*

A page has unity if the elements seem to belong together and relate to one another. When the elements are exploded—flung apart—the page usually lacks unity. Bringing elements together in a group provides unity

FIGURE 12.3 ▼   Rhythm

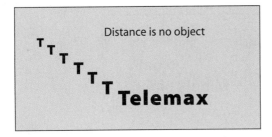

FIGURE 12.4 ▼   Unity

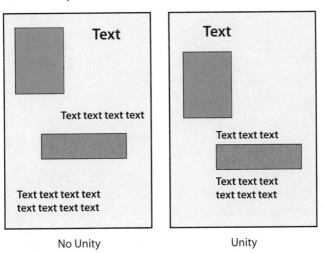

through proximity. Unity can also be achieved by aligning the borders of elements and by repeating elements, values, and colors. Figure 12.4 demonstrates these techniques.

▲ *5. Break the Rules*

The above four rules were made to be broken. A page that is perfectly balanced and unified, with the same elements repeated and the title enlarged for emphasis, can be boring. Bring tension and drama into your design with asymmetrical, off-balanced elements. Establish boundaries and then cross them. Do this deliberately and carefully, not randomly. The poet Robert Frost once commented that he wrote the first version of some poems in perfect iambic pentameter, and then went back and roughed up the meter. If your design looks too settled, shake it up. Figure 12.5 provides an example.

FIGURE 12.5 ▼ Break the Rules

Graphic design expert Robin Williams (1994) offers two pieces of advice that might prevent you from creating a boring page:

1. Keep things out of the corners and the middle of the page. In this way, you can prevent a simple boxy look. Williams advises beginning designers to avoid centering titles as well.

2. **When setting two different things next to each other, make them very different.** *Small contrasts look like mistakes. For example, when changing text from a heading to the running text, change serif type and value (darkness, thickness)—not just size. Two pictures, one half the size of the other, look better next to each other than two pictures nearly the same size. And notice how much better this text block looks than #1, which has only a contrast of size between the advice and the explanation.*

▲ 6. Borrow and Play

Did we say five principles? We lied. To learn those five principles you need a sixth: Borrow ideas from others and toy around with them. Steal from your environment—the writing on the wall, the woods across the river. Get in a playful mood, teeter on one foot, "lose it." See what comes up. Professional designers try out many versions and revisions before arriving at the final page. Go with the pros.

ASSIGNMENTS FOR 12.1

1. *Identify Principles* In a memo report to your instructor, explain how each of the preceding figures (12.1 through 12.5) manifests the particular principle it is supposed to illustrate.

2. *Analyze an Ad* In a memo report to your instructor, analyze an advertisement from a magazine in terms of the six principles of design discussed in this section.

3. *Block Out Examples* Using geometric shapes and Greeked text, create six pages illustrating each of the six principles of design discussed in this section.

4. *Design a T-Shirt or Cap* Create a design for a T-shirt or a cap advertising an organization, company, or product. Pay particular attention to design principle #6. Review the discussion of icons in section 7.5.

12.2 Flyers, Polybags, and Posters

These three types of documents allow you to give full play to the principles of design discussed in section 12.1. Flyers are single-sheet announcements, usually using only one side of the page. When you return to your car after shopping in the mall to find a page of paper under your windshield wiper, you've been "flyered."

Polybags are disseminated at trade shows. When you visit a booth, you pick one up and drop it in the canvas or plastic bag obtained at the entrance to the show. A polybag typically uses both sides of a single page and describes a product line. Polybags often use slick paper and photographs to showcase products. (See Figures 7.17 and 7.18 in Chapter 7.)

A poster, like a flyer, makes announcements on one side of a page, but a poster is much larger. It's meant to be posted on a wall and read from a distance. Lettering is therefore usually oversized, but not always. Small words can intrigue readers, drawing them closer to the poster and into its art.

Pittsburgh Telemax has been distributing polybags for many years and is just now starting to design posters (Figure 12.2) and T-shirts (Figure 12.3) for distribution at trade shows.

ASSIGNMENTS FOR 12.2

Note: For these assignments you can use your fictional company or Pittsburgh Telemax or a company from the list in assignment 13.2(5) in Chapter 13.

1. *Create a Flyer* Create a flyer to announce a sale on one or more of your products.

2. *Create a Poster* Create a poster advertising your products or company, or announcing your presence at an upcoming trade show.

3. *Create a Polybag* Create a polybag to advertise your product or product line. Put technical details on the back side.

12.3 ⟩——— Brochures

Brochures are used to promote interest in an organization and its services. They can function like sales letters promoting a product. They can also serve as instructional literature: Six Steps in Baking Bread; How to Unclog a Drain; Healthy Eating Habits. They can be handed out or left in piles at appropriate sites to be picked up by anyone interested. Or they can be mailed, with the back panel serving as the "envelope front."

The sections below discuss basic principles for creating effective brochures.

▲ 1. Folding the Brochure

Brochures are always folded. Typical folds include these:

- **Four-Panel** Fold a piece of $8^1/2 \times 7$ inch paper in half, lengthwise.

- **Six-Panel** Fold a piece of $8^1/2 \times 7$ inch paper widthwise in the following manner. First turn one-third of the paper inward from the right side. Then turn one-third inward from the left side, completely overlapping the already-turned-in panel.

- **Accordian** Start with a long strip of paper and fold panels into a stack of squares in the following manner. Start at the bottom, fold upward to create a double layer, then fold the double layer under the strip to create three layers, then fold those three layers upward over the top of the strip, and so on. This procedure can also be used to create an accordion of narrow vertical panels. Use the accordion fold when you need a large number of panels.

▲ 2. Designing the Brochure

Design your brochure panel by panel. On the cover panel, display the title of the brochure or the name of the organization (Figure 12.6). In the case of an organization, include the address and phone number, unless that text would interfere with the aesthetics of the cover. In any case, display

FIGURE 12.6   ▼   Front Panel of a Brochure

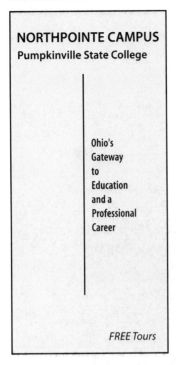

the address and phone number prominently in the brochure where the reader can easily find them.

The inside panels provide details. It is tempting to stuff your brochure with information, but you should avoid a crowded look. Write each panel in blocks of text, leaving white space and visuals in between.

Remember that when a reader opens a brochure, at least two panels will be visible. You have to design those two to fit together—to achieve unity. Consider crossing the border between the panels with part of the design, as in Figure 12.7. That helps to tie the panels together.

In Figure 12.7, rhythm and balance are provided by the text, and asymmetry and border crossing are achieved through the arrangement of the pictures. Consistent with the Robin Williams rule of making contrasts big, the text headings use a relatively large, boldfaced sans-serif font to distinguish them from the smaller, unemphasized serif font used for the running text.

Following the Robin Williams rule of avoiding the middle, the center of balance for the large set of pictures is above the center of the page, and the large-print phone number appears below the center. This "heavy" phone number provides weight to help vertically balance the smaller

FIGURE 12.7 ▼ Interior Panels of a Brochure

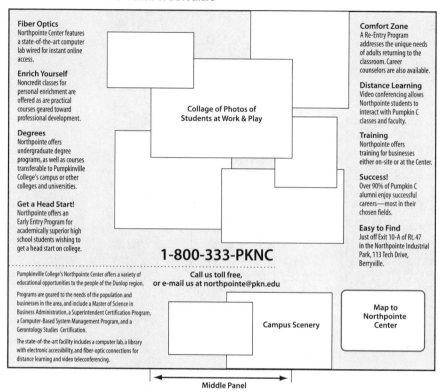

Fiber Optics
Northpointe Center features a state-of-the-art computer lab wired for instant online access.

Enrich Yourself
Noncredit classes for personal enrichment are offered as are practical courses geared toward professional development.

Degrees
Northpointe offers undergraduate degree programs, as well as courses transferable to Pumpkinville College's campus or other colleges and universities.

Get a Head Start!
Northpointe offers an Early Entry Program for academically superior high school students wishing to get a head start on college.

Collage of Photos of Students at Work & Play

Comfort Zone
A Re-Entry Program addresses the unique needs of adults returning to the classroom. Career counselors are also available.

Distance Learning
Video conferencing allows Northpointe students to interact with Pumpkin C classes and faculty.

Training
Northpointe offers training for businesses either on-site or at the Center.

Success!
Over 90% of Pumpkin C alumni enjoy successful careers—most in their chosen fields.

Easy to Find
Just off Exit 10-A of Rt. 47 in the Northpointe Industrial Park, 113 Tech Drive, Berryville.

1-800-333-PKNC

Pumpkinville College's Northpointe Center offers a variety of educational opportunities to the people of the Dunlop region.

Programs are geared to the needs of the population and businesses in the area, and include a Master of Science in Business Administration, a Superintendent Certification Program, a Computer-Based System Management Program, and a Gerontology Studies Certification.

The state-of-the-art facility includes a computer lab, a library with electronic accessibility, and fiber-optic connections for distance learning and video teleconferencing.

Call us toll free,
or e-mail us at northpointe@pkn.edu

Campus Scenery

Map to Northpointe Center

◄——— **Middle Panel** ———►

bottom portion of the brochure with the picture-heavy top. From a horizontal perspective, the phone number is centered in the middle panel; so, to add asymmetry, the dotted line below it extends only to the left. Notice that this line ties two panels together by crossing a border, and that the middle and right panels are tied together at the bottom by the alignment of the campus-scenery picture with the map.

▲ 3. Rhetorical Concerns

Pay attention to your purpose when writing blocks of text. If your brochure is designed to promote interest, then point out interesting facts and services—don't saturate the brochure with information. But if your brochure is designed to provide complete information (such as how to do something), then carefully plan the content to make sure that it is comprehensive.

Be sensitive to your reader. If older people will be reading the brochure, don't use small font sizes.

Some brochures contain a tear-out panel to be filled in with information and then mailed to the organization. In such cases, the reader will lose whatever information appears on the back of the tear-out panel, so don't put important information there, such as the organization's address and phone number.

ASSIGNMENTS FOR 12.3

1. *Analyze a Brochure* Find a brochure on campus and analyze it in a memo to your instructor. Indicate how and why the brochure is effective, or not effective, in terms of both design and content.

2. *Create a Brochure Mock-up* Create a mock-up of a brochure that (a) promotes a club or sporting team or some other organization on your campus, (b) educates about an academic program at your school, (c) advertises a product, or (d) explains how to do something. Your brochure doesn't have to be "camera ready" for printing, but it should show your understanding of the principles discussed in this section. Cut and paste text blocks and pictures and do the fold.

12.4 >——— Creating Web Sites for Marketing Purposes

Today almost every organization has its own Web site that talks about the organization and advertises its products or services. In section 9.5, we discussed Web site design in general, as well as online documentation. Here, we emphasize that the principles of design discussed above in section 12.1 should be applied to the development of attractive Web pages.

For marketing sites especially, you should prefer a shallow hierarchical structure that takes readers quickly to their destination. Figure 12.8 shows both a good and a bad structural design. In the good design, the reader can access many pages directly from the main menu on the homepage and most of the remaining pages at the second level beyond the homepage. In the bad design, the reader has to click to a third level or further to access more than half the pages.

The tree diagram offers a good method for planning Web sites. An example is provided in Figure 12.9, which shows the design of a Web site for Center in the Woods, a senior center in Pennsylvania. The long horizontal line represents the main menu on the homepage. You can see how that plan works itself out by visiting the site at **www.cup.edu/citw.**

Table 12.1 shows the maintenance table for the Center in the Woods site. The left column, "Page," lists the homepage as well as the pages

FIGURE 12.8 ▼   Good and Bad Structural Designs for a Web Site

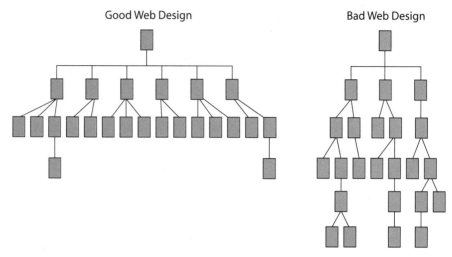

Note: Both designs have 23 links off the homepage, but the good design does not require readers to travel through many links to find what they are looking for.

accessible from the menu on the homepage. The "HTML" column lists the HTML file name for each of these pages. The "Frequency" column states how frequently each page needs to be updated. The "Situations" column indicates the conditions affecting updating, as well as other notes. And the "Links" column lists the links that appear on each page.

ASSIGNMENTS FOR 12.4

1. *Analyze a Web Site*   Find a commercial Web site advertising an organization's services or products. In a memo to your instructor, analyze the site in terms of the aesthetic and structural guidelines that appear in this chapter. In what ways does the site follow those guidelines and in what ways does it deviate? How effective are the deviations?

2. *Create a Plan*   Create a tree outline, as in Figure 12.9, for a Web site for your fictional company or for a school team, club, or service. Consider your purposes and your audiences.

3. *Create Mock Pages*   Create three of the pages, on paper, for your design in assignment 12.4(2). Try to make each printed page small enough to fit on

a computer screen. Indicate words or buttons programmed as links by using underlining or a color different from that of the running text.

4. ***Create a Maintenance Table***   Create a maintenance table for the site you planned in assignment 12.4(2).

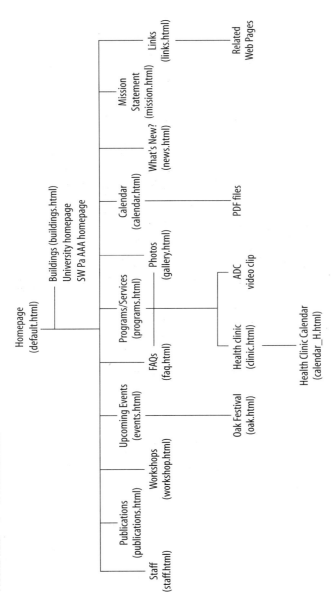

FIGURE 12.9 ▼ A Web Site Plan

TABLE 12.1 ▶ Web Site Maintenance Table

Page	HTML	Frequency	Situations	Links
Homepage	default.html	As needed	Adding a new page; e-mail address changes	programs.html, calendar.html; mission.html; news.html; events.html; workshop.html; publications.html; links.html; faq.html; stuff.html; gallery.html; links to Cal U and the AAA
Programs and services	programs.html	As needed	Adding or deleting a new program or service	gallery.html; clinic.html (calendar_H.html); ADC video clip
Calendar	calendar.html	Monthly		download Adobe Acrobat Reader; PDF files
Mission statement	mission.html	As needed		
What's New?	news.html	As needed	Better be checked monthly	
Upcoming Events	events.html	Monthly		oak.html
Workshops	workshops.html	As needed	Better be checked monthly to add or change	
Publications	publications.html	As needed	A new publication; contact person changes	
Links	links.html	As needed	A new link	Menu of links
FAQs	faq.html	As needed	New questions	
Staff	staff.html	As needed	Changes in personnel	
Photos	gallery.html	As needed	Changes in photos	
Health Clinic Calendar	calendar_H.html	Monthly		

13 *Letters and Reports*

Technical writers routinely write a variety of business documents. This chapter describes and illustrates strategies and formats for several common types of business letters and reports.

13.1 ▷— AMA Letter Format

Pittsburgh Telemax uses the American Management Association (AMA) block-style format for business letters (Box 13.1).

Some of the potential features of business letters are not visible in Box 13.1. Here are some additional possibilities:

▲ 1. Page Numbering

Letters that run more than one page require page numbering. At Telemax, writers place the numbering at the top left, preceded by the reader's name and the date:

> Fred Jones
> January 23, 2000
> Page 2

▲ 2. The Salutation

The salutation is the formal greeting: Dear Mr. Jones. If you don't know the name of the person who will be reading your letter, you should make every effort to find out. If necessary, call the organization and ask: "Who's in charge of such and such?" If finding a name is impossible, you may be able to use a generic title instead:

> Dear Sales Representative:

A modern way of dealing with this problem is to simply leave out the salutation altogether. When business writers do that, they sometimes emphasize the **Re:** line by boldfacing it or printing it in a slightly larger font size, as in Box 13.2.

BOX 13.1 ▼ **AMA Block Style**

8000 Boulevard of the Allies,
Suite 4
Pittsburgh, PA 15219-3555
(414) 555-8972
hstone@pittsburghtelemax.com

July 2, 1999

Dr. Marcus Dunlevey
Associate Dean of Liberal Arts
Pumpkinville College
Pumpkinville, OH 44102-8899

Re: Our presentation on the **Communicator DL 1000** system at Pumpkinville College

Dear Dr. Dunlevey:

This letter is to confirm our visit to your campus next Wednesday, July 28, at 2:00 to make a PowerPoint presentation on the Telemax Communicator DL 1000 system. We hope that all the members of the Campus Computer Committee will be able to attend.

The presentation will last about thirty minutes, after which a Telemax technician will answer technical questions.

We look forward to meeting with your committee.

Respectfully,

Howard Stone
President, Pittsburgh Telemax

MM/pmw

▲ 3. The Closing

The model letter uses *Respectfully* for its polite closing line. Other possibilities include *Sincerely, Sincerely yours, Best regards,* and *Yours truly.* Note that in two-word expressions the second word is not capitalized.

After the polite closing line, leave four or five blank lines for a signature; then type the sender's name.

▲ *4. Writer's and Typist's Initials*

A technical writer may be asked to draft a letter for a superior. For instance, Marge Mendoza wrote the letter from Howard Stone that appears in Box 13.1.

When the person writing the letter is someone other than the person signing it, the writer's initials follow the closing in upper case, as in Box 13.1 (*MM* for Marge Mendoza). When the person typing the letter is someone other than the person signing the letter, the typist's initials follow the closing in lower case, also as in Box 13.1 (*pmw* for Pat Maynard Walcomb). These initials keep track of who was involved in the production of a document. Some organizations always put the writer's initials after the closing, even if the signer and the writer are the same person. Telemax forgoes that superfluous initialing.

▲ *5. Other Post-Closing Information*

The letters *cc* followed by one or more names indicate that copies of the letter are going to those people. The letters *cc* used to mean "carbon copy" from the days of typewriters; they now mean "courtesy copy." Example:

Sincerely,

George Waite

George Waite
cc   Fred Humes
    Mary Spigott

When sending a copy privately to someone not on the *cc* list, use *Bcc* (blind carbon copy), followed by the person's name at the bottom of the private copy only, below the *cc* list.

Enc. or *Enclosure* indicates that other material is included in the envelope and that the receiver should look for it.

P.S., meaning "Post Script," introduces a note on a subject other than the ones covered in the body of the letter.

Letters and Reports

13

ASSIGNMENTS FOR 13.1

1. *Analyze a Letter* One way to study business letter format is to note the variations that arise in actual business letters. Obtain an actual business letter (not a sales letter) from your mail or elsewhere and compare its format with the AMA format shown in Box 13.1. In a memo to your instructor, detail the similarities and differences. Include a photocopy of your letter.

2. *Practice Letter* Demonstrate your knowledge of business letter format by writing a letter to your instructor requesting a letter of recommendation. In the first part, identify yourself and make your request in general terms. In the second part, provide details for inclusion in the recommendation. In the third part, indicate where the recommendation should be sent, and by what deadline. Then thank your instructor.

13.2 >——— Routine Letters

Certain problems that require business letters arise repeatedly in the professional workplace, and business writers have worked out strategies for solving them. Technical writers should learn these strategies for basic business letters such as the request, the complaint, the response to a complaint, the good-news message, the bad-news message, and the sales letter.

The general organizational strategy for business letters is to visualize the content in three parts:

1. **The Beginning.** Orient the reader, first by identifying yourself, if necessary, in terms of your role in the situation: a customer, someone responding to a letter, someone seeking information. (Do not state your name.) Continue the orientation by indicating the general purpose of the letter, so that the reader knows why you are writing.

2. **The Middle.** Provide details. Include persuasive arguments, if appropriate.

3. **The End.** Tell the reader what you want the reader to do, or what you will do (this is called the "action statement"). Finish with a polite closing phrase, such as "I look forward to hearing from you."

Box 13.2 demonstrates this basic structure.

Most business communications call for a style that is mildly formal, without being stuffy. The tone should be polite, rational, and optimistic, regardless of the situation. In your first communication at least, assume that your reader is a rational, intelligent person of good will—even if you suspect otherwise. If necessary, you can adopt a cooler, more formal tone in later communications, but you should never stop being polite and reasonable.

Certain types of letters use specific strategies:

BOX 13.2 ▼ Complaint Letter Showing Three-Part Structure

October 27, 2000

682 Brewer Boulevard
Brownsville, PA 15417

Customer Service Department
Tinsoft Corporation
P.O. Box 987
Buffalo, NY 14240

Re: Request for missing contents of Tinsoft Workshop Plus package

1. Orientation	I am a Tinsoft customer who purchased Tinsoft Workshop Plus but got the Standard version instead.
2. Details Narrative	I purchased the Plus version in order to get the Tin Can database program, which I had heard was excellent. From the shelf of a bookstore, I selected a box whose cover stated that it contained Workshop Plus. Please examine the photocopied box cover attached to this letter. Note that an icon for Tin Can appears among the infographics representing the programs included. Note also that the box cover identifies the contents as the Plus version of Tinsoft Workshop, the version that includes Tin Can. When I opened the box at home, I found that it did not contain Tin Can, but a voucher for the program. I sent in the voucher, and in response I received a letter (enclosed) from your company saying that the voucher had expired.
Logical argument	When Tinsoft customers select a Tinsoft product from a retailer's shelf, they should have confidence that the package will contain what the cover on the box says it contains. That's a universal principle of trust between company and customer, one that both parties depend on and take for granted. The next time I try to purchase a Tinsoft product, how am I supposed to know what is inside the Tinsoft box, if I cannot rely on the cover? I can't take the box from the shelf and tear it open in the store to see if it contains any outdated vouchers.
3. Action statement	Please send me the contents missing from your Workshop Plus package—that is, the Tin Can database program. Thank you.

Sincerely,

Betty Moranda

Betty Moranda

Enclosures

▲ 1. Complaints

Supply enough information for the reader to assess your situation. Be precise. If complaining about a product, identify the product by its full name and, if it has one, its product number. Provide sufficient detail so that the person you are writing to can understand what happened and can identify those involved in any incident. If complaining to someone at a service company such as a heating oil company, supply your customer account number to make it easy for the reader to find the right file.

Keep your cool. Assume that the reader regrets your inconvenience and wants to rectify the situation.

Box 13.2 provides an example of a complaint letter.

▲ 2. Response to Complaints

If you are at fault, and you are not concerned about being sued, apologize at the beginning and again at the end of the letter. Do not make excuses, but describe how the problem arose and what you are doing to guarantee that it doesn't occur again. At the beginning or the end, state what you will do for the reader to make things right.

If you are not at fault, do not apologize. Commiserate. Express regret that your reader has a problem. Be helpful, if you can. If appropriate, direct the reader to someone who can solve the reader's problem.

Box 13.3 shows two different responses to the same complaint.

▲ 3. Requests

As part of your orientating statement, make your request in general terms. In the middle, provide persuasive arguments for fulfilling the request. In the middle and final sections, supply details that will help your reader fulfill the request. In the final section, make it clear what you want the reader to do. If time is a factor, mention any deadline that you have to meet and, therefore, that the reader has to meet.

Except for very routine requests ("please send me a copy of your free catalog"), you should try to use the *you-* or *we-*perspective. (See section 4.4 for an explanation of these terms.) Never demand or complain in a request letter.

Box 13.4 provides an example of a request letter.

▲ 4. Good-News Messages

Always state the good news up front; don't make the reader wait for it. State your pleasure at being able to pass on this good news. In the middle, provide details about the good news. When praising someone, details make you sound sincere. If appropriate, work in a sales pitch for your company.

BOX 13.3 ▼   **Two Responses to a Complaint**

Admitting Fault

Orienting statement, which includes an initial apology and the good-news statement

We apologize for the inconvenience that our voucher program caused you. You will be receiving a copy of Tinsoft in the next few days, at no charge.

Admission of error and what the company is doing to correct the situation

You are right that the packaging of our Tinsoft Workshop, at that time, was flawed in that it could lead a customer to believe that a copy of Tin Can was included in the box. We have since become more sensitive to the implications of text and icons on our packages.

A final apology and a soft sales pitch (the mollified reader might now view the company with respect)

Again, we apologize for your inconvenience, and we hope that you will continue to consider Tinsoft products for your computing needs.

Rejecting a Complaint

Orienting statement with expression of sympathy, but no apology

We regret that you have been inconvenienced by our voucher program, which was used to introduce the Tin Can database program during its first months on the market. However, we cannot provide you with a free copy of Tin Can.

Explanation of how the customer is wrong

You are right that the packaging of our Tinsoft Workshop, at that time, used the phrase "Tinsoft Workshop Plus" and displayed an icon representing Tin Can. However, the package also displayed, in a prominent boxed paragraph, a statement that the package contained a voucher for the Tin Can program that was "good through June 1999."

A second expression of sympathy, followed by the bad news, followed by a solution to the problem (discount purchase of the program)

We are sorry if you overlooked that notice when you made your purchase. However, we cannot give away a program that we now sell to the general public. If you would like to purchase Tin Can, we will sell it to you direct, at a cost below retail. Please send $125.00 to our sales manager, James Harlow, and he will promptly mail you a copy of the program.

Polite sign-off, which consists of a third expression of sympathy, followed by a soft sales pitch

Again, we regret any misunderstanding or inconvenience. We hope that you will continue to consider Tinsoft products for your computer needs.

13 **Letters and Reports**

BOX 13.4 ▼   A Request Letter

Dear Dean Morganstein:

Orienting (identifying) statement includes the request in general terms	I am a graduating senior at Pumpkinville College, majoring in journalism. At the moment I am finishing up a full-semester internship at the *Miami Herald*. When I return this spring, I would like to get your permission to make a course substitution in order to graduate at the end of the spring semester.
Details of the request	Specifically, I need to substitute Article Writing II for a required course, Ethics in Journalism, which is offered only in the fall. I missed Ethics this fall because of the internship. I realize how important professional ethics are, and therefore I intend to write articles on that subject in the Article Writing II course, if you allow me to take it as a substitute.
You perspective	I have a job offer to start in June at the *Miami Herald*, one of our nation's greatest newspapers, provided I graduate on time. I know that Pumpkinville College is proud of the achievements of its students and likes to advertise their success. Surely a journalism student landing a job at a newspaper like the *Miami Herald* makes our journalism program look good.
Polite sign-off followed by a deadline	Thank you for considering my request. During the week before final spring registration begins, I will stop by your office to find out your decision.

You may need to qualify the good news or to include some bad news as part of the whole message. Save that for the middle or last section, and then restate the good news at the very end so that the text finishes on a positive note.

Box 13.5 provides an example of a good-news message.

▲ 5. Bad-News Messages

When the reader is expecting your letter and knows that it will bring either good or bad news, present the bad news immediately. For example, "Thank you for interviewing for the junior technical writer position at Pittsburgh Telemax. Unfortunately, we cannot offer you a position at this time." Then provide an explanation for the bad news: "Several of the other applicants were already experienced in the kind of technical writ-

BOX 13.5 ▼ Good News-Bad News Messages

<table>
<tr>
<td></td>
<td>

Good News

Dear Ms. Ciampi:

</td>
</tr>
<tr>
<td>Good news up front</td>
<td>We accept your bid to create new manuals for our SBD line of security systems.</td>
</tr>
<tr>
<td>Reminder of the details of the agreement</td>
<td>For a fee of $6500, you will update the existing two manuals and create a third manual for our new guard-dog training program. The work will begin on October 12, 2000. You will submit an interim draft of all three manuals for review on or before November 21, 2000. You will submit the final version of all three manuals on or before December 20, 2000.</td>
</tr>
<tr>
<td>Action statement</td>
<td>Please report to Angela Davis at our New York office on October 12. She will provide you with the old manuals and will arrange for you to interview appropriate personnel.</td>
</tr>
<tr>
<td>Action statement</td>
<td>Please confirm your intention to undertake this job by calling or e-mailing Ms. Davis within the next few days.</td>
</tr>
</table>

<table>
<tr>
<td></td>
<td>

Bad News

Dear Mr. Gumble:

</td>
</tr>
<tr>
<td>Orientation

Buffer describing the requirements the reader is not meeting</td>
<td>Thank you for participating in Northern Tallahassee Hospital's puppy visit program. Our patients look forward to these visits. The puppies soothe those who are suffering and reduce the stress of illness. Because puppies are small and their bite weak, patients can hold them without fear of being hurt, even though the dogs are still teething. That is an important consideration.</td>
</tr>
<tr>
<td>Bad news in detail</td>
<td>We have enjoyed the company of your dog, Thunderwolf. However, at forty pounds, he is getting too big for our program. He doesn't quite know his strength, and his bite broke the skin of an elderly patient last week.</td>
</tr>
<tr>
<td>Action statement providing an upbeat closure</td>
<td>Please reapply for our puppy visit program the next time you acquire a small puppy. Thanks again for your contribution.</td>
</tr>
</table>

13 Letters and Reports

ing we do at Telemax, so we have hired one of them." If the reader is not expecting bad news, begin with a buffer. A buffer is not so much a delaying tactic as a means of creating a context that will make the bad news seem reasonable, perhaps inevitable, and possibly not the fault of the writer or reader: "As you know, our profits have been declining for two years now. Like many companies, we need to cut back on recently hired staff. Therefore, regretfully, we cannot renew your contract for next year." If appropriate, try to be helpful: "Our Human Resources Department can help you find a new position, and I will write you a strong recommendation."

See Box 13.5 for an example of a bad-news message.

▲ *6. Sales Letters*

A sales letter is a persuasive message sent to potential customers to persuade them to try your product or service. Such letters also go out to

FIGURE 13.1 ▼ Sales Letter for a Product

TOTAL COMPUTER
Your complete microcomputer supplier

March 15, 2000

"The Internet Takes Forever!"

If that's how you feel, it's probably time to update your computer system.

Yet you're also probably frustrated by the fact that the computer you bought just three years ago needs to be updated. We've got an answer to that.

Introducing...

Free Update

of any TC100 computer bought between March 15 and May 1, 2000

If you buy a TC100 computer from us before May 1, we'll update the memory and processor speed for free in the year 2002. Come to the store for details, or send in the enclosed certificate to reserve your TC100 and get a full written explanation of our creative new approach to keeping you up-to-date at no cost.

Total Computer
1134 Market Street
Heidelburg Beach, FL 33141
(305) 555-7865   Open 9–9 Mon–Sat

existing customers or contributors to maintain their loyalty and interest, and to past customers or contributors to attempt to win them back. Here are some guidelines for content:

▌ *Possibilities for the Beginning:* Many people automatically toss away sales letters without reading them. In the beginning section, therefore, you need to grab the reader's attention and interest. You may have only a second or two to succeed, so begin with a statement about your product or service, or about the reader's needs, designed to make the reader want to continue reading. You can highlight your attention grabber by setting it off dramatically. The model letters in Figures 13.1 and 13.2 both use attention grabbers.

FIGURE 13.2 ▼ **Sales Letter Seeking a Donation**

ELK HOLLOW PUBLIC LIBRARY
R.D. 6 Elk Hollow, PA 15378 (414) 555-4567

March 28, 2000

Dear Friend of the Library:

A MAJOR LIBRARY PROGRAM IS SINKING—WE'RE REACHING FOR YOUR HAND!

Your support has made a difference in the past and it can do so again. Thanks to you and other regular contributors, we now bring in the new best sellers as soon as they make the *NY Times* list. We have adult reading classes and we have a reading program for children.

Unfortunately, the children's program is at risk!

Our reading instructor, Mary Tobbs, who was doing this work for no pay, has retired. We have not been able to find a volunteer with the appropriate background, and we are going to have to hire someone—or drop the program!

In addition to your regular contribution of $50, we are asking for an additional $25 this year to specifically finance the children's reading program. Last year, this program:

• Helped 14 children with reading difficulties improve 2 or more grade levels.
• Helped 5 non-readers get started on the road to reading.

As you know, a child who is significantly behind in reading will almost certainly fail in school. These are the children of our own small community, and we don't want any of them to become losers when it comes to education!

Please fill out the enclosed information card and send me your check for $75 made out to the Elk Hollow Public Library. The children and I thank you!

—Louise Bellsworth, Library Director

13 Letters and Reports

■ *Possibilities for the Middle:* Promote your product or service, showcasing its worth. Dispel any worries or objections that might occur to readers.

■ *Possibilities for the End:* Tell your readers what you will do for them and/or what you want them to do. For example:

To get a month's free sample, fill in the enclosed card and mail it before July 1.

Sales letters, because of their enthusiastic tone, may seem undisciplined; however, there's more control behind them than one might think. Here are some guidelines for effective sales letters:

■ Analyze your audience. Determine who your likely clients are. Focus on what will appeal to them. Don't try to appeal to the whole world.

■ Don't libel your competition. That can turn off prospective customers. Use a serious tone when making accurate comparisons between your product and competing products.

■ Don't mention the shortcomings of your products or services. Stay positive. At the same time, don't deceive the reader about what you're selling. Don't make offers your company can't fulfill.

Figures 13.1 and 13.2 provide examples of two kinds of sales letters.

ASSIGNMENTS FOR 13.2

1. *Request Letter Scenarios*   Respond to one of these request scenarios.

   a. Write a letter to one of your instructors requesting that you be allowed to take an exam late because, as secretary of the Business Club, you feel obligated to attend the annual club trip to a conference in Bimini, and the date of this conference conflicts with the exam date.

   b. Your fictional company has just received a very large order from your state government and you will need to get some supplies or parts on credit. (Invent details.) Unfortunately, as a matter of policy, your supplier doesn't give credit. Write a letter to your supplier asking for credit for this order. Use the *we*-perspective.

2. *Complaint and Response-to-Complaint Scenarios*   Respond to one or the other of these paired complaint and response-to-complaint scenarios.

   a. You just bought a computer screen saver, Puppies at Play, for your computer at work at a price of $15.00, and you are dissatisfied with the product. The program has no timing control, and the pictures flash on the screen in sequence, one after another, much too rapidly. You don't get to enjoy the pictures. If you had known that the pictures were timed this way, you would not have purchased this screen saver. You want a full refund. Write an e-mail message to the company from which you purchased the product, asking how you should proceed to return it. You purchased it by visiting the company's Web site, entering your credit card number, and then downloading the program. The company's name is Computer Planet, at **www.complanet.com**.

b. As the owner and sole employee of Computer Planet, you have received the complaint letter mentioned in the previous assignment. The customer purchased one of your inexpensive screen savers, which indeed has no timing control. Only your $30 savers allow users to control the timing of the pictures. That fact is stated in the paragraph in the Web ad describing and contrasting the features of the $15 and $30 models. To avoid customer disappointment, you allow those who visit your Web site to test the screen savers in advance of buying them. Because the customer downloaded the product, the product cannot be returned and you cannot give a refund. Write an e-mail message in response to the complaint refusing to grant the refund.

c. You were asked to recommend specs and a local vendor for new computers for the five secretaries in your building. After conducting a product comparison study, you recommended the CC100 model from a local outfit, DigiMaster. A week after installation, two of the hard drives crashed, resulting, in one case, in the loss of data. Write a complaint letter to DigiMaster. Be clear about what you want the company to do.

d. As the manager of DigiMaster, you received the complaint letter mentioned in the previous assignment. Admitting fault, write a response.

3. *Good-News Scenarios* Respond to one of these good-news scenarios.

a. As the DDM for Telemax, you are pleased to inform Sally Bryant, president of EcoCore, that you will be able to give EcoCore, at no charge, a revised and improved version of the documentation for your TeleTalk I teleconferencing system, which EcoCore is using. Your staff did this revision after field-testing the old documentation at EcoCore's site. In addition, you will soon be offering online documentation for this product—also at no charge. Write the good-news letter.

b. After interviewing five good candidates, you have selected Billie Lazzaro as your new junior technical writer. Write Lazzaro a good-news letter informing her of your decision. Provide her with details about when to show up to work and who to report to. Request a letter of intent on her part indicating whether she wishes to accept your offer.

4. *Bad-News Scenarios* Respond to one of these bad-news scenarios.

a. As the DDM for a high-tech company in your area, you run a summer internship program for college students studying to become technical writers. You generally hire two college students who will be seniors next year to work on updating documentation for a product undergoing an upgrade to a new version. This is a complex activity, since every small change in the product requires many changes in the documentation. You are flustered, then, when your best friend's daughter, Jennifer Lacross, applies for the job. Jennifer just completed her sophomore year as an art major. Judging by her resume and cover letter, she writes adequately for a college student, but not at the professional level you require from interns working on a real project. From the tone of her letter, she seems confident that you will hire her. Write a letter to Jennifer, whom you know well enough to address by her first name, rejecting her for the position. Don't treat this as a routine rejection of a job application. Use a buffer, creating a context for the bad news.

b. A freelance proofreader, Lemar Lutz, left a number of errors in one of your company's manuals (invent details). You had an informal arrangement with Lutz for another project, but no contract has yet been signed. Write Lutz a letter explaining why you will not be using his services in the future.

c. You have been assigned to evaluate a newly hired technical writer, Herbie Starbuck, who, you learn, does a great job in producing text but has some personal habits that are starting to irritate others. Starbuck doesn't listen well at meetings, he tries to push his own views too strongly, and he shows less than full respect for older managers when talking behind their backs. (Invent additional or alternative details of your own, if you wish.) Write an evaluation, in memo form, addressed to the department head, Jan Wu, with a copy to Starbuck.

5. *Create a Sales Letter for a Product* Create a sales letter for a product made by your fictional company, or choose a fictional product and company from this list:

a. A do-it-yourself professional hair curler from the Home Hair Care Co.

b. A set of knives from Total Kitchen

c. A fireplace screen from American Log Fires

d. A tree, a bush, grass sod, or flowers for landscaping from Greg's Garden

e. An automobile seat cover from Wheels Ahead

   f. A flea collar from Pet Please

   g. An exotic beer from Suds City

   h. A walking shoe from What's Afoot

   i. A child-care video from Marriage, Inc.

   j. A piece of computer software from the SoftSell Co.

   k. A poetry series from Literati Publishers

   l. A high-powered bullet from His & Hers Ammo

   m. A leather-bound Ranch Bible from Christian Country Products

6. *Create a Sales Letter Appealing for Donations* Write a sales letter appealing for donations to your favorite cause or a fictional cause. This list may inspire you:

   a. Save the Florida Salt Water Crocodile

   b. Buy and Preserve American Desert Land

   c. Research to Defeat the Common Cold

   d. Books for Prisoners

   e. Guns for Kutjurzians

   f. Adopt a Village in Sumariland

   g. Help Our Local Tornado Victims

   h. Homes for the Homeless

13.3 >—— Report Formats and Organizational Plans

Sometimes technical writers find themselves participating in the writing of long reports. Such documents can run to book length or even many volumes. The primary author is usually an engineering manager or a business manager or some other SME. The technical writer as "professional writer" may be called in for polishing or document design.

In a book like this one we do not have room to explore the long report in detail, but we can make a few points about it. First, we define the long report as one of sufficient size and complexity that it has a table of contents. Two common types are the final report on research and the feasibility study. Both often follow the problem-solution organizational pattern (Box 13.6). Research reports also frequently use the scientific organizational pattern (Box 13.7).

BOX 13.6   ▼   A Problem-Solution Structure for Long Reports

1. Background to Problem or Need
   • Where the problem or need occurs
   • Causes
   • Consequences of not solving the problem or meeting the need

2. False Solutions
   • Solutions that have failed, and why
   • Solutions that might be anticipated but will fail, and why

3. Your Solution

4. Why Your Solution Will Work

5. Plan for Implementation, Including Estimated Budget

Note: This structure is also useful for internal proposals to improve an organization.

BOX 13.7   ▼   A Scientific Structure for Long Reports

1. Introduction
   • A review of related studies
   • Statement of the hypothesis
   • Discussion of the value of your research

2. Procedures
   • Description of the instruments used
   • Description of human participants, if any
   • The story of what you did to gather information

3. Results
   • Presentation of quantifiable data (often in tables)
   • Report on qualitative (non-numerical) information

4. Conclusions
   • Interpretation of results
   • Recommendations for action or further study

ASSIGNMENT FOR 13.3

1. *Examine a Long Report* Examine the table of contents (TOC) of a long report and write a short memo report to your instructor about it. What kinds of front and back matter does it include? Looking only at its TOC, determine whether or not the report follows a problem-solution pattern. If so, what is the evidence? If not, what organizational plan does it seem to follow?

13.4 >—— Routine Short Reports

Short reports are sometimes called "memo reports" when they are formatted as memos. They have the usual memo heading, followed by one or more pages of text. However, some short reports partially imitate long reports at the beginning in that they have a title page and even a preface or formal introduction.

The immediate audience for short reports is usually your supervisor, although higher authorities may have to approve any recommendations that you make and others in the organization may have to carry out those recommendations. Write for all relevant audiences. As with long reports, make the organization of your short report modular, with headings for each section.

The sections below describe specific kinds of short reports.

▲ 1. The Incident Report

Many organizations require incident reports whenever there is a serious accident, an unusual breakdown of machinery, or any other unfortunate, unforeseen occurrence.

First you investigate the incident at the site; then you write the report.

You begin the report by answering the "journalist's questions": Who, What, Where, When, and How. You then make a judgment about fault, determining whether any person or process is to blame. In the concluding section, you make recommendations about what your organization should do to handle the present situation and to avoid this problem in the future.

▲ 2. The Work Report

Unlike the incident report, which deals with unusual events, the work report focuses on normal work activities and their outcomes. Whenever police officers make an arrest, for example, they must fill out a "police report," which is a kind of work report. A police report records the circumstances of the arrest, including interviews with witnesses. Such reports are an important part of the effort to successfully prosecute criminals.

Compliance reports are another kind of work report. A civil engineer working as a city employee who monitors housing and commercial development around a lake, for example, would regularly submit reports detailing whether or not the various construction companies are compliant with environmental laws.

Work reports often follow templates. They involve a fill-in-the-blanks or fill-in-the-boxes kind of writing. Box 13.8 shows an Adult Day-Care Center daily report. The use of a template reduces the possibility that the recorder will leave out any required information.

▲ 3. The Product Comparison Report

Purchases within organizations usually require a product comparison to make sure that the right product is being purchased at the best price. Let's suppose that your company needs another multimedia projector for sales presentations. As a technical writer between projects, you have been

BOX 13.8 ▼ Routine Work Report

DAILY CARE REPORT

Date: *April 4, 2000*

Participant: *Evelyn Coopers*

Recorder: *Josh McDaniel*   **Position:** *ADC Director*

Observation:

She seems fine. Her health seems stable. As usual, she had difficulty concentrating on one activity for very long. However, she did stay in the Jeopardy game for 30 minutes, the longest she has participated to date. She enjoyed doing housework and being in the garden. She didn't want to go home when Cathy came to pick her up (it took 20 minutes to convince her to get in the car).

Arrival:	*9:00 Dave (her son) drove her.*
Pickup:	*4:00 Cathy (her daughter-in-law) picked her up.*
Rx:	*Coumadin at lunch; Laxative at lunch*
Blood pressure:	*10 am 180/100; 3 pm 185/110*
Bathroom:	*11:00 am, 1:00 pm, 3:30 pm*
Meals:	*Lunch—tomato soup, chicken salad sandwich, and lemon pudding Snack—a glass of ginger ale and 3 sugar cookies*
Activities:	*Participated in the Jeopardy game for 30 minutes; folded washed towels; talked with Barb (activity volunteer) about her childhood; walked in the garden area and watched volunteers planting vegetables.*

assigned to make a product comparison report. Your first step would be to create a product comparison table to help you clearly see the alternatives. This table would become part of your report.

To make a product comparison table, you would follow this procedure:

1. Develop a list of desired features, based on interviews with the sales personnel.
2. Create a list of products to compare by perusing catalogs or visiting office equipment stores.
3. Put the names of the products in the stub of a table (i.e., in the leftmost column), and list the features in the column headings across the top of the table.
4. Fill in the matrices of the table.

See Table 7.1 in Chapter 7 for an example of a product comparison table.

Having made your decision about which product you will recommend, you would then write the report, following this organization:

Executive Summary   An executive summary is a short section at the beginning of a report meant to be read by the decision maker. This may be the only part of the product comparison report your supervisor reads before signing off on the purchase, especially if the purchase is minor and your supervisor trusts your judgment. The summary should consist of a statement of the problem and your recommendation, including cost. You might also want to add a brief statement justifying your decision:

> Our sales staff needs another multimedia projector to carry out its increased number of on-site sales presentations. Roger Williams asked me to make a recommendation for this purchase. After examining five popular projectors, I recommend the Maximus DT 9450 at a cost of $4,955. The Maximus is highly portable and relatively inexpensive, with adequate features for the job.

Description of the Products   Begin with any products that are unacceptable. State why they are so. Move from the least desirable to the most desirable, ending with a description of the product you recommend. Describe the products in terms of how their features meet the requirements. Indicate which products could serve the purpose, in case your supervisor, for whatever reason, doesn't want to purchase the one you recommend. Refer to the table as early in the section as possible.

Conclusion and Recommendation   Your conclusion is your interpretation of the data gathered. You might conclude that system B is as good as system A but less expensive. Explain why it is as good a system. Or you might conclude that system C is only slightly more expensive than all the others, but offers many more useful features. Explain why the features are useful.

Your recommendation tells the reader what to do. There should be a logical connection between your conclusions and your recommendation. Don't praise one product to the hilt and then recommend another.

▲ 4. The Internal Proposal

Despite the word *proposal,* an internal proposal begins as a report on a problem, which you then follow up with a proposed solution. It has more in common with short reports than with the external proposals described in Chapter 8, so we discuss it here. The problem-solution approach shown in Box 13.6 works well for this kind of persuasive report. Box 13.9 provides an example of an internal proposal.

In problem-solution argumentation, you may wish to emphasize your understanding of the nature of the problem rather than the solution. Often, once the problem has been defined, the solution is obvious. For example, suppose a department isn't working efficiently. If the problem is lack of personnel, the solution is to bring in more people; if the problem is inadequate equipment, the solution is to get more equipment. In that kind of situation, once you have convinced your readers that your interpretation of the problem is accurate, you can usually get them to accept your solution.

In other instances, everyone might agree on the nature of the problem and the importance of the problem, but disagree on the best solution. Then your argument would focus on why your solution would work and why other solutions wouldn't. In still other instances, you may have to do both: argue for your interpretation of the problem and then argue for your solution over others. When planning your proposal, begin by determining which of those approaches you should pursue.

▲ 5. The Progress Report

If you are engaged in a long project, your original timetable for completion will probably include the submission of progress reports at specified intervals. If not, submit such reports anyway. Progress reports usually go only up the hierarchy. That creates a problem because everyone involved in a project, not just the bosses, should be kept informed of the status of the project. To solve that problem at Telemax, Louis Frapp has developed a Project Status Table (Table 13.1), based on a table developed by G. Lanyi (1994). Frapp sends this Project Status Table via interoffice mail to

BOX 13.9 ▼ **Internal Proposal**

To: Dean Schuler
From: J. Powel
Date: March 16, 2000
Re: The need for a new printer in the English Department
         Computer Classroom

Location of the problem

The new computer classroom in Victory Hall is working out very well. The teachers are developing new teaching methods day by day, and the students, according to a recent survey, strongly support lab classes in English.

General nature of the problem and the consequences of not solving it

However, we are having a problem with printing that threatens to seriously limit the whole lab-classroom approach to writing courses.

The Problem

Detailed explanation of the problem

Our lab classroom has only one printer. Although it is a large laser printer that prints very quickly, it cannot keep up with the demand. As the close of each class approaches, many students begin to print their documents at the same time. This creates a queue. Adding to the problem is the fact that our lab is on the university network, which means that students in other labs can—and do—access our printer, creating further delays in printing.

Detailed explanation of the consequences of not solving the problem

Students in the Victory Hall lab sometimes find themselves waiting ten minutes for their papers to emerge from the printer. Many of them have to choose between being late for their next class or failing to collect their work and turn it in to the professor, who may have to leave to teach elsewhere.

Proposed Solution

A false solution that might be imagined and why it won't work, and a false solution that has been tried without success

We could remove the Victory Hall printer from the university network, but that would eliminate access to the Internet. The Internet is too important a research tool to give up. We have tried arranging for lab workers to collect papers and take them to professors' mailboxes, but that approach has not been dependable.

The proposed solution

I recommend that the university purchase a small, $400 laser printer that we could attach to the professor's computer in the lab, off the network. When the big printer gets overloaded, students who are not yet in the queue can print individually at the professor's computer.

Why the proposed solution will work

We borrowed a printer from the English Department office and tried out this solution in one composition class and it worked.

TABLE 13.1   ▼   Project Status Table

Manuals for Communicator III+ Project Status Table
Work Completion Dates (1999)

	Plan	1st Draft	Review	2nd Draft	Editing	Final Review
Installation Manual	Feb 16	Apr 6	Apr 12	May 12	May 16	May 20
System Maintenance Manual	Feb 14	Apr 12	Apr 25	May 3	May 18	
Module Manuals	Feb 19	Apr 14	Apr 23			
Instrument User's Guide	Feb 28	Apr 22	May 1	May 17		

project participants on a regular basis. The dates in the table represent the completion of various stages for each manual. For example, as the table shows, the Installation Manual was finished on May 20, but the Module Manuals haven't yet progressed beyond the review of the first draft.

Progress reports that go up the hierarchy typically follow this organizational pattern:

1. a description of where you stand in the overall project, in terms of whether or not you are on schedule

2. a description of any problems that need to be addressed (such as a lack of cooperation from departments whose input you rely on)

3. a description of what your next steps will be.

You should also include decisions that have been made, early results, and any other information that your reader wants to have as early as possible.

Progress reports have an important CYA function, as Lanyi points out:

> The fact that you routinely communicate with your superiors about these matters is no substitute for progress reports. People's memories tend to fail them miserably when suddenly you are called on the carpet by the powers that be and someone has to take the blame for a delay. (1994, p. 87)

▲ 6. The Trip Report

There are many reasons for which you may have to travel on company time, at company expense. For example, you may travel to meet with customers or business partners, to examine or exhibit products at trade shows, or to attend educational conferences or workshops. For any such travel, you will probably be required to submit a trip report upon your return.

Your trip report communicates what you accomplished or learned. At a trade show, you may convince new distributors to handle your product line, or you may discover that a competitor has a new product with attractive features that your product lacks, or you may pick up gossip about industry trends, or you may meet a vendor who can supply your company with parts at a more attractive price than you are now paying. At a convention, you may learn about new, experimental processes or products under development that would be useful to your company. At a conference, you may encounter new theoretical ideas or hear about recent research in your profession. At a workshop, you may learn practical skills of use to your professional work.

Writing a trip report is a way of sharing new information and ideas with your supervisor and with interested co-workers who did not make the trip.

Begin the report by describing when you traveled, where, and for what purposes. Then provide the details of what you learned that would be of interest to your readers. Conclude with recommendations, if appropriate. You may have to attach a record of your expenses.

ASSIGNMENTS FOR 13.4

1. *Incidence Report* As Director of Student Microcomputer Facilities at your school, you are the person whom student lab workers call whenever there is a breakdown of machinery or some other serious incident. Invent an incident and write up an incident report for your boss, the Director of Computer Services.

2. *Work Report* Recall a job that you have held, or consider any student job on campus, for which a routine work report might be useful. Create a template for such a report.

3. *Product Comparison* Your office needs one of these items: filing cabinet, L-shaped secretarial desk, answering machine, or an item of your own selection. Your supervisor, Len Zuber, has asked you to do the necessary research on this piece of office equipment and to present him with a product comparison report recommending a purchase. Write a report compar-

ing three brands on the basis of at least four important characteristics, including price. Use catalogues, visit stores, talk to secretaries—do whatever you have to do—to obtain your data. For your report, create a table and refer to it in your text.

4. *Internal Proposal* Write a memo report addressed to one of your instructors proposing an improvement in a course you are taking, or have taken, from that teacher. Use the problem-solution approach. Submit the report to your technical writing instructor.

5. *Progress Report* Write a progress report on a project you are doing (or have done) this semester. Assume that you are halfway through with the project. Address your memo report to the instructor for whom you are doing the report, but submit it to your technical writing instructor. If you are not engaged in a project this semester, think of an imaginary one and invent the details of your report.

6. *Trip Report* (a) Assume that you were sent by your fictional company to a national trade show in Miami to demonstrate one of your products through a slide show that you helped create. You were also there to look for distributors of this product. Write a trip report describing your degree of success. (b) Assume that you were sent by Pittsburgh Telemax to a workshop on a subject related to technical writing, such as cross-cultural communication or project management. Write a trip report describing what the workshop was like and what you learned that would be of interest to other employees, especially the technical writers, at Telemax. Refer to materials that you brought back with you. (You may have to do some research about the topic of the workshop in order to complete this assignment.)

14 *Job Search*

Technical writing is a hot profession. Positions are available, the starting salaries are high, and the future looks good. When searching for a job, however, you should look beyond the paycheck and signing bonus to the career path. This applies to everyone, not just technical writers. Some companies allow no advancement, and the technical writer (or graphic artist or Web designer or computer programmer) at these companies may be perceived as a low-level technician. It might make sense to take such a position in order to pay off college loans and get some experience to beef up your resume, but know what you are stepping into. If possible, when visiting for an interview, talk to other employees at the organization who are doing your kind of work. Ask how they like working there. If you're replacing someone, try to find out why he or she left. Don't be afraid to ask blunt questions during your interview. You have a right to know the whole score before you accept a job offer.

The rest of this chapter looks at the process of getting that job offer. Job search involves four processes:

1. finding job openings and places to send your application
2. preparing and sending a resume and cover letter
3. selling yourself during an interview
4. sending post-interview letters.

This chapter covers all those processes except interviewing. We recommend that you visit your school's placement office for interview tips and practice.

14.1 > Finding Job Opportunities

Personal contacts remain one of the best ways to get a job. Through conferences, internships, and summer work, you can get to know professionals working in your field. Also, take advantage of "friend of a friend" personal networks.

In the absence of personal contacts, you will have to find job opportunities on your own. The rest of this section discusses how you can do that using electronic and print resources.

▲ *1. Using Electronic Databases to Learn About Job Search*

The computer indexes available in most post-secondary school libraries can put you in touch with periodicals and books that will help you in your job search. By entering key words like **job search**, you can use those indexes to find articles in periodicals like the *National Business Employment Weekly* and *Job Choices* and to locate useful books on writing resumes and doing Internet job searches.

The Internet itself provides sites for learning about job search techniques, for gaining information about companies and professions, for finding job advertisements, and for connecting with job search companies. Here's an example of a learning site available at the time of this writing:

Resume Articles at **http://canada.careermosaic.com**

▲ *2. Job Ads in Print*

Your nearest big city publishes at least one newspaper with advertisements for jobs in various professions. At any large chain bookstore, you can buy newspapers from around the country. Trade journals in your profession also advertise jobs.

▲ *3. Job Ads on the Web*

Most major newspapers have a Web site that publishes a limited edition of the newspaper, including job ad pages. You can often guess the site address: **www.nytimes.com** (for the *New York Times*), **www.latimes.com**, **www.washingtonpost.com**, and so forth.

Box 14.1 shows some of the general Web sites that advertise jobs. In addition, you can find sites that advertise jobs for particular professions; Box 14.2 provides some examples. To find such sites, use search engines to search for key words related to your profession, such as **technical writer** or **professional communications jobs** or **nursing jobs**. (See Chapter 3 for a detailed discussion of Internet research.)

BOX 14.1 ▼ **General Job-Ad Sites**

JobTrack www.jobtrack.com
For students and recent college grads.

Career Center www.careers.org
For students and recent college grads. Includes internships.

America's Job Bank www.ajb.dni.us
Provides links with public employment services, employers' job sites, and a private placement agency's site of 706 listings.

NationJob Online Jobs Database www.nationjob.com
Lists various jobs by category in "Specialty Pages"

The Monster Board www.monster.com
Includes a section for entry-level jobs.

Yahoo Classified classifieds.yahoo.com

Helpwanted.com www.helpwanted.com

JobWeb www.jobweb.org

Job Bank USA www.jobbankusa.com

Monster Research Companies www.occ.com
A well-organized site with interesting articles on campus issues.

Career Mosaic www.careermosaic.com/cm/jobs.html
A unique site for college students with a writing clinic for resume writing. Includes job listings.

4Work www.4work.com
Includes jobs for volunteers, internships, and part-time jobs. Allows you to leave your e-mail address to be notified of job vacancies.

Careerpath news.careerpath.com
Lists the latest help-wanted ads from many newspapers.

Career Magazine www.careermag.com
Each day, downloads and indexes all of the job postings from the major Internet jobs newsgroups.

Federal Jobs Digest www.jobsfed.com
Provides updates on vacancies in federal government jobs.

Cool Works www.coolworks.com
Provides information on jobs in ski resorts, Club Med, cruise ships, and national parks.

Summer Jobs www.summerjobs.com/do
Not limited to summer jobs.

Job Smart www.jobsmart.org
A good site if you are looking for a job in California.

Career City www.careercity.com
Provides links to hundreds of other sites of interest to job seekers.

Job Hunt www.job-hunt.org

14 Job Search

BOX 14.2 ▼ Examples of Jobs by Major

Bio Online's Career Center bio.com/hr
For biology majors.

100 Careers in Wall Street www.globalvillager.com/villager
For business majors.

Corporation for Public Broadcasting www.cpb.org/jobline
For communication/media majors.

Comrise Technology www.comrise.com/joblink.html
For computer science and technology majors, including engineers, system analysts, and programmers.

Westech Virtual Job Fair www.vjf.com
For computer science and technology majors.

Jobs Jobs Jobs www.jobsjobsjobs.com
For computer science and technology majors.

1-800 Network www.1800network.com
For computer science and technology majors.

Education Jobs Marketplace www.edjobs.com

Engineering Jobs www.engineeringjobs.com

Environmental Careers Organization www.eco.org
For environmental science majors. Includes internships and jobs.

MedSearch Healthcare Careers www.medsearch.com
For healthcare majors, such as nursing, therapy, and pharmacology.

Social Work and Social Services Jobs on Line gwbweb.wustl.edu/jobs
Social work majors.

▲ *4. Company Joblines*

Joblines are recorded phone messages that companies leave for job seekers. If you call an organization's jobline, the message will provide you with up-to-date information on job openings within that organization, including the necessary qualifications and who you should write to at what address.

A useful list of jobline phone numbers can be found in Marcia Williams and Sue Cubbage's book *The National Job Hotline Directory*. The authors list organizations by state as well as by profession. The 1998 edition of their book provides about 6,000 phone numbers.

ASSIGNMENTS FOR 14.1

1. *Find a Print Advertisement* Find a job ad or internship opportunity from a print source. Choose one that you could logically apply for now or upon graduation. Submit the advertisement to your instructor along with a statement of how you meet, or will meet, the qualifications called for in the advertisement.

2. *Find a Web Advertisement* Do assignment 14.1(1), but find an advertisement on the Web.

3. *Use a Company Job-line* Find a company jobline and call the number. Write down the job title and required qualifications for a job that interests you. Submit a memo report to your instructor.

14.2 >—— Preparing Your Resume

A resume is a summary of your qualifications that you submit in application for a job or job interview. (If you are completely unfamiliar with resumes, take a quick look at Box 14.3 before reading further.) You mail your resume, along with a cover letter (discussed in section 14.3), to an employer in response to a job advertisement or any clue you may have about a job opening. You can also post your resume on Web sites designed for that purpose; such sites are routinely perused by companies in search of employees, especially for high-tech jobs.

Many companies advertise on the Internet, and many can receive resumes electronically.

The printed resume should be neatly produced on high-quality white paper using a laser printer. Busy resume readers look for reasons to reject an application, so make sure there are no proofreading or grammatical errors in your resume.

Resumes usually run one or two pages, though professionals with wide experience may justifiably produce longer documents. The standard telegraphic style for resumes encourages brevity. The traditional resume should use sentence fragments beginning with strong verbs: *Maintained, Managed, Supervised, Administered, Evaluated, Created, Initiated, Installed, Increased, Produced, Improved, Developed, Modernized, Launched, Conducted, Sold, Operated, Wrote, Published, Delivered, Scheduled, Negotiated, Solved,* and so forth.

Noun phrases are also effective: *Memberships: French Club, Student Government, Sports Association.* In fact, in the scannable resume (discussed below in section 14.2[4]), strong nouns are preferable to strong verbs.

14 Job Search

BOX 14.3   ▼   Reverse-Chronological Resume: Strong School

Wendy Smith

214 Elm Street, East Rutland, VT 05701
(612) 555-9080 / wsmith@whammy.com

EDUCATION

Bachelor of Arts in English, 3.5 GPA
Holybroke College, East Rutland, VT

- Minor in computer science
- Took courses in database management and accounting
- Spent two summers in Europe, traveling extensively

COLLEGE ACTIVITIES

- Chair of the Computer Science panel at the Humanities Conference, senior year
- Student government representative, two years
- Residence Hall Council, one year
- President of Shakespeare Club, one year
- Treasurer of Phi Alpha Psi service sorority, three years
- First-string women's intercollegiate tennis team, three years

AWARDS AND HONORS

- Won prize for Best Composition, freshman year
- Recipient of Queenie Smith Scholarship for Women
- Nominated for English Major of the Year, junior year

EXPERIENCE

1996–1998   Black Bear Steak House, East Rutland, VT
             Waitress and cashier
             - Set up the restaurant's new computerized accounting
               and database system for a consulting fee

1995   Volunteer work: Rutland Recreation Committee
             - Organized summer activities for 6- to 10-year-olds
             - Helped arrange cultural events for the city

You may wish to create a general version of your resume to carry in the trunk of your car for distribution at opportune moments, for instance, when you run into someone at a picnic who is looking for a person with your qualifications). However, when responding to job advertisements, you should adjust your resume to fit the job. For example, the fact that you took two years of Spanish in college may not even show up in one version of your resume, but it would be highlighted in another version targeted for a summer job as a playground coordinator in a neighborhood with a large Spanish-speaking population.

BOX 14.4 ▼ **Reverse-Chronological Resume: Strong Work**

Larry Fernandez

980 Front Street
Albany, NY 12387
(453) 675-9076

OBJECTIVE: Management position working with animals

SUMMARY: Experienced pet store clerk. Junior-year environmental science major with management minor. Know how to keep books and records and how to manage workers.

WORK EXPERIENCE

1996–Present   Animal lab assistant for Biology Department, SUNY Albany
 • Helped students with animal experiments
 • Maintained lab animals

1992–1995   Clerk, Grindstone Pet Mart, Aldo, NY 13429
 • Performed all maintenance jobs required for a wide range of animals, including birds, cats, dogs, rabbits, snakes, lizards, and frogs.
 • Sold animals and pet care products.

1991–1993   Waiter, Butchy's Restaurant, Stewart, NY 13427

EDUCATION

Seventy-six credits toward degree in biology. Twelve credits in business. State University of New York, Albany. Courses taken include:
 • General zoology   • Business administration
 • Comparative vertebrate anatomy   • Accounting I and II
 • Ethology   • Marketing

HOBBY

Trained my Newfoundland for water trials; entered her in competitions.

Resumes can follow either of two organizational patterns: reverse-chronological (Boxes 14.3 and 14.4) or functional (Box 14.5). Both types are discussed below. Many applicants combine the two (as in Box 14.6).

▲ 1. Resume Headings and Initial Sections

Your heading should include your name (in big type), address, and phone number. If you are leaving college soon, provide a "permanent" address and phone number where you can be reached until you settle in elsewhere. If possible, include an e-mail address and fax number.

BOX 14.5 ▼ Functional Resume

Larry Fernandez

980 Front Street, Albany, NY 12387 (453) 675-9076

Goal: Pet Store Manager

ANIMAL EXPERTISE

Three years' experience in pet store:

- Maintained a variety of animals, including birds, cats, dogs, rabbits, snakes, lizards, and frogs.
- Sold animals and pet care products.

As a biology major (junior-year status), took courses in zoology, comparative vertebrate anatomy, and ethology

MANAGEMENT EXPERTISE

As management minor in college, took courses in

- Business administration
- Accounting I and II
- Marketing

EMPLOYMENT

1996–Present	Animal lab assistant in Biology Department, SUNY Albany
1992–1995	Clerk at Grindstone Pet Mart, 11 Hoover Way, Aldo, NY 13429
1991–1993	Waiter at Butchy's Restaurant, 453 McClellen Street, Stewart, NY 13427

EDUCATION

Seventy-six credits toward degree in biology. Twelve credits in business. State University of New York, Albany.

Beneath the heading you may wish to have an OBJECTIVE statement, indicating the kind of work you are looking for. Include an OBJECTIVE statement only if you wish to limit your application to a certain kind of work and would not be interested in other offers. For example, you may be interested in doing engineering work only—that is, not sales or business management—within an engineering firm. Box 14.4 provides an example of an OBJECTIVE statement.

You may also include a SUMMARY OF QUALIFICATIONS section (also called SUMMARY or MAJOR QUALIFICATIONS). This section creates interest, motivating the reader to seriously examine the rest of your qualifications. Again, Box 14.4 provides an example.

▲ 2. Reverse-Chronological Resumes

The reverse-chronological resume is the most popular. It has the advantage of being familiar to all resume readers. This format begins with a heading and then presents educational and work experience in reverse-chronological order—that is, starting with the latest experiences and going backward to the earliest. Box 14.3 shows the kind of reverse-chronological resume most college students produce. Applicants with more experience and fewer college activities would present work experience first and education second, as in Box 14.4.

A number of additional sections are possible: ACTIVITIES, MEMBERSHIPS, HONORS, AWARDS, MILITARY SERVICE, CHARITABLE WORK, PERSONAL INTERESTS, HOBBIES, and so forth. You can use conventional headings like those, or invent your own to match your experience and accomplishments.

Anything that indicates an ability to communicate effectively should be highlighted. Communication skills are valued in almost every profession. A list of your hobbies or personal interests can demonstrate that you get along with others and that you are an energetic, active person with a life beyond TV and computer games. Organizations generally prefer to hire outgoing, social people.

▲ 3. Functional Resumes

The functional resume is designed around statements of your abilities. Education and work experience are included briefly at the end to verify your claims. Your headings can name "skills" (WRITING SKILLS, MANAGEMENT SKILLS); they can name "expertise," as in Box 14.5; or they can name roles (WRITER, MANAGER).

The advantage of a functional resume is that it pulls out of your education and experience those abilities that the employer is likely to be looking for, and it highlights those abilities by placing them up front. If you were to follow the reverse-chronological organization, your most impressive job, or the educational experience most relevant to the job you are applying for, might get buried in the middle of a list. The functional resume, on the other hand, gives you control over where in the resume your strongest and most relevant credentials will appear.

BOX 14.6 ▼ Combined-Pattern Resume

Louis Frapp

9008 Beasel Street	Home telephone: (412) 555-7382
East McKeesport, PA 15035-1616	e-mail: Frapp@Telemax.net

EDUCATION

School	Degree	Dates	QPA	Major
University of Pittsburgh	B.S.	6/85–12/91	3.86	Computer Science

- Nominated to Honors Program
- Maintained membership in Phi Chi Theta, national business fraternity

School	Degree	Dates	QPA	Major
Duquesne University	M.A.	9/80–8/83	3.80	English

- Awarded one-third academic scholarship
- Awarded graduate teaching assistantship

School	Degree	Dates	QPA	Major
Branworth Polytechnical Institute	B.A.	9/75–5/80	3.83	English/Technical Writing Track

- Awarded graduate assistantship
- Served as chapter president of Sigma Tau Delta, National English Honor Society
- Received English Faculty Award as senior
- Received Minor Major Scholarship Award as junior

EXPERIENCE

Organization	Dates	Supervisor	Phone
Mansford Communications, Inc.	6/98–present	Don O'Brien	(742) 555-8014

- Develop user documentation for telecommunications line-test systems

Organization	Dates	Supervisor	Phone
Pittsburgh Telemax, Inc.	7/94–present	Marge Mendoza	(412) 555-4000

- Develop user documentation for audio and multimedia teleconferencing bridges
- Write proposals
- Develop PowerPoint presentations, press releases, promotional literature, and other marketing materials
- Train teleconferencing system administrators and end-users
- Designed the original Telemax World Wide Web pages

Organization	Dates	Supervisor	Phone
Rockmore Corporation, Inc.	9/83–3/94	Lou Marshal	(800) 555-7433

- Provided telephone support for field office computer systems
- Traveled to and trained at fields offices and at home office
- Developed applications documentation and online documentation
- Maintained Pittsburgh field office database

Organization	Dates	Supervisor	Phone
Duquesne University English Department	1/81–5/82	Melissa Monk	(412) 555 6420

- Taught freshman composition and literature courses
- Took part in various department activities and meetings

Organization	Dates	Supervisor	Phone
California State College (now California University of PA) English Department	9/70–5/80	Bill Yahner	(412) 555 4070

- Conducted writing conferences with students
- Participated in a seminar on the teaching of writing led by the director, Dr. Yahner

BOX 14.6 ▼ **Combined-Pattern Resume**

SKILLS

Communications

- Technical writing and editing: maintenance manuals and instruction guides for the electronics, software, and telecommunications fields
- Graphics: drawing and painting, importing and exporting, conversion
- Projects: proposals, reports, forms, instructions, templates
- Newsletter: desktop publishing, including compostion, layout,and editing
- Telephone: customer service, scheduling and dispatching, negotiations

Programming and coding
- World Wide Web scripts written in HTML, Perl, and JavaScript
- Database applications written in Access, dBASE IV, and Foxpro
- Word processing macros written in WordBASIC and Visual BASIC for applications
- School projects in various languages, including Modula-2, ADA, Pascal, Fortran, COBOL, BASIC, prolog, Smalltalk, C, and VAX assembly

Database management
- Design relational database system, including indexes, views, reprots, and queries
- Maintain database files, including snapshots and backup sets
- Perform ad-hoc queries using RQBE, SQL, and Xbase commands
- Update database file structures and indexes
- Translate file formats using word processing macros as well as import and export filters

---

SOFTWARE (most familiar listed at top)

Programming	Spreadsheet	Database	Communications
Visual BASIC	MS Excel	MS Access	Windows 95 Utilities
Perl	Lotus 1-2-3	Foxpro	Procomm Plus 95
Borland C++			

Word Processing	Drawing	Graphics	Operating Systems
MS Word 97	CorelDraw	Corel PhotoPaint	Windows 95/3.1/DOS
FrameMaker 5.5	Visio	PhotoFInish	UNIX, SCO UNIX

HARDWARE   (most familiar listed at top)

Machines	Printers	Modems	Scanners
PentiumPro	Panasonic Laser	SmartLink K56	Optic Pro 4800P
VAX mainframe	HP LaserJet 4P, 4si	Hayes Accura 144	CompletePC

AFFILIATIONS
- Senior Member, Society of Technical Communications

FURNISHED UPON REQUEST
- References, portfolio, demo diskettes

14 Job Search

▲ 4. Scannable Resumes

Before you post your resume on the Web, or e-mail or mail it to a potential employer, you must decide whether to send a conventional resume or a scannable resume. Many large employers, both government agencies and private corporations, use scan-and-search software to make the first review of resumes sent to their organizations. This software scans the text of a submitted resume into its database of resumes, converting it to ASCII; then it searches the resume for key words related to the required qualifications for the job. To compete with other applicants, you will have to compose your resume so that the scanning software is likely to find the key words that the employer told the program to look for. This leaves you playing a guessing game. While a human reader will recognize synonyms for designated key words, the scanning software will not.

The best way to play the key-word guessing game is to list key words in a KEYWORD SUMMARY section at the beginning of your resume, using nouns instead of verbs as your strong words. The traditional resume, as we have said, calls for strong verbs to demonstrate what you can do: Supervised ten employees, Taught Lotus 1-2-3, Improved the purchasing process. But scan-and-search software programs look for nouns: supervisor, teacher, purchaser.

Your scannable resume must, however, be more than a list of nouns naming software you know (CAD), or job titles you have held (technical writer), or your qualities (skilled manager). If your resume is selected by the scanning software, a real person will then read it. Your scanned ASCII resume must appeal to the human mind as well as to the computer program. It should make sense, and it should be attractive and easy to read. See Box 14.7 for an example of a scannable resume.

If you are printing your scannable resume and mailing it to the employer, avoid these characteristics, which interfere with the scanning process:

▮ nonwhite paper

▮ italics, underlining, and other font manipulations

▮ crowding of text (use white space liberally)

▮ exotic fonts (Helvetica is best)

▮ small type (use 12 to 14 point).

ASSIGNMENTS FOR 14.2

1. *Reverse-Chronological Resume* Find a job ad or internship opportunity from a print or online source. Choose one that you could logically apply

BOX 14.7 ▼ Scannable Resume

MARIA STROPPOLO
1536 Ginger Street
Newton, PA 17865
(413) 765-9087
mstroppolo@aol.com

KEYWORD SUMMARY

Manager whose innovations led to increased profits. Experienced in employee training, purchasing, bookkeeping. Volunteer work as professional writer. Know DOS / Windows and Mac word processing software.

EXPERIENCE

Assistant manager for Clarkstown, PA, Mobile gas station (1996–present)
—Did paper work for gasoline and store product sales
—Constructed time-saving process for the daily checkout
—Trained new employees
—Arranged work shifts for new employees

Manager of Bolton's Fish Market, Clarkstown, PA (1992–1996)
—Supervisor for 8 employees
—In charge of ordering all products
—In charge of bookkeeping
—Initiator of a lunch bar on the premises, which yielded excellent profits

Volunteer for the Clarkstown SENIOR TIMES magazine (1990–present)
—Write responses to inquiries and complaints from subscribers
—Research and write articles at the request of the editor

EDUCATION

B.A. Management, Pumpkinville College, 3.2 QPA
24 credits, Clarksville Junior College, 3.4 QPA

---

for now or upon graduation. Write an appropriate reverse-chronological resume targeted for that job.

2. *Functional Resume* Do assignment 14.2(1), but create a functional resume.

3. *Scannable Resume* Do assignment 14.2(1), but create a scannable resume.

14.3 ≻——— Job Search Letters

This section discusses cover letters and other correspondence related to your job search.

▲ 1. Cover Letters

You should never mail a resume without including a cover letter that introduces yourself, states that you are applying for a job, and develops your qualifications. Even if responding to a job advertisement that merely says "Send resume to . . .," send a cover letter with it.

At some point you should use a phrase like "As my resume indicates . . ." to connect your claims with the resume itself. And since the resume will be enclosed, you must refer to it by putting the word *Enclosure* at the bottom-left side of your cover letter, two spaces below the signature.

The cover letter should be seen as an opportunity to sell yourself unabashedly. Tell the reader what you can do for the target organization. Tell the reader what you have done for other organizations you have worked for. Describe your character—hard-working, reliable, enthusiastic, competent, or whatever adjective seems appropriate, provided that it accurately reflects your nature.

Here is a breakdown of the content:

▌ **Beginning:** At the outset, introduce yourself (I am a recent college graduate with a major in chemistry looking for a job in . . .). If responding to an advertisement, say so (I am interested in the opening you advertised in the *Miami Herald* for "an experienced school counselor" . . .). Mention any contacts you have with the organization (I am a friend of Louise Shelton, a secretary in your main office . . .). Identify yourself in terms of your general qualifications (As my resume indicates, I am an experienced professional writer . . .).

▌ **Middle:** Here is where you try to sell yourself by showing how your qualifications match those mentioned in the advertisement. You can use a bulleted list, as in a resume, or you can just talk about yourself in traditional paragraphs. Refer to your education and experience. If possible, use phrases from the advertisement:

> Your advertisement calls for a writer with "experience in electronic marketing." I worked for two summers in the marketing department of a large Atlanta real estate agency. During that time I wrote and maintained Web site listings, as well as text describing the agency's services.

BOX 14.8 ▼ Cover Letter

CONFIDENTIAL

March 30, 2000

500 Graham Avenue
Partridgeville, OR 48390

Box 76389
c/o *Duff Daily News*
967 Main Street
Princeton, OR 48390

Re: Web site maintenance position

I am applying for the Web site maintenance position advertised in the March 28th edition of the *Duff Daily News*. I have a computer science degree from Oregon State University and a 15-credit graduate certification in multimedia technology. As an undergraduate, I worked for two years as an intern at a local Senior Center where I helped develop their Web site.

As my enclosed resume shows, I carried out a range of duties at the Senior Center, where I wrote marketing documents and edited reports and business letters.

Your advertisement indicated a desire for computer skills. In addition to my computer science degree and my multimedia certification, I have a thorough knowledge of word processing, desktop publishing, and advanced database software. At the Senior Center I was in charge of the computer network and all database management. At my present job, I function as a general computer expert, helping various departments with their networking and software problems.

If my qualifications interest you, I am available for an interview on Wednesday or Friday afternoons. I can take short phone calls at work: (745) 555-9042. I have an answering machine on my home phone: (745) 555-8796. I can also be reached any time via e-mail: keye@techno.com.

My salary requirements are in the $30K to $40K range, depending on workload and responsibilities. Thank you for your consideration.

Sincerely yours,

Louise Keye

Louise Keye
Enclosure

▌ **End:** State what you want your reader to do—specifically, to set up an interview. Make that easy by including your phone number and stating when you can be reached. End with a "thank you" of some sort. Here is a typical conclusion:

> If my qualifications interest you, I would like to discuss this position further in an interview at your location. You can reach me at (412) 555-8976 after 3:00 PM, or you can leave a message on my answering machine. I can take time off work for an interview on any day during the next several weeks.
>
> Thank you for taking the trouble to consider me for this position.

Box 14.8 provides an example of a cover letter.

▲ *2. Follow-Up, Acceptance, and Rejection Letters*

A few days after a job interview, especially one that you think was successful, send the interviewer a follow-up letter (Box 14.9). The purpose of this letter is to remind the interviewer of your qualifications and to emphasize your interest in working for the organization. A three-part follow-up letter might follow this pattern:

▌ **Beginning:** Thank the interviewer for taking the time to interview you and provide you with information about the organization. Mention your admiration for the organization.

▌ **Middle:** Remind the interviewer of your qualifications and explain how they fit what you learned about the organization during the interview. Mention some detail about the organization that impressed you.

▌ **End:** Reassert your interest in working for the organization. Finish with a friendly, optimistic sign-off.

Suppose you get a job offer. After deciding whether to accept or reject the offer, immediately write back to the organization, informing it of your decision. An acceptance letter states at the outset that you are pleased to take the job. Make clear what you are agreeing to by restating any condition of employment mentioned in the letter offering you the job, such as salary, rank, or date on which the employment begins. End with a friendly sign-off.

If you don't want the job, write a rejection letter. As a matter of decency, quickly inform the organization that it needs to find someone else. As a practical matter, never burn bridges to possible employers by arrogantly ignoring their offer.

BOX 14.9 ▼ Follow-Up Letter

June 18, 2000

440 Market Street
Apt. 7B
Coaltown, PA 15411

Ms. Jackie Bartlett
Production Supervisor
Parkway Foods
4000 Dunning Avenue
Bolton, PA 14734

Dear Ms. Bartlett:

I enjoyed my interview with you and Mr. Schrader at Parkway Foods last Monday, and I want to thank you for taking the time to show me around the facilities. I was impressed by the physical plant and the energetic, professional work force. Parkway strikes me as the kind of place where my diligent work style can get full play.

I especially liked the mingling of line workers with their managers at lunch and the pre-work meetings at which problems are discussed. Supervisors at Parkway are indeed able to benefit from these friendly interchanges.

If you have any questions about my resume, please call me at (565) 873-5555, or e-mail me at jminx@aol.com.

Sincerely,

James Minx

James Minx

In your rejection letter, begin by stating that although you admire the organization you cannot accept its job offer. Then explain why. Perhaps you have already accepted an offer elsewhere, or the salary offered isn't high enough and you intend to keep looking for a job that pays more. Be honest. End with a friendly sign-off, possibly wishing the organization good luck in its job search. Box 14.10 shows the content for an acceptance letter and a rejection letter.

BOX 14.10   ▼   Acceptance and Rejection Letters

Acceptance

Dear Ms. Bartlett:

I am pleased to accept your job offer for the position of Communications Manager at Parkway Foods. As your letter states, this job pays $42,500, plus the benefits described in the booklet you gave me at my interview.

You asked if I can begin by August 10. I will have no problem starting on that date. Tomorrow I will give two weeks' notice to my present employer, and that will leave me almost a week to get settled in the Bolton area. In fact, I hope to come in a day or two early to handle the paperwork with the personnel department and perhaps meet a few more of my co-workers.

I am looking forward to working for Parkway Foods.

Rejection

Dear Ms. Bartlett:

I just received your letter offering me the position of Communications Manager at Parkway Foods. Regretfully, I must decline the offer because I have already accepted a job at another company.

I am flattered to have received your offer. Parkway struck me as an excellent employer, and I enjoyed the interview with you and Mr. Schrader. I wish you luck in filling the Communications Manager position.

ASSIGNMENTS FOR 14.3

1. *Cover Letter* Find a job advertisement and write a cover letter that would fit the stated job requirements.

2. *Follow-up Letter* Assume that you were interviewed for the job you applied for in assignment 14.3(1). Write a follow-up letter.

3. *Acceptence and Rejection Letters* Write acceptance and rejection letters for the job you applied for in assignment 14.3(1).

References

Anson, P. A. H. (1998). Exploring minimalistic technical design today: A view from the practitioner's window. In J. M. Carroll (Ed.), *Minimalism beyond the Nurnberg Funnel* (pp. 91–117). Cambridge, Mass.: MIT Press.

Archee, R. K. (2000, February). New ideas for Web searchers. *Intercom, 47,* 40–41.

Axtel, R. E. (1993). *Do's and taboos around the world.* New York: John Wiley.

Barclay, R. O., & Pinelli, T. E. (1998). Writing in the aerospace industry. In J. A. Lutz & C. Gilbert Storms (Eds.), *The practice of technical and scientific communication: Writing in professional contexts* (pp. 49–60). Stamford, Conn.: Aplex Publishing.

Bedford, M. S., & Stearns, F. C. (1987). The technical writer's responsibility for safety. *IEEE Transactions on Professional Communication, 30*(3), 127–131.

Bever, T. G. (1982). Regression in the service of development. In T. G. Bever (Ed.), *Regressions in mental development: Basic phenomena and theories* (pp. 153–188). Hillsdale, N.J.: Lawrence Erlbaum.

Buffington, N., Diogenes, M., & Moneyhun, C. (1997). *Living languages.* Upper Saddle River, N.J.: Blair Press.

Bush, D. (1999, September/October). Better to be consistently wrong? *Intercom, 46,* 38, 42.

Cannon, L. (1997, July 21). Prosperity, with a Latin beat. *Washington Post National Weekly Edition,* p. 33.

Carroll, J. B., Davies, P., & Richman, B. (1971). *The American Heritage word frequency book.* Boston: Houghton Mifflin.

Carroll, J. M. (1998). *Minimalism beyond the Nurnberg Funnel.* Cambridge, Mass.: MIT Press.

Chicago Manual of Style, 14th ed. (1993). Chicago: University of Chicago Press.

Clement, D. E. (1987). Human factors, instructions and warnings, and products liability. *IEEE Transactions on Professional Communication, 30* (3), 149–156.

Crump, E., & Carbone, N. (1998). *Writing online: A student's guide to the Internet and World Wide Web.* Boston: Houghton Mifflin.

Ede, L. (1984). Audience: An introduction to research. *College Composition and Communication, 35,* 140–154.

Ede, L., & Lunsford, A. (1984). Audience addressed/Audience invoked: The role of audience in composition theory and pedagogy. *College Composition and Communication, 35,* 155–171.

Etz, D. V. (1992). Confucius for the technical communicator: Selections from *The Analexts. Technical Communication, 39,* 641–644.

Fisher, G. (1992). *Mindsets: The role of culture and perception on international relations.* Yarmouth, Maine: Intercultural Press, Inc.

Flesch, R. (1949). *The art of readable writing.* New York: Harper & Row.

Follett, W. (1966). *Modern American usage.* New York: Warner Books.

Fry, E. B. (1988). Writability: The principles of writing for increased comprehension. In B. L. Zakaluk, L. Beverly, & S. J. Samuels (Eds.), *Readability: Its past, present, and future* (pp. 77–95). Newark, Del.: International Reading Association.

Gunning, R., & Kallan, R. A. (1994). *How to take the fog out of business writing.* Chicago: Dartnell Corporation.

Hargis, G. (1998). *Developing quality technical information: A handbook for writers and editors.* Upper Saddle River, N.J.: Prentice-Hall.

Haswell, R. (1988). Error and change in college student writing. *Written Communication, 5* (9), 479–499.

Hayhoe, G. (1999). Technical communication: Trivial pursuit? *Technical Communication, 46,* 23–25.

Horn, R. E. (1990). *Mapping hypertext: The analysis, organization, and display of knowledge for the next generation of on-line text and graphics.* Waltham, Mass.: Info-Map.

Horn, R. E. (1992). *Strategies for developing high-performance documentation.* Waltham, Mass.: Info-Map.

Horton, W. (1993). Let's do away with manuals . . . before they do away with us. *Technical Communication, 40,* 26–34.

Horton, W. (1994). *The icon book: Visual symbols for computer systems and documentation.* New York: John Wiley & Sons.

Johnson, D. R. (1999, June). Copyright issues on the Internet. *Intercom, 43,* 16–17.

Kemnitz, C. (1991). How to write effective hazard alert messages. *Technical Communication, 38*(1), 68–73.

Kirkman, J., Snow, C., & Watson, I. (1978). Controlled English as an alternative to multiple translations. *IEEE Transactions on Professional Communication, 21,* 159–161.

Kirsch, G., & Roen, D. H. (1990). *A sense of audience in written communication.* London: Sage.

Koren, L., & Meckler, R. W. (1989). *Graphic design cookbook.* San Francisco: Chronicle Books.

Kroll, B. M. (1984). Writing for readers: Three perspectives on audience. *College Composition and Communication, 35,* 172–185.

Kucera, H., & Francis, W. N. (1967). *Computational analysis of present-day American English.* Providence, R.I.: Brown University Press.

Landy, A. (1994). Managing a headcount-based documentation group. In G. Lanyi, *Managing documentation projects in an imperfect world* (pp. 160–169). Columbus, Ohio: Batelle Press.

Lanham, R. A. (1981). *Revising business prose.* New York: Charles Scribner's Sons.

Lanyi, G. (1994). *Managing documentation projects in an imperfect world.* Columbus, Ohio: Batelle Press.

Lazarus, A., MacLeish, A, & Smith, H. W. (1972). *Modern English: A glossary of literature and language.* New York: Grosset & Dunlap, Inc.

Lutz, J. A., & Storms, C. G. (Eds.). (1998). *The practice of technical and scientific communication.*

Lynch, P. J., & Horton, S. (1999). *Web style guide.* New Haven: Yale University Press.

Meyer, E. K. (1997). *Designing infographics.* Indianapolis: Hayden.

Microsoft Corporation. (1995). *The Microsoft manual of style for technical publications.* Redmond, Wash.: Microsoft Press.

Miller, A. R., & Davis, M. H. (1990). *Intellectual property rights: Patents, trademarks, and copyright.* St. Paul, Minn.: West Publishing.

Murdick, W. (1996). What English teachers need to know about grammar. *English Journal, 85* (7), 39–45.

Murdick, W. (1999). *The portable business writer.* Boston: Houghton Mifflin.

Ogden, C. K. (1968). *Basic English: International second language.* New York: Harcourt, Brace, & World, Inc.

Parsons, S. O., Seminara, J. L., & Wogalter, M. S. (1999). A summary of warnings research. *Ergonomics in Design: The Magazine of Human Factors Applications, 7*(1), 21–31.

Pinkerton, L. F. (1990). *The writer's law primer.* New York: Lyons & Burford.

Porter, J. E. (1987). Truth in advertising: A case study. *IEEE Transactions on Professional Communications, 30,* 182–189.

Redish, J. C., & Schell, D. A. (1989). Writing and testing instructions for usability. In B. E. Fearing & W. K. Sparrow (Eds.), *Technical writing: Theory and practice* (pp. 63–71). New York: Modern Language Association.

Rew, L. J. (1999). *Editing for writers.* Upper Saddle River, N.J.: Prentice-Hall.

Richards, I. A. (1943). *Basic English and its uses.* New York: W. W. Norton.

Rockas, L. (1992). *Styles in writing.* Lexington, Mass.: D. C. Heath.

Roger, V. O. (1990). *A whack on the side of the head.* New York: Warner Books.

Rude, C. D. (1994). Managing publications according to legal and ethical standards. In O. J. Allen & L. H. Deming (Eds.), *Publications management: Essays for professional communicators* (pp. 171–187). Amityville, N.Y.: Baywood.

Sakiey, E., & Fry, E. (1979). *3,000 instant words.* Providence, R.I.: Jamestown Publishers.

Schriver, K. A. (1997). *Dynamics in document design: Creating texts for readers.* New York: John Wiley & Sons.

Siebert, L., & Ballard, L. (1992). *Making a good layout.* Cincinnati: North Light Books.

Smart, K. L., Seawright, K. K., & DeTienne, K. B. (1995). Defining quality in technical communications. *Technical Communication, 42,* 474–481.

Smith, P. (1997). *Mark my words: Instruction and practice in proofreading,* 3rd ed. Alexandria, Va.: EEI Press.

Strate, L., & Swerdlow, S. (1987). The maze of the law: How technical writers can research and understand legal matters. *EEI Transactions on Professional Communication, 30* (3), 136–148.

Sutcliffe, A. J. (1996). How (and why) to create an in-house style manual. In *Stet again! More tricks of the trade for publications people.* Alexandria, Va.: EEI Press.

Talishain, T., & Nystrom, J. (1999). *Official Netscape guide to Internet research,* 2nd ed. New York: Netscape Press.

Tarutz, J. A. (1992). *Technical editing: The practical guide for editors and writers.* Reading, Mass.: Perseus.

Thomas, M., Jaffe, G., Kinkaid, J. P., & Stees, Y. (1992). Learning to use simplified English: A preliminary study. *Technical Communication, 39,* 69–73.

Van de Meij, H., & Carroll, J. M. (1998). Principles and heuristics for designing minimalist instruction. In J. M. Carroll (Ed.), *Minimalism beyond the Nurnberg Funnel* (pp. 19–53). Cambridge, Mass.: MIT Press.

Washington, D. A. (1993). Creating the corporate style guide, process and product. *Technical Communication, 40,* 505–510.

Williams, M., & Cubbage, S. (1998). *The national job hotline directory.*

Williams, R. (1994). *The non-designer's design book.* Berkeley: Peachpit.

Williams, R., & Tollett, J. (1998). *The non-designer's Web book.* Berkeley: Peachpit.

Zakaluk, B. L., & Samuels, S. J. (1988). *Readability: Its past, present, and future.* Newark, Del.: International Reading Association.

List of Illustrations

Index